AF600229

THE CATHOLIC UNIVERSITY OF AMERICA
STUDIES IN CANON AND CIVIL LAW

Number 39

THE CANONICAL JURISTIC PERSONALITY WITH SPECIAL REFERENCE TO ITS STATUS IN THE UNITED STATES OF AMERICA

A DISSERTATION

Submitted to the Faculty of Canon Law, Catholic University of America, in Partial Fulfillment of its Requirements for the Degree of Doctor of Both Laws

BY

BRENDAN FRANCIS BROWN, A.B., LL.M., J.U.L.
OMAHA, NEBRASKA.

The Catholic University of America
Washington, D. C.
1927.

Nihil Obstat:

✠ Thomas Joseph Shahan, S.T.D., Censor Deputatus.

Imprimatur:

✠ Michael J. Curley, D.D., Archiepiscopus Baltimorensis.

Washington, D. C., May, 1927.

PREFACE.

This dissertation, a comparative legal study, aims to present the fundamentals of ecclesiastical corporate organization, one of the most important phases of juridical personality. It approaches this subject from the historical, philosophical and juridical viewpoints, and uses the conclusions thereby obtained to clarify the legal position occupied by the Church in the United States. Three juridical schemes have been considered in this connection, namely, the Civil Law of the European Continent, Canon Law and Anglo-American Law. Emphasis has been placed upon the status of the ecclesiastical corporation in this country; the last six chapters are devoted to this consideration. Adjudications involving the major Church denominations in this country have been used in the development of this section. It is hoped that the present undertaking, however limited it may be, will serve to suggest the utility of comparative studies in Civil and Ecclesiastical Law. Just as greater proficiency in the English language is produced by the study of foreign tongues, so in like manner is the American jurist able to improve his knowledge of American law by the consideration of other juristic systems. The substantial unity of Universal Jurisprudence is manifest.

The writer takes this occasion to express his gratitude to the Right Reverend Thomas J. Shahan, S.T.D., LL.D., Rector of the Catholic University of America, for his many kind favors and to Francesco J. Lardone, S.T.D., J.U.D., through whose encouragement the writer was inspired to continue his work in Canon and Roman Laws. He also gratefully acknowledges the valuable assistance rendered by those illustrious professors under whose personal direction this work was produced.

CONTENTS

CHAPTER I.

SCOPE AND SIGNIFICANCE OF THE SUBJECT.

Corporate organization represents one of the supreme achievements of highly civilized society. The substantial benefits to be derived from such a legal mechanism have been recognized both by Church and State, which have in turn adapted the corporate scheme to their respective needs. The relation between Church and State may be gleaned by an analysis of the position which the State assumes toward the ecclesiastical juristic personality. This generalization is limited neither by temporal nor geographical variations. It covers the situation which obtains today in the United States. True, the corporate aspects of the Church in this country have not been widely discussed; it is a domain which few have traversed. Yet in the determination of the temporal rights and obligations of the Church before the law, it is of extreme importance to understand the status and forms of the ecclesiastical legal personality. More particularly, the problem reduces itself to this: What view does the Church take of the canonical personality, and how does that idea compare with the recognition actually accorded this juristic person in the United States? This implies a statement of the legal standing which the Church is justly entitled to enjoy, and the practicability of obtaining such a status under the present constitution of American society and government.

In general, it is the Catholic attitude to regard the Church and Holy See as moral persons by virtue of divine law;[1] to consider the inferior ecclesiastical moral persons, for example, individual churches, as possessing this character of juridical personality from the Church; and to de-

[1] Canon 100.

clare that in both instances these legal personalities enjoy certain inalienable rights and privileges apart from the State. But in the United States, the Church, as such, is not recognized as a juridical personality endowed with civil rights.[2] This is true in both public and private law. This legal mentality seems to be an inheritance from the English common law, where there prevails the "Concession Theory" of corporations,[3] namely, that the State is the creator of corporations, a legal principle which coincides with the Hobbes philosophy of the superiority of the State.

There is, then, in the United States, a conflict between Church and State in the matter of public and private corporate law. But in practice this clash of theories is softened by the State's allowing Catholics the right to practice their religion without molestation, and as citizens of the United States to exercise indirectly the corporate rights which are directly denied the Church by refusal to recognize her corporate capacity. The practical consequences of corporate personality are chiefly in the realm of Church ownership of property and its administration.[4]

The vigilance of the Church in the United States in this respect is indicated by the directions of the Third Plenary Council of Baltimore with reference to the holding of ecclesiastical property.[5] Insistence upon proper civil recognition may also be found in the formulations and Pastoral Letter of the Second Plenary Council of Baltimore. To quote from the latter document: "While cheerfully recognizing the fact, that hitherto the General and State Governments of our country, except in some brief intervals of excitement and delusion, have not interfered with our ecclesiastical organization or civil rights, we still have to lament that in many of the States we are not as yet permitted legally to make those arrangements for the security of Church property, which are in accordance with the

[2] Tyler, *American Ecclesiastical Law,* §110.

[3] Blackstone, *Commentaries,* I, 472.

[4] Strong, *Relations of Civil Law to Church Polity,* 40.

[5] *Acta et Decreta, Con. Plen. Balt.,* III, Tit. IX, Cap. iii, n. 275.

canons and discipline of the Catholic Church. In some of the States, we gratefully acknowledge that all is granted in this regard that we could reasonably ask for. The right of the Church to possess property, whether churches, residences for the clergy, cemeteries, or school houses, asylums etc., can not be denied without depriving her of a necessary means of promoting the end for which she has been established. We are aware of the alleged grounds for this refusal to recognize the Church in her corporate capacity, unless on the condition, that, in the matter of the tenure of ecclesiastical property, she conform to the general laws providing for this object. * * * These laws, however, * * * are the expression of a distrust of ecclesiastical power as such * * * [6]" This was written more than half a century ago, yet it substantially summarizes the legal position which the Church occupies in this country today.

This "distrust of ecclesiastical power" is simply a modern phase of the age-old conflict between Church and State. The Church and its law, however, have contributed immensely to the development and refinement of civil jurisprudence.[7] As humanity emerged from the crude social background of primitive civilization and scaled the summit of governmental achievement, the supreme necessity of law was recognized. Man everywhere formulated laws in all his various relationships. The nature of these laws was determined by his particular needs and by the precise character of the activity which was to be regulated. As a result, such legal systems as the Greek, Roman and other civil types of jurisprudence were evolved. These were agencies of the State seeking to preserve order and promote the best interests of itself and its members. In history, there grew up along with these systems of civil law another juridical scheme whose province was ecclesiastical and whose purpose was to guide the exterior activity of the

[6] *Con. Plen. Balt. II, Pastoral Letter,* 215; cf. also, *Acta et Decreta Con. Plen. Balt.* II, Tit, IV, Cap. i, n. 182 to 204.

[7] Desmond, *The Church and The Law,* 14.

Church to its proper end. This aggregation of legal principles is called Canon law.[8]

This system of jurisprudence occupied and continues to occupy a unique place in the development of juridical thought. One of the world's oldest legal systems, Canon Law has played an important role in influencing practically the whole juristic tendency of western civilization. It has affected the jurisprudence of continental Europe.[9] It was a prominent factor in the formation of English common law and incidentally of Anglo-American jurisprudence.[10] From the end of the eleventh century, the legal procedure of Roman law was reformed by Canon law. Beginning with that epoch, two great compilations of law stand out in bold relief, silhouetted against the sky of occidental progress, the law of the Emperors, i. e., the *Corpus Juris Civilis,* and the law of the Popes, or the *Corpus Juris Canonici,* consisting of the *Decretum Gratiani,* the *Decretals of Gregory IX,* the *Decretals of Boniface VIII,* the *Clementinae* and the two *Extravagantes.*[11] Ecclesiastical law was a vital influence in the preservation of Roman civil law upon the Continent.[12] In England, the development of Chancery Courts, the conception of individual responsibility, the abolition of such crude forms of justice as trial by combat and fire, and the growth of democracy in government were largely the result of the refining influence of Canon law.[13]

But while it is possible and indeed desirable that Church and State, civil and ecclesiastical law, should function harmoniously together, history proves that the State, that perfect society whose aim is to procure the temporal welfare of its members, jealous of its jurisdiction, has challenged every assumption of temporal power which the Church has found necessary to insist upon in the furtherance of her

[8] Augustine, *Commentary on the New Code of Canon Law,* I, 2.
[9] Sherman, *Roman Law in the Modern World,* I, §225.
[10] Pollock and Maitland, *History of English Law,* I, 113.
[11] Sohm-Ledlie, *Institutes of Roman Law,* 139.
[12] Sherman, *o. c.,* I, §225.
[13] Pollock and Maitland, *o. c.,* I, 104.

primary purpose. In the field of both public and private law, the antagonism of the State toward the Church has found expression in such national policies as complete separation of Church and State, State superiority in all matters, and finally positive enmity expressed by such tyrannical measures, as forcible expulsion of religious and confiscation of ecclesiastical property. The American policy is one of qualified liberalism.

The promotion of the welfare of humanity should be the mutual task of Church and State, each sovéreign in its respective domain. But the coöperation of the State has often been lacking. The annals of ecclesiastical and civil law evidence the bitter struggles between these two societies, in the realm particularly of public law and politics. Like a scarlet skein, the record of these struggles is traceable across the pages of the past. From the earliest time it began, manifesting itself in such climaxes as the edicts of Diocletian and the Valerian persecutions. The latter struck at the very core of the Christian religion by the declaration that it was a dangerous corporation, inconsistent with the best interests of the State. The same grasping attitude on the part of the State is found in subsequent events.[14] The imperial successors of Constantine attempted to intermeddle with dogma and to trespass upon the domain of Church discipline.[15] There were times when the Merovingians and Charles Martel under the guise of patronage infringed upon the property rights of the Church.[16] The untrammeled exercise of legitimate rights by the Church was interfered with by the Italian renaissance, and the resurrection of intense nationalism in England and France. The Avignon captivity, the Western Schism and the so-called Reformation were subsequent developments. State absolutism may be seen in the effort to establish the "episcopal system," which would permit civil authority to usurp

[14] Augustine, *o. c.*, II, 202.
[15] Permaneder, *Handbuch des Kirchenrechts*, I, 62.
[16] Scherer, *Handbuch des Kirchenrechts*, I, 32 seqq.

episcopal prerogatives, at least with reference to Protestants. "Territorial systems" sought to regulate arbitrarily the religion of a territory by recourse to the superior authority of the State. The Church's independence was weakened by compromises and concordats. Even the so-called Catholic systems as Josephinism, Febronianism and Gallicanism were temporal transgressions upon affairs strictly ecclesiastical.[17]

But it is not in the realm of politics that it is proposed to examine the relation of Church and State, but rather in the strictly legal domain of the conflict between Canon and Civil law viewed as juristic systems. In other words, the canonical juristic personality with special reference to its status and recognition in the United States will be considered. The American constitutional attitude of separation of Church and State has to large extent determined and fixed the corporate rights of the Church in this country. This political background, therefore, has lent a distinctive color to the Church's rights under American civil law. The structure of ecclesiastical organization is in no small measure based upon the canonical juristic personality, a conception necessarily of compelling significance to both the canonist and the civil lawyer.

In our own country, it is in the field of corporate law that the distrust of ecclesiastical power is most emphatically manifested by the State. Here, there is no repetition of such iniquitous laws as the mortmain statutes which prevailed in England under Edward I and Richard III, restraining statutes which violated ecclesiastical property rights by constituting religious corporations "dead hands" (mort main), incapable of receiving property.[18] Nor is there today in this country an application of laws violating the rights of the Church such as obtained in European countries during the reign of Maximilian I, Ferdinand II, Leopold I, Charles VI, Maria Theresa and Joseph II. Here,

[17] Augustine, *o. c.*, I, 208.

[18] Brabandere, *Juris Canonici et Juris Canonico-Civilis Compendium,* I 54.

there is no counterpart of the political jockeying and diplomatic intriguing which flecks the whole history of the old world. But there is a rivalry between Church and State in some quarters which has come to mean an insistence by the Church of her rights under American law, and an effort by the State to subordinate the ecclesiastical corporate status as far as possible. The clash is fundamentally in the field of private law. Thus, there are states that do not recognize religious corporations, and in states where such corporations are allowed, the exercise of their rights is so restricted that the Church has deemed it advisable to avoid incorporation. In the following pages, an analysis will be given of the fundamental conceptions of the canonical juristic personality, first, from the ecclesiastical viewpoint, and secondly, from the standpoint of the civil law which prevails in the United States.

CHAPTER II.

THE ROMAN JURIDICAL PERSONALITY AS THE PREDECESSOR OF THE CANONICAL.

The history of juridical personality is not the history of a "rule of law" but of a "form of thought", which generates persons other than human beings. The first manifestation of this form of thought goes back into the dim twilight of the past where the imagination of primitive men began to paint anthropomorphic pictures of an aggregation of individuals.[1] But that philosophy did not find application with resultant legal consequences until a much later date. The evolution of a juristic person in the strictly legal sense is the product of a highly developed jural mentality. It was that marvellous legal growth known as Roman law which evolved this intricate legal conception, i. e., of a person existing only in contemplation of law.[2] This juristic notion of the Romans was later absorbed by Canon law and transfused into the body of the law of the European continent and from there into the English common law. From this latter source, it has entered American jurisprudence. It is, therefore, necessary to begin with the rise of juridical personality in that system of law which gave to the world's jurisprudence the idea of the corporate entity.[3]

The notion of juristic personality is not to be found in the earlier Roman law. The power to possess rights was in the beginning extended only to individual, natural persons.[4] It is true that these could unite to form societies, for example, clubs and trade guilds,[5] but these were orig-

[1] Pollock and Maitland, *o. c.*, I, 471.
[2] Wernz-Vidal, *Jus Canonicum*, II, 25.
[3] Sohm-Ledlie, *o. c.*, 187.
[4] *Ibid.*
[5] *Digest* 47, 22, 4; Ricobono, *Fontes Juris Romani Ante-Justiniani*, Introduction.

inally not legal persons, for the property had to be vested in one or more of the members themselves.[6] No legal personality attached to the association itself. This property was regarded as the separate property of the individuals. The idea of organization was rudimentary.[7] Proprietary capacity was not referable to the *societas, collegium,* or *sodalitas* in ancient times. Corporate law at that period, if it could be called such, was restricted to the contemplation of collections of individuals, who as individuals were capable of maintaining certain legal relations with each other and with society in general.

What has thus far been said refers to the *jus privatum* of the Romans, the law for citizens which did not concern itself with other than natural persons.[8] The *jus civile privatum* was applied to the *civis,* but it did not apply to the *Civitas Romana,* the Roman State, which was identical with the totality of the Roman people. This latter occupied a plane analogous to that of the national gods in respect to the ownership of property. The property of both the gods and the State was described as *res extra commercium,* in contradistinction to *res privatae.* In private law, the property of the State was no one's property; it could not be owned by anyone: "Quae publicae sunt, nullius videntur in bonis esse, ipsius enim universitatis esse creduntur."[9] In fact, it could not constitute the subject matter of ordinary transactions. Thus, the individual *cives* were not regarded as the common owners of the public lands of the State, which in turn was not in the domain of private law but rather possessed an element of juridical personality of its own.

The principle that the Roman State, a "persona juridica perfecta,"[10] was outside the domain of private law in refence to the ownership of property (*ager publicus et aerar-*

[6] Sherman, *o. c.,* II, §537; Law of XII Tables, viii, 27.

[7] Taylor, *Corporations,* §1.

[8] Sherman, *o. c.,* II, §537.

[9] Gaius II, 11.

[10] Cavagnis, *Institutiones Juris Publici Ecclesiastici,* I, 7.

ium) was extended to include all proprietary dealings. Redress by the private individual against the State was not possible through legal procedure, but only by an administrative process.[11] While it has been suggested above that the Roman State possessed an element of personality,[12] it must be remembered that Roman jurists at that time did not consider the State as a juridical person in the sense in which that expression is used today. The State was looked upon as something transcendent so far as the private law was concerned,[13] for the private law recognized only private property.

There was another type of *res publicae,* called the *res sacrae,* or property dedicated to the gods. This was also outside the realm of private law and incapable of being owned by individuals.

Under the earlier Roman law, therefore, only the natural person could be *capax,*[14] the subject of rights, and of course, obligations, within the domain of the *jus privatum;* and only the State could enjoy a similar privilege in the field of the *jus publicum* and *jus sacrum.*

The evolution by which public property, *res publicae,* with the exception of common property in the very strictest sense as intended for the common use of all, became a subject of private law was due to the growth of municipal government, which took place toward the end of the Republic. These municipalities began to enjoy in some measure the status of persons in private law. The theory was further developed by allowing lawful societies, such as the *collegia, sodalitates, universitates* to have a certain proprietary capacity, and thereby acknowledging them as legal persons in the realm of private law.[15] Eventually, the Roman State came to be regarded as a person in private law in respect to the *fiscus,* although it continued to enjoy a num-

[11] Dernburg, *Römisches Recht,* I, 97.
[12] *Code* 10, 1; *Dig.* 49, 14.
[13] Wernz-Vidal, *o. c.,* II, 26.
[14] Sohm-Ledlie, *o. c.,* 187.
[15] Sohm-Ledlie, *o. c.,* 189.

ber of fiscal exemptions which evidenced its previous separation from the restrictions of Roman private jurisprudence. The theory of juristic personality, therefore, came to be recognized in imperial Roman law.[16]

The historical background of the public and private juridical person affords an interesting study. The public corporation was the first type of Roman juristic personality, for example the *fiscus, civitas, municipium.* In ante-Justinian law, Rome carried on her extensive governmental scheme by incorporating cities and towns, which were governmental units. In Justinian law, legal personality in public law reached an even higher pinnacle of importance. Three types of municipalities existed in Italy after the termination of the Latin War in 338 B. C.: colonies, *municipia,* and allied cities. Uniformity of government among these organizations was introduced towards the end of the Republic; and the work of extending the dominion of Roman municipal government was carried on by the Emperors. The Roman State, a perfect society, sovereign and independent of private law, served as the model for the administration of government in the cities of Italy before the end of the early Empire. With the development of the theory of juridical personality by the Roman jurists, these municipaliaies[17] began to be allowed to exercise certain corporate rights, especially with regard to the ownership of property, by virtue of their similarity to the Roman State, but they were dependent upon the latter as a *pupillus* upon his *tutor.*[18]

The Roman State in its proprietary capacity was known as the *fiscus.*[19] During the period of the Republic, the *aerarium populi Romani* or the *aerarium Saturni* was the single public treasury of the Romans,[20] but there grew up about

[16] *Ibid.*

[17] Dernburg, *o. c.,* I, 98.

[18] Walsh, *History of English and American Law,* §115; *Dig.* 46, 48, 49; Wernz-Vidal, o. c., II, 26.

[19] *Dig.* 49, 14.

[20] Smith, *Dictionary of Greek and Roman Antiquities,* I, 860, *fiscus.*

the time of the Empire a dual treasury, that of the Senate called the *Aerarium* and the one belonging to the Emperor known as the *Fiscus Caesaris* or simply *fiscus*. The Emperor was regarded as a trustee in whom was vested the title of public property, with this limitation, that he was bound to fulfill his trust in the interests of the State. "Res fiscales quasi propriae et privatae principis sunt."[21] This *fiscus* assumed the character of juridical personality upon the same theory that such a character was referable to the cities and municipalities; but there was a dissimilarity in this, that because of the relation of the *fiscus* to the Emperor it had various privileges and exemptions. The *fiscus* was administered by representatives of the Emperor. Modern authors disagree as to the corporate character of the *fiscus;* its exact nature is generally the subject of much discussion.[22]

Not only was Roman administrative life in a large measure carried on by means of the public corporation, but the essential character of society itself at a certain period was vitally affected by even the private corporation. This type of corporation had its origin in the old religious associations or *sodalitas,* which was at first looked upon rather as a loose organization corresponding to our modern idea of partnership; but later some of them became incorporated.[23] History indicates that in the period of Justinian law, Roman society was developing a caste system. New social purposes were arising.[24] Society was all divided into well defined classes and the social organization of the State was reared upon various types of corporations.

As Roman society began to be more and more organized into classes, so the conception of juristic personality expanded. Just as an individual could not be without his

[21] Ulpian *Dig.* 43, 8, 2 and 4.

[22] Buckland, *Elementary Principles of Roman Private Law,* 56; *A Text Book of Roman Law,* 177; Morey, *Outlines of Roman Law,* 263; Mommsen, *Römisches Staatsrecht,* II, 998.

[23] Savigny, *System des heutigen Römischen Rechts,* II, §86, 88.

[24] Dernburg, *o. c.,* I, 98; Sherman, *o. c.,* II, §911.

familia, so too, he must belong to a certain class. The State, as it were, functioned through *personae morales,* and the juridical person was beginning to form the bed-rock stratum of the whole Roman social structure. Serfs, professional men, bakers, artisans, boatmen and the like were organizing into corporations, and such persons had to belong to these organizations.[25] The corporate principle which had evolved with respect to the *municipia,* towns and villages began to be applied to these mercantile and industrial corporations, the predecessors of the guilds.[26]

The Sources do not explicitly refer to the corporation by that name, but employ terms which convey the notion of a corporation. It appears that the strictly technical expression for the idea of corporation is *universitas personarum.*[27] Ordinarily the term *corpus* is used to denote a corporation and the word *corporati* is occasionally used to signify the same conception: "Cessante omni ambitione, omni licentia quingentorum sexaginta trium *collegiatorum* numerus maneat nullique his addendi mutandive vel in defuncti locum substituendi pateat copia, ita ut judicio tuae sedis sub ipsorum praesentia *corporatorum* in eorum locum, quos humani subtraxerint casus, ex eodem quo illi fuerant *corpora* subrogentur; nulli alii *corporatorum* praeter praedictum numerum per patrocinia immunitate concessa."[28]

The word *collegium* occurs thus: "Animadvertendum autem, quod praetor hoc edicto generaliter et in rem loquitur nec adicit a quo gestum: et ideo sive singularis sit persona, quae metum intulit, vel populus vel curia vel *collegium* vel corpus huic edicto locus erit."[29] This word occurs in the oldest known Roman corporation inscriptions.[30] Literally, (*con,* with, and *lego,* select), it meant an organiza-

[25] Bonfante, *Storia del Diritto Romano,* II, 21, 22.
[26] Walsh, *o. c.,* §115.
[27] *Dig.* 46, 47, 49; *Dig.* 2, 4, 10, 4.
[28] *Code* 4, 63, 5.
[29] *Dig.* 4, 2, 9, 1.
[30] Waltzing, *Etude historique sur les corporations professionelles,* III, 1.

tion of persons united for any common scheme.[31] At first, the term was used to indicate those loose voluntary organizations of persons which did not possess legal personality.[32] *Collegium* did not, therefore, always indicate that the organization possessed legal personality, thus, the early religious associations of the Romans were designated *collegia*,[33] and the first mercantile guilds were known by the same name, before there was any possibility that they were juridical persons. The name was retained, however, when these organizations did become juristic persons, and was eventually referable to all private and some quasi-public corporations.

The Justinian Sources refer to *societas* thus: "Mortuo reo promittendi et ante aditam hereditatem fide jussor accipi potest, quia hereditas personae vice fungitur, sicuti municipium et decuria et *societas*.[34] Industrial corporations even before their incorporation were designated as *societates*. References to *sodalitates* in the sense of clubs may be found in the Sources: "Mandatis principalibus praecipitur praesidibus provinciarum, ne patiantur esse collegia **sodalicia** neve milites collegia in castris habeant."[35] Mention is made of sodales: "**Sodales** sunt qui ejusdem collegii sunt: quam Graeci 'etaireian' vocant."[36] In Code 1, 2, 22 pr., *consortium* is spoken of: "Sancimus res ad venerabiles ecclesias vel xenones vel * * * si quid aliud tale *consortium* descendentes ex qualicumque curiali liberalitate sive inter vivos sive mortis causa sive in ultimis voluntatibus habita lucrativorum inscriptionibus liberas immunesque esse; lege scilicet, quae super hujusmodi inscriptionibus posita est, in aliis quidem personis suum robur obtinente in parte autem ecclesiastica vel aliarum domum, quae piis consortiis deputatae sunt, suum vigorem pietatis intuitu mitigantes."

[31] Pauly-Wissowa, *Real-Encyclopadie, collegium,* 380 seqq.
[32] Smith, *o. c.,* I, 470, *collegium.*
[33] Sherman, *o. c.,* II, §544.
[34] *Dig.* 46, 1, 22.
[35] *Dig.* 47, 22, 1 pr.
[36] *Dig.* 47, 22, 4.

There were various types of private corporations. The *collegia templorum*[37] were associations of religious persons, such as Vestal Virgins and Priests. Pagan Rome assigned a patron deity to each of its private corporation.[38] Artisans formed associations which were known as *collegia pistorum, naviculariorum* etc.[39] Political societies,[40] at first organizations for recreation and friendly intercourse, were later hot beds of conspiracy and political intrigue,[41] which necessitated drastic action by the government.[42] They were ultimately dispersed by a law of the Senate.[43] In the imperial period, the poorer classes organized mutual benefit associations which took the name of *collegia tenuiorum,* chiefly intended as a means of insuring the members decent burial.[44] But membership in these organizations was restricted so that a person could belong to only one of them. Dues were paid and monthly meetings held. They were open to noncitizens and even slaves who had permission from their respective masters.[45]

There is no express statement in the Sources, *Corpus Juris Civilis,* that these corporations were actually endowed with juridical personality. But it is a fact, in the opinion of Romanists, that the Roman jurists had been successful in making great strides in legal development and considered the *universitas* as a new subject in law, distinct from the individual incorporators taken either singly or collectively.[46] The Roman Sources afford numerous references which unmistakably indicate that the *persona moralis* existed, although the Roman law, avoiding definitions as it usually does, nowhere explicitly states the precise nature

[37] *Dig.* 32, 38, 6.
[38] Sherman, *o. c.*, II, §539.
[39] *Dig.* 3, 4, 1 pr.
[40] *Dig.* 47, 22, 1.
[41] Cicero, ad. Quint. Frat. ii, 3.
[42] Dernburg, *o. c.*, I, 99.
[43] Smith, *o. c.*, II, 979, *universitas.*
[44] *Dig.* 47, 22, 1 pr.
[45] Smith, *l. c.*
[46] Hohenlohe, *Papstrecht und Weltliches Recht,* 28.

of a corporation. But juridical personality is inferable from situations in which these corporate organizations exercised such personal rights and privileges as the right to sue and be sued, to contract, to own property and the like, in their own name, independently of the rights of the members by which the body was constituted:[47] "Si quid universitati debetur, singulis non debetur; nec quod debet universitas, singuli debent."[48] The Pandects even granted that it was possible for members to commit theft on corporate property.[49]

It is interesting, as well as useful, to examine the Sources themselves and analyze some of the rulings which have been formulated therein as to the law applicable to a given set of facts involving some corporate right. Suppose that a boatman died intestate and that he had no heirs. His property would go to the corporation and not escheat to the State: "Si quis navicularius sine testamento & liberis vel successoribus defunctus est: hereditatem ejus non ad fiscum, sed ad corpus naviculariorum, ex quo fatali subtractus est, deferri praecipimus."[50] The same law applied where a curial was concerned: "In testatorum curialium bona, si sine herede moriantur, ordinibus patriae eorum adipisci praecipimus."[51] In the case of artisans' corporations, it seems that the estates of intestate members without heirs were turned over to their fellow incorporators after the prior rights of creditors had been satisfied: "Si quis fabricensis sine liberis vel legitimo herede decesserit non condito testamento: ejus bona, cujuscunque summae sint, ad eos pertinere (sancimus) qui velut creditores decedentium attinentur, qui fisco pro intercepto respondere coguntur. Hoc enim facto contingit, ut Reipublicae ratio salva permaneat & fabricenses collegarum suorum solatiis perfruantur, qui damnis ac detrimentis retinentur ob-

[47] *Dig.* 3, 4, 7, 1.
[48] *Dig.* 40, 3, 1; Hohenlohe, *o. c.*, 29.
[49] Hohenlohe, *Papstrecht und Weltliches Recht*, 28.
[50] *Code* 6, 62, 1.
[51] *Code* 6, 62, 4.

noxii."[52] A legacy left to a corporation of professional men was held to be valid: "Si quis sacro senatui vel curiae civitatis vel officio, quod magnis potestatibus vel iis quae in provinciis sunt ministerium praebet, vel medicorum professorumve vel advocatorum corpori vel militibus vel ejusdem artis opificibus vel clericis vel uno verbo si cuicumque non illicito corpori quid relinquerit, valet relictum, et si quidem simpliciter collegii vel legionis mentionem fecerit."[53] Soldiers were not allowed to have organizations while under military discipline; this might be fatal to the security of the government. "Mandatis principalibus praecipitur praesidibus provinciarum, ne patiantur esse collegia sodalicia neve milites collegia in castris habeant."[54] Burial corporations could levy a monthly assessment: "Sed permittitur tenuioribus stipem menstruam conferre, dum tamen semel in mense coeant, ne sub praetextu hujusmodi illicitum collegium coeat."[55] In reference to churches (*ecclesiae*), asylums for foreigners (*xenones*), monasteries (*monasteria*), homes for the poor (*ptochotrophia*), asylums for foundlings (*brephotrophia*), for orphans (*orphanotrophia*) and old people (*gerontocomia*), it seems that Roman law was wont to protect the rights of these corporations, especially in the instance of legacies and inheritances: "Sancimus res ad venerabiles ecclesias vel xenones vel monasteria vel ptochotrophia vel brephotrophia vel orphanotrophia vel gerontocomia vel si quid aliud tale consortium descendentes ex qualicumque curiali liberalitate sive inter vivos sive mortis causa sive in ultimis voluntatibus habita lucrativorum inscriptionibus liberas immunesque esse."[56]

Although numerous other instances may be cited to demonstrate the recognition of the corporate conception in the Sources, yet it is not defined anywhere, nor do Roman jurists of any age speak of what are now called "juristic

[52] *Code* 6, 62, 5.
[53] *Code* 6, 48, 10.
[54] *Dig.* 47, 22, 1 pr.
[55] *Ibid.*
[56] *Code* 1, 2, 22 pr.

persons" by that name.[57] But they did recognize associations of persons which collectively as a group exercised rights and assumed duties which did not vest in the members as such but rather in the body. The expression "juristic person" or "juridical personality" was evolved by later law, but this idea was presented by such terms as *collegium, universitas, municipium,* and the like.[58]

The breadth of the corporate field is so large that it affords numerous classifications of juristic persons depending upon the angle from which they are contemplated. They may be distinguished according to their activity into public, such as the *fiscus, civitas, municipium, ecclesia* and the like, and into private, such as the *collegium tenuiorum* or *medicorum* and so forth. Numerous types of private corporations have been cited and explained above. If private corporations be considered from a different viewpoint, they may be divided into those with a public interest, such as the *gerontocoma* (old peoples' home) and private corporations with only a private interest, such as the *collegia tenuiorum.* But a far more important division is possible. This division is an outgrowth of a distinction according to the structure of the juristic person.

Of all the possible classifications, the structural distinction appears to be the most fundamental. This would divide the artificial person into two classes; first, the corporation, and secondly, the institution or foundation.[59] The institution was a public undertaking generally, while a foundation arose from goods devoted to private purposes of a charitable character.[60] Modern authors regard the former class as including those juridical persons which were constituted from a collectivity of physical persons, and they were known as *universitates personarum.* The latter were the result of a collection of goods, or property and

[57] Buckland, *Elementary Principles of Roman Private Law,* 56.

[58] Mitteis, *Römisches Privatrecht,* 339 seqq.

[59] Smith, *o. c.,* II, 980, *universitas.*

[60] Dernburg, *o. c.,* I, 94.

were called *universitates bonorum.*"[61] In general, corporations were organizations of natural persons which enjoyed the capacity to own property, enter into obligations and the like, as a municipality or *civitas,* while institutions were collections of property endowed with proprietary capacity, such as a hospital, orphanage and the like.

The historical background of the *universitas personarum* has been suggested above. It remains to discuss briefly the historical development of the institution. This type of juridical entity was not known as a legal person in the ante-Justinian law. Although at the time of Justinian there was springing up some kind of distinction between the corporation and the institution, yet before his time all juristic persons were known as corporations.[62] The institution had its origin, just as did the corporation, in the acticity of the Roman State. At the beginning of the Empire, the Emperors sanctioned charitable foundations to take care of the material needs of the poor children of Italy. Such State institutions were in fact the application of a portion of the *fiscus* to charity. In private law, citizens were unable to duplicate such an undertaking, but it was possible for them to deed or will property to an already existing corporation and in the bequest to make known the object for which the property was given. Such a bequest was in the nature of a quasi-foundation. There was an obligation upon such a corporation to dispose of the property in the manner prescribed by the donor, yet there was not created any new juridical personality. So far, then, as the earlier Empire was concerned, the only foundations recognized were State undertakings, functioning by grace of the Emperor.

But at the time of Justinian, the institution appeared in three forms: (1). There might be a *persona in individuo.* The institution was thought of as a fund administered by an individual person; and the connection between the in-

[61] Sohm-Ledlie, *o. c.,* 195.
[62] *Ibid.* 197.

dividual and the fund was necessary. This is indicated by the following quotation from the *Digest:* "Annuam pecuniam ad ludos civitati relinquit quibus praesidere heredes voluit: successores heredum negant se debere, quasi testator tamdiu praestari voluisset, quamdiu praesiderent heredes: quaero igitur an, cum praesidendi mentionem fecerit, ad tempus fideicommissum an perpetuo praestari volverit. * * *"[63] (2). The institution might have its *persona* in a corporation. The *bona* were left to a corporation which administered them, but the property was not thought of as capable of standing alone: "Quidem in testamento ita scripsit: reipublicae Graviscanorum lego in tutelam viae reficiendae, quae est in colonia eorum usque ad viam Aureliam: quaesitum est, an hoc legatum valeat * * * potest tamen videri tanta summa legata, quanta ei rei sufficeret: si modo non apparet aliam fuisse defuncti voluntatem aut ex magnitudine ejus pecuniae aut ex mediocritate facultatium, quam testatrix relinquit: tunc enim officio judicis, secundum aestimationem patrimonii et legati, quantitas definiri potest."[64] Or, (3). The institution might be a foundation in the strict sense, standing alone as an independent person. It is this notion of the institution at the time of Justinian which is not clear and certain. But it is evident that it was in the period of Justinian that juristic persons were gaining fuller maturity.

Institutions were not common in Rome before Christianity became the State religion, though by grace of the Emperor or Senate temples were allowed to inherit property in their own right.[65] It was in the later days of the Empire that foundations resulting from the generosity of private persons came to be regarded as foundations in the legal sense. Impetus was given to the creation of institutions by the favorable attitude of Constantine toward Christianity which fostered charitable and religious under-

[63] *Dig.* 33, 1, 6.
[64] *Dig.* 31, 30.
[65] *Ulp. Reg.* 22, 6.

takings.[66] These foundations continued to approach more and more the character of the *persona moralis.*

In the above description of the institution, it must be remembered that the theoretical position of later Romanists is assumed, who by close examination of the facts of the past have constructed a legal doctrine which they reasonably presume to have a basis in the Sources. At the period of Justinian, it was not yet possible to speak with assurance about the personality of the institution. The idea of the foundation was just arriving. The mentality of the lawyers of that epoch was just beginning to accept the conception of the institution as a separate entity. It was not possible at the time of Justinian to specify the elements of the foundation because the idea of this type of corporate entity was just starting and it was frequently not very clear whether it was distinct from the corporation. Under Roman law, legal thought developed the juridical personality in the field of the *universitas personarum,* chiefly, making the substratum of the legal person (*collegium*) a plurality of persons. As a matter of fact, it was actually Canon law which developed the theory of the *universitas bonorum,* personifying the common ideal end to which masses of property, money and land had been dedicated.[67]

Since the Church developed under Roman law, it is not surprising that ecclesiastical jurists took the idea of juridical personality from the Roman law,[68] and adapted it to their own needs. The Sources indicate that ecclesiastical organizations were given recognition as juridical persons under Justinian law and this was doubtless a vital factor in the development of juridical personality in the ecclesiastical law of that time. Just as in Roman law there were juridical persons based on individual physical persons and others resulting from accumulations of property, so too, there was a similar division in ecclesiastical law and the

[66] *Code* 1, 2, 23; 1, 3, 35, 46.
[67] Hohenlohe, *o. c.,* 29.
[68] Wernz-Vidal, *o. c.,* II, n. 26.

early history of the canonical juristic personality may be traced by considering the rise of the ecclesiastical *personae moralis* from these two viewpoints.

With respect to the Church under Roman law, the question arises whether it was a corporation or a foundation. The most reasonable answer to this is that the Church was considered a mixed type, so to speak, that is, it was a corporation or an institution, depending upon the particular point of view. If it was regarded as a collection of persons, and here reference is made not to the Universal Church but to individual congregations, then, under Roman law, the Church was considered a corporation. But if it was viewed as an administrator of property, in other words, not merely as a body of individuals, but as an aggregate of assets, and this conception was very possible, then, the Church might be deemed an institution.

In the following passage, the Church is referred to as a collection of persons and hence as a corporation: "Si quis sacro senatui vel curiae civitatis vel officio quod magnis potestatibus vel iis quae in provinciis sunt ministerium praebet, vel medicorum professorumve vel advocatorum corpori vel militibus vel ejusdem artis opificibus vel clericis vel uno verbo si cuicumque non illicito corpori quid relinquerit, valet relictum."[69] Again: "Habeat unusquisque licentiam sanctissimo catholicae venerabilique concilio decedens bonorum quod optavit relinquere."[70] But when the Church is spoken of here as a corporation, it is to be understood that the Church was regarded as a distinctive type of corporation, different in an essential feature from other Roman corporations. Although the Church as a corporation would be required to have a plurality of members, like other corporations, yet it did not need the approbation or approval of the State, since the State recognized the sovereignty of the Church. Other passages from the works of Justinian may be offered indicating that the Church was

[69] *Code* 6, 48, 10.
[70] *Code* 1, 2, 1.

often viewed as an institution, thus: "Ea enim, quae ad beatissimae ecclesiae jura pertinent vel posthac forte pervenerint, tamquam ipsam sacrosanctam et religiosam ecclesiam intacta convenit venerabiliter custodiri, ut, sicut ipsa religionis et fidei mater perpetua est, ita ejus patrimonium jugiter servetur illaesum."[71] But the treatment of the history of the canonical juristic personality will be undertaken in the following chapter.

[71] *Code* 1, 2, 14, 2.

CHAPTER III.

THE HISTORY OF THE CANONICAL JURISTIC PERSONALITY.

The Church Universal is a moral person by divine right. She has the inalienable right to establish inferior moral personalities as efficient mediums for the fulfillment of her divine mission, as effective instruments, therefore, for the accomplishment of all those ends, whether spiritual or temporal, which contribute to the accomplishment of the purpose divinely ordained.[1] This is fundamental. It is, therefore, not the purpose of the present chapter to show that the above conception was the result of an historical growth or evolution, or that the civil law by a gradual process was ultimately willing to concede such power to the Church, but rather to indicate, first, how this inalienable right, namely, moral and legal personality, was invariably insisted upon by the Church, and secondly, to show the variations in the recognition accorded this right by occidental civil law.

The idea of attributing personality to the Church as such, i. e., as applied to her as the mystical body of Christ existed at the very beginning of the Church.[2] The notion of mystical personality flowed from the thought that Christ is the Head of the Church, the faithful are its members, and His personality, as it were, pervades the Church, in the words of the Scriptures, "all days even unto the consummation of the world."[3] As early as 829, the Council of Paris[4] reflected St. Paul's theory of the mystical personality

[1] Cappello, *Institutiones Juris Publici Ecclesiastici*, I, 217.
[2] Cor. I, XII, 12; XII, 27; Eph. 1, 22, 23; 4, 16.
[3] Matt. XXVIII, 20.
[4] Mansi, *Collectio Conciliorum*, XIV, 537.

of the Church: "Primum igitur quod universalis sancta Dei ecclesia unum corpus manifeste esse credatur, ejusque caput Christus, apostolicis oraculis approbamus." The same view is thus expressed by Aquinas: "multi homines ex Adam derivati sunt tanquam multa membra unius corporis."[5]

A brief historical examination reveals that the Church not only claimed a mystical but also a moral personality. At the Church's inception, its Divine Founder conferred upon the Church all the requisites of such personality,[6] and the successors of Peter have universally upheld this right in their promulgations. Thus, the view of the inadequacy of a merely invisible unity, with resulting need for a visible monarch, the successor of St. Peter, was expressed by Gregory VII. The Papal Succession has been unanimous in its insistence upon the moral personality of the chair of Peter, and upon all the consequences which such personality implied. Among these consequences are, first, the right to employ the most perfect and effective form of human organization (the juristic person) to facilitate the work of evangelization, administration of the sacraments and the like, and secondly, the right to exercise a measure of temporal power, not a temporal power which would usurp the rightful province of the State, but one which was necessary for the fulfillment of the Church's divine mission. In the words of Cappello: "In rebus temporalibus quae vel per se vel per accidens necessariae sunt ad finem spiritualem, Ecclesia plenam exercet potestatem et societas civilis cedere debet."[7]

The universal claim of the Popes to exercise temporal power within such limitations, and its actual exercise is in the nature of an historical proof of the continued insistence by the Church upon its inalienable right to moral person-

[5] *Summa Theologica,* II, 1. q. 81. a. 1; cf. also III, q. 8. a. 1 and 2.

[6] *Infra* pp. 57, 58, 77.

[7] Cappello, *o. c.,* I, 217, prop. VI.

ality.[8] Innocent III in numerous places has emphasized the universality and thus the moral personality of the Church.[9] Thus, he wrote: "Quod non solum in Ecclesiae patrimonio, super quo plenam in temporalibus gerimus potestatem, verum etiam in aliis regionibus, certis causis inspectis, temporalem jurisdictionem casualiter exercemus."[10] The *unum corpus mysticum*" is referred to by Boniface VIII in his famous Bull, *Unam Sanctam,* of 1302,[11] in which he in substance stresses the moral personality of the Church, by declaring that all the faithful are under the Pope who exercises both spiritual and temporal power ("utrumque gladium habet"). The principle of Unity and hence of moral personality which was enunciated in the *Unam Sanctam* had been the view of all the predecessors of Boniface VIII, and his work was a re-statement of that principle.[12] The Bull *Unam Sanctam* has been here cited simply as an historical incident to show the existence of the Church's moral personality at that period, not for the purpose of illustrating the extent of the temporal power of the Church.[13]

Papal documents, therefore, suggest the historical background of the canonical juristic personality of the Church, in that they show that the Church was a corporate subject of rights and duties with the Papacy as the heart of the or-

[8] Gierke, *Political Theories of the Middle Ages,* notes 10, 11, 12. Gierke, however, fails to interpret the actually intended attitude of the Church toward the civil power at the period of which he treats.

[9] C. 34, X, *de electione et electi potestate,* I, 6; c. 6, X, *de majoritate et obedientia,* I, 33; c. 13, X, *de judiciis,* II, 1; c. 13, X, *qui filii sint legitimi,* IV, 17.

[10] C. 13, X, *qui filii sint legitimi,* IV, 17.

[11] C. 1, *de majoritate et obedientia,* VIII, 1 in Extrav. Comm.

[12] Cavagnis, *Institutiones Publici Ecclesiastici,* I, 215.

[13] Indeed, the Bull was written in reference to certain peculiar conditions of government in Medieval Western Europe and must be interpreted accordingly; cf. Kirsch, *Unam Sanctam* Catholic Encyclopedia, XV, 127. The "two sword" theory and the "two-headed monster" hypothesis (Gierke, *o. c.,* note 68) are simply analogies (Cavagnis, *o. c.,* I, 215), not exact statements of the Catholic theory of the relation between Church and State. (Cappello, *o. c.,* I, 217).

ganization.[14] And it was the Church Universal. founded by Christ, which profoundly influenced legal thought and from which were borrowed the legal elements of that type of juristic personality known as the institution.[15] It has been said that corporate jurisprudence in Medieval times was affected by the conception of mystical personality.

It is impossible to speak of the recognition of the personality of the Church Universal during the first three centuries of the Empire due to the illicit status which the Roman Emperors ascribed to the Church. But Constantine gave religious liberty to the Christians, and the Church became a *religio licita*[16] in the eyes of the Roman law, and began to exercise corporate rights both of a spiritual character, i. e., the Church was recognized as a perfect, sovereign society with the right to utilize *personae morales inferiores* for the spreading of the Gospel, administering the sacraments etc., and also corporate rights of a temporal nature, such as the holding of property and the like, through the medium of corporations and institutions. The exercise of such rights has continued although it was often necessary for the Church to make concordats with the State at various times: thus, the Concordat of Worms in 1122;[17] and the necessity has arisen many times subsequently, even up to the present time.[18] But the sovereignty of the Papacy and incidentally its legal personality is of necessity acknowledged by the State, when the latter in its sovereign capacity enters into a conventual agreement of this kind.

The Church Universal is not a person in the domain of private law; it has a personality in public law, otherwise the element of Catholicity would be taken away.[19] The historical background of the personality of the Church Uni-

[14] C. 6, X, *de electione et electi potestate,* I, 6.

[15] Hohenlohe, *o. c.,* 29.

[16] Kirch, *Enchiridion Fontium Historiae Ecclesiasticae Antiquae,* n. 314 seqq.

[17] *Raccolta Di Concordati tra la Santa Sede e le Autorita Civili,* 18, 19.

[18] AAS., XVIII, 279.

[19] Schulte, *Die Juristische Persönlichkeit,* 42.

versal has been suggested above. Such personality was of divine ordination; hence, it was absolute and admitted of no evolutionary change, with the progress of time, although there was an evolutionary transformation with reference to the recognition of this right by the civil authority. The Church having the nature of moral personality by direct, divine conference also possesses the right to establish what the *Codex Juris Canonici* now refers to as "ceterae inferiores personae morales."[20] History does not reveal an evolutionary growth of this conception; the right to create these inferior moral parsons, which then share in the divine character of the Church Universal is innate; but history evidences the first efforts of the Universal Church to exercise its divine right to establish these inferior moral persons, also the development of the outward form of such personalities and finally their recognition by the State.

With respect to the outward form of the juristic personality, it may be said that Canon law borrowed the idea of the *universitas personarum* from the Roman law and in turn stimulated the legal conception of the institution, also a product of Roman law but not extensively developed by the latter juristic scheme. Christianity introduced a social consciousness into the individualistic Roman law. This influence was reflected several centuries later upon the codification of Roman law by Justinian in the *Code* provisions for foundations and institutions to care for foundlings, the aged and the like.[21] The institution is, therefore, the most distinctively ecclesiastical type of juristic personality. Hence the origin and historical development of this form of juristic entity will be considered, from the Canonical, Roman, English, and American legal points of view respectively.

1. Canon Law. Common ownership of property was the rule among the early Christians. It belonged to no one

[20] Canon 100, §1.

[21] Hohenlohe, *o. c.*, 29.

Church. Indeed the early synods of Nice 325,[22] Ancyra 314,[23] Neo-Caesarea 314,[24] Constantinople 381,[25] and Ephesus 431[26] formulate no laws with regard to the regulation of Church property. But as soon as the early Christian Councils began to forbid the sale of Church property, except by episcopal action, the basis was laid for the erection of inferior canonical juristic personalities of the institutional type. These personalities were to facilitate the spiritual mission of the Church and also to assist her in her temporal affairs, which in turn were intended to subserve the spiritual. It was provided in canons 7 and 8 of the Synod of Gangrae 324[27] that the Bishop or one appointed by him shall have the right to dispose of Church property. The same is to be found in canons 24 and 25 of the Council of Antioch 340,[28] and canon 25 of the Oecumenical Council of Chalcedon.[29] The ecclesiastical Sources indicate that the Church exercised the right of holding and inheriting property.[30]

The Bishops as successors of the Apostles represented the Church Universal in their respective dioceses. With the spread of the Church, therefore, and the erection of bishoprics, there immediately arose dioceses, whose juridical essence from the very beginning consisted in this: that the territory and the faithful living in that territory were

[22] Mansi, *o. c.*, II, 637.

[23] *Ibid.* 513.

[24] *Ibid.* 539.

[25] *Ibid.* III, 521.

[26] *Ibid.* IV, 567.

[27] *Ibid.* II, 40.

[28] Mansi, *o. c.*, II, 65.

[29] *Ibid.* 1, 257.

[30] C. 1, 2, 3, X, *de precariis*, III, 14; c. 1, X, *de commodato*, III, 15; c. 1, 2, X, *de deposito*, III, 16; c. 1 to 7, X, *de emptione et venditione*, III, 17; c. 1 to 4, X, *de locato et conducto*, III, 18; c. 1 to 9, X, *de rerum permutatione*, III, 19; c. 1, 2, X, *de feudis*, III, 20; c. 1 to 8, X, *de pignoribus et aliis cautionibus*, III, 21; c. 1 to 5, X, *de fidejussoribus*, III, 22; c. 1 to 4, X, *de solutionibus*, III, 23; c. 1 to 10, X, *de donationibus*, III, 24; c. 1 to 20, X, *de testamentis et ultimis voluntatibus*, III, 26; c. 1 to 3, X, *de successionibus ab intestato*, III, 27; c. 1 to 14, X, *de sepulturis*, III, 28; c. 1 to 35, X, *de decimis, primitiis et obligationibus*, III, 30.

subject to the Bishop.[31] But the geographical division of the ecclesiastical territory was merely a matter of feasibility, and had nothing to do with the juridical character of the bishopric, which sprang rather from the fact that it constituted the domain where the Bishop exercised his episcopal duties. Nor did the existence of the faithful constitute the material element of the juristic personality of the diocese.[32]

The ecclesiastical Sources afford evidence that the bishopric was referable to the office and not to the bishop in his private capacity.[33] They are also explicit in showing that the Episcopal Church was a juridical personality with spiritual and temporal rights, the latter including ownership, inheritance and the like. Thus, in c. 16, X, *de foro competenti,* II, 2: "Conquestus est nobis (venerabilis frater noster) Bononiensis episcopus, quod potestas et commune Bononiense temporalem jurisdictionem, quae in * * * * * * quibusdam (aliis) castris et villis ecclesiae Bononiensis competit pleno jure, et in **cujus** quasi possessione fuisse acesse dignoscitur per violentiam usurpare praesumunt." It appears to be a valid legal interpretation that the Church in Bologna must have been personified to attribute to it possession, as Gregory IX did above, and the unity which legal personality always implies is clearly indicated by the use of the singular form, *cujus* which refers to ecclesiae, which in turn is considered as a juridical entity capable of exercising certain rights for the violation of which relief is sought. This passage also shows that the personified Church has rights in a *causa mixti fori,* namely, to be heard in a competent ecclesiastical tribunal, and to receive redress, a status enjoyed only by "persons."[34] The redress

[31] Schulte, *o. c.,* 29.

[32] Dernburg, *o. c.,* I, 99.

[33] C. 4, 5 (*Aquilejensis*), 18, 19 (*Capuana*), 20 (*Vigoriensis*), 23 (*Moguntina*), 25 (*Wintoniensis*) ecclesia, X, *de electione et electi potestate,* I, 6.

[34] Santi, *Praelectiones Juris Canonici,* II, 15.

sought was *per censuram ecclesiasticam.*[35] Numerous other passages may be cited to lend cumulative force to the above arguments.[36]

The diocese was the first instance of the ecclesiastical juristic person. There followed other forms, as the parish, cathedral chapter, and the *mensa episcopalis,* but these derived their personality from the position which they occupied toward the Bishop.[37] The system of ecclesiastical juristic personality was, therefore, greatly extended with the further growth of Christianity. Parishes arose and these too became complete juristic entities with capacity to exercise all necessary corporate rights. They were actually legal personalities in the strict sense, distinct from the Cathedral Church, yet obtaining their personality by virtue of their ecclesiastical relation to the Cathedral Church.[38]

Eventually, the *mensa episcopalis,* too, became distinct from the other property of the Cathedral Church.[39] The *mensa episcopalis* was the revenue for the support of the episcopal household, as distinguished from the *bona mensae episcopalis,* and the *bona fabricae ecclesiae.* It became personified with the development of ecclesiastical law.[40] The juridical personality of the *mensa episcopalis* is evident from a number of ecclesiastical documents,[41] which forbid Bishops to treat ecclesiastical property as their own, justifying such a regulation by reference to the Council of Car thage and the Canons of the Apostles.[42] Moreover, the Bishop as a private, physical person, was not the owner of these things, to judge from the form of oath which he took

[35] Schmalzgrueber, *Jus Ecclesiasticum Universum,* Tom. III, lib. II, tit. II, n. 1.

[36] Cf. c. 5, X, *de in integrum restitutione,* I, 41; c. 13, D. 28; c. 6, C. 16, qu. 3.

[37] Dernburg, *o. c.,* I, 99.

[38] Schulte, *o. c.,* 37.

[39] Schulte, *o. c.,* 39.

[40] *Ibid.* 48.

[41] Conc. Trident., sess. XXV, *de ref.,* c. 11, n. 1 and 2; Mansi, *o. c.,* I, 706; Waterworth, *Canons and Decrees of the Council of Trent,* 253 seqq.

[42] *Ibid.*

upon being consecrated: "Possessiones vero ad mensam meam pertinentes non vendam, nec donabo, neque impignorabo."[43] This limitation showed that no right to these things inhered in the Bishop as a physical person, but that the rights were vested in the personified *mensa episcopalis* for which the Bishop acted as representative, under the supervision of the Pope; and conversely, obligations against the *mensa episcopalis* were not referable to the Bishop as an individual person.[44] The Bishop, however, had the right of usufruct.[45]

Finally, the care of the poor came to be left to private enterprises, more or less distinct from the Cathedral Chapter, and so arose the various institutions, hospitals, asylums and the like.[46] This evolution was very gradual. It is, therefore, impossible to find any clear cut decrees or legal documents concerning the matter. Authors are disagreed as to whether the property belonged to the Church or to the institute.[47] These institutions were under the supervision of the Bishop. There were some institutions and foundations, however, which were exempt from his control, such as those under the direction of the Emperor, and certain other institutions which were only loosely united to the Church by virtue of the terms of the foundation.[48] The Council of Trent insisted that *piae causae* should be administered and supervised by the proper ecclesiastical authority, making allowance, however, for certain exceptions.[49]

[43] Schulte, *o. c.*, 48, note 21; cf. c. 2, *de religiosis domibus, ut episcopo sint subjectae*, III, II, in Clem.: providing for the reformation of the administration of hospitals and the actions of the rectors; c. 15, X, *de testamentis*, III, 26: where the personality of the institution is specifically mentioned and where the rights of the bishop are specified; c. 17, 20, X, *de testamentis*, III, 26; c. 11, 15, X, *de foro competenti*, II, 2; c. 26, X, *de verborum significatione*, V, 40.

[44] Schulte, *o. c.*, 50.

[45] C. 17, X, *de praebendis et dignitatibus*, III, 5.

[46] Dernburg, *o. c.*, I, 103; Schulte, *o. c.*, 39.

[47] Schulte *o. c.*, 40.

[48] *Ibid.* 55.

[49] To quote from Conc. Trident., sess. XXII, *de ref.*, c 8: recorded in Mansi, *o. c.*, I, 686: "Episcopi etiam tanquam sedis apostolicae delegati, in casibus a jure concessis omnium piarum dispositionum tam in ultima

II. Roman Law: From the viewpoint of civil law, the idea of legal personality seems to be associated always with the existence of an enduring medium which can permanently hold and administer property, i. e., in civil law tenure of property and legal personality seem to be correlative. Roman civil law may be said to have acknowledged the personality of the Church and its inferior moral persons as soon as the Church, as an enduring unit, was conceded the right to own and administer property and to protect that property by recourse to the proper tribunals.[50] After the Christian persecutions, Roman law was most favorable to the Church, admitting its right to control its own affairs (*res ecclesiasticae*); and also its capacity to make laws concerning them. Roman law, then, made no effort to intrude upon ecclesiastical legislation, for the Church was regarded as a sovereign juridical personality.[51] Roman law understood that if the Church was to fulfill her divine mission, she must not be hampered by the laws of the State.

Explicit legal approval was given the Church by the Edict of Licinius, which established the basis upon which

[50] Schulte, *o. c.*, 9.

[51] *Ibid.* 2.

---

voluntate quam inter vivos sint executores; habeant jus visitandi hospitalia, collegia quaecunque ac confraternitates laicorum, etiam quas Scholas sive quocunque alio nomine vocant, (NON TAMEN QUAE SUB REGUM IMMEDIATA PROTECTIONE SUNT, SINE EORUM LICENTIA) eleemosynas montis pietatis sive caritatis, et pia loca omnia, quomodocumque nuncupentur, ETIAM SI PRAEDICTORUM LOCORUM CURA AD LAICOS PERTINEAT, atque eadem pia loca exemptionis privilegio sint munita; ac omnia, quae ad Dei cultum aut animarum salutem seu pauperes sustentandos instituta sunt, ipsi ex officio suo juxta sacrorum canonum statuta cognoscant et exsequantur, non obstantibus quacunque consuetudine, etiam immemorabili privilegio aut statuto." Cf. Conc. Trident., sess. VII, *de ref.*, c. 15; Mansi, *o. c.*, I, 653 and Waterworth, *o. c.* 262; there directions are given as to what is to be observed in regard to hospitals, and by whom and in what manner the negligence of administrators is to be punished. Cf. also Conc. Trident., sess. XXII, *de ref.*, c. 11, recorded in Mansi, *o. c.*, I, 686; Sess XXII, *de ref.*, c. 6, in Mansi, *o. c.*, I, 686; Sess. XXV, *de ref.*, c. 4, in Mansi, *o. c.*, I, 707, and in Waterworth, *o. c.*, 259; Schulte, 55, 56, notes 39, 40. Pious undertakings were in most instances carried on by religious; cf. c. 1, 2, X, *de deligiosis domibus, ut episcopo sint subjectae,* III, 36.

recognition of the ecclesiastical legal personality was grounded. That personality was *ipso facto* admitted as soon as the State acknowledged the Church's capacity, as an enduring unit, to possess and administer property.[52] Thus, in both public and private law, the Church Universal in the former and its inferior moral persons in the latter, came to be recognized as juristic personalities in the law of Rome.

What specific historical evidence may be submitted to indicate that Roman law recognized the juristic personality of the diocese? Institutions, orphanages and the like in accordance with the prescriptions of Roman jurisprudence had their *oeconomi,* who were appointed by the Bishop. The *Novels* declare that these were representatives of the Bishop, to whom they must render yearly inventories.[53] The Roman Sources provided that the Bishop should appoint defenders,[54] and determine the annual expenses of the Church,[55] that he should act as judge in law suits pertaining to ecclesiastical property;[56] that he might enforce promises made to the Church or *pia causa*[57] bring action of *rei vindicatio,* and execute instruments made in favor of the Church. If a person willed property to the Church, it remained for the Bishop to determine to what particular Church it was to go.[58] The appointment of corporate administrators if not provided for in the bequest of the donor was entrusted to the Bishop.[59] If only the property was left, and no mention made of the management, the Bishop could appoint managers.[60] Should a donor appoint managers, but expressly prohibit the Bishop from administering the property, yet the Bishop would still have control.[61] In-

[52] *Ibid.* 37.
[53] *Nov.* 123, 23.
[54] *Nov.* 15, 1.
[55] *Code* 1, 2, 25, 6.
[56] *Code* 1, 4, 13.
[57] *Code* 1, 2, 15.
[58] *Code* 1, 2, 13; *Code* 1, 3, 27; *Code* 1, 3, 41.
[59] *Nov.* 131, 11.
[60] *Code* 1, 3, 45 pr.
[61] *Nov.* 131, 9.

deed, it was founders' attempts in certain cases to exclude the Bishop from any interference with charity that lead Justinian to enact a law that such a direction should not nullify the Bishop's right in general to supervise the administration. Schulte declares that in consideration of all these episcopal powers Roman law may be presumed to have regarded the diocese as a juridical entity.[62]

Roman law extended complete juridical personality to all ecclesiastical legal entities. Thus, the right to own and administer property was acknowledged.[63] Ecclesiastical institutions,[64] including *piae causae* had the right to inherit property, according to Roman law.[65] But foundations in the narrow sense, i. e., which were not referable to the Cathedral Church were not considered as juristic persons.[66]

Under Justinian law, the Church exercised complete jurisdiction with respect to the supervision, and administration of legacies, and over all those projects which were inherently ecclesiastical, as also over all those things that pertained to charitable undertakings, such as the *pia causa.* The Church represented all charities. As the State perceived that everyone trusted the Church, the State itself, therefore, reposed confidence in ecclesiastical management, and the Bishop, as the duly authorized representative of the Church, had the immediate control of the property.[67] In the later Empire, under Roman law, when property was willed or dedicated to some charitable purpose, such as the support or care of orphans, the infirm etc., there was at once automatically brought into existence a new subject of legal rights and duties, namely, the poor-house, or orphanage. But according to the viewpoint of Roman law, such charitable bequests were in the nature of ecclesiastical property, to the extent that these *piae causae* were under

[62] Schulte *o. c.,* 14.
[63] *Code* 1, 2, 11 to 13; *Code* 1, 3, 20 to 23.
[64] *Nov.* 123, 13.
[65] *Code* 8, 54, 34, 1.
[66] Schulte, *o. c.,* 22.
[67] Buckland, *A Text Book of Roman Law,* 179.

the control of the Bishop or his duly appointed representatives.[68] They were ecclesiastical institutions. Since the Church was recognized as such by the State, these institutions were civil also. The *pia causa* received its legal personality automatically, as it were, without any explicit conference by the authority of the State, simply by the founder's dedication of things of value to charitable uses, and *ipso facto,* its control was vested in ecclesiastical authority. Since both Church and State institutions were public, the above rule was in conformity with the theory that only public institutions could have a legal personality.[69]

Roman law, then, generally regarded all foundations *ad piam causam* as ecclesiastical institutions and did not recognize any that there were separate from Church and State. The personality of the ecclesiastical body was recognized, for the Church was regarded as a public corporate body. The founding of an institute or the willing of property to any definite purpose of an ecclesiastical or pious character was *per se* valid. If these wills demanded an executor he was under the supervision of the Church. In case a will was made for the purpose of founding a hospital, this was regarded by Roman law as an actual founding of the hospital, which was generally connected with religious orders.[70] The civil law of Rome extended the same unqualified recognition of legal personality to institutes for the sick, poor etc., as was given to those of a conventual or monastic type. Of course, some of these institutes exercised only limited legal privileges, and did not enjoy full legal personality.

Piae causae are usually under the civil law of the country in which they exist, except in those States which recognize the legal personality of the Church, so that *piae causae* are ecclesiastical institutes except in those countries where

[68] Sohm-Ledlie, *o. c.,* 198.

[69] *Ibid.*

[70] Schulte, *o. c.,* 57, note.

the civil law declares otherwise. The scarcity of Source references and private treatises on the subject of the private legal personality of such ecclesiastical bodies and undertakings under Roman law is attributable to the fact that the right of the Church in this respect was not questioned.

III. English Law. American jurisprudence is grounded upon the English common law; hence, it is advantageous to approach the status of the canonical juristic personality in the United States by examining its status in English law. The conception of the canonical legal personality found its way into England eventually. Indeed, it was largely through the influence of ecclesiastics and the Canon law that the principle of the corporation was made a part of the English common law.[71] The notion brought forward by the Catholic Church that the Church is Christ's mystical body has been credited with influencing profoundly legal thought in England, and with shaping the corporate mentality there among jurists.[72] Kent[73] admits that the principles of English corporate law were taken from the Romans and applied after the conquest of Britain by Rome, but ignores the influence of the Church, though somewhat inconsistently stating that the two main divisions of corporations in England were the ecclesiastical and lay. It is generally agreed that the conception of legal personality in modern jurisprudence is due to the influence of Canon law and ecclesiastics.[74]

Following Roman jurisprudence, the English common law conferred corporate charters first, upon municipalities, and secondly, upon such bodies as the trade-guilds.[75]

[71] Blackstone, *Commentaries,* I, 471; Walsh, *o. c.,* 20; Williston, *History of Business Corporations before 1800* in *Sel. Essays,* III, 197, 198; Brentano, *History of the Guilds.*

[72] Pollock and Maitland, *o. c.,* I, 479.

[73] Kent, *Commentaries,* II, 270.

[74] Pollock and Maitland *o. c.,* I, 489.

[75] Thus the Weavers' Guild became a corporation during the reign of Henry III, the Goldsmiths' in 1327, Mercers' in 1373, Haberdashers' in 1407, the Fish-Mongers' in 1433, Vintners' in 1437, the Tailors' in 1466. These were followed by the great international trading corporations of the 16th century.

The terms "corporation" and "body corporate" first appeared in public documents during the reign of Henry IV.[76] Before the time of Hobbes, reference was made to a *corpus morale et politicum* by John of Salisbury.[77] Common law jurists were confronted with the idea of the corporation definitely in the reign of Edward IV,[78] and the conception was precipitated by virtue of an ecclesiastical issue. Mere aggregations of men, such as townships and guilds were contrasted with incorporated communities of an ecclesiastical character, such as convents and chapters.[79] It became recognized in England that the Pope could incorporate friars and the like, and the idea was taken over by the common law which applied the same principles to mayors and communities.[80] But the anthropomorphic idea lingered in England, so that a "head" was required; thus, "the ideal person is not the Convent of St. Albans, the Chapter of Lincoln, the Commonalty of Norwich, but the Abbot and the Convent of St. Albans, the Dean and Chapter of Lincoln, the Mayor, Sheriffs and Commonalty of Norwich.[81] About 1429 the English common law seemed to be tending away from the juristic personality idea,[82] but it gradually reappeared, and this through the profound effect which Bracton made upon English jurisprudence.

Bracton was the contemporary of Innocent IV, who is generally credited with having been the first jurist to give final form to the corporate theory, and doubtless it was from him that Bracton acquired many of his principles of corporation law as applied in England. Before that time, it is doubtful whether the Italian jurists, though having the advantage of the *Corpus Juris Civilis* and parts of the *Cor-*

[76] Kent, *Commentaries,* II, 271, note.

[77] Pollock and Maitland, *o. c.,* I ,471.

[78] Year Book, Edward IV; case of Abbot of St. Benet's (Hulme) v Mayor and Commonalty of Norwich, four times reported, Y. B. 21 Edw. IV f. 7, 12, 27, 67.

[79] Y. B. 20 Edw. IV. f. 2 (Pasch. pl. 7).

[80] Y. B. 14 Hen. VIII, f. 3 (Mich. pl. 2).

[81] Pollock and Maitland, *o. c.,* I, 474.

[82] Y. B. 8 Hen. VI, f. 1 (Mich. pl. 2).

pus Juris Canonici had a complete notion of the *universitas,* as it is now understood by Romanists. It was actually the canonists of the 13th century that were making a definite, conscious legal distinction between the *societas* and the *universitas,*[83] between the partnership and the corporation. Bracton, commonly referred to as England's greatest lawyer, was an ecclesiastic, well versed in ecclesiastical law and well acquainted with the writings of the Roman lawyers and the Canonists, "from whom he adopted greater helps than the language in which they wrote."[84] He works out the corporate conception of the *universitas* by following the reasoning of the Justinian Institutes,[85] though he has been criticized for trying to adapt Roman law to English society which differed materially from that of the Romans.[86] And he prefers to exclude ecclesiastical organizations from the notion of the *universitas.*

The canonical legal personality played an important role upon the stage of English history. Aethelbert, at an early date, referred to "God's property and the Church's twelvefold."[87] There was thus springing up in England a recognition of canonical personality on the theory that the property was held by the Saint or by God Himself in a fictitious way. This may be gleaned from the tone of the Anglo-Saxon charters and Domesday Books.[88] These bring out that the same situation was developing in legal circles in England as was going on upon the continent, namely, the Bishop's See was becoming personified and regarded as capable of exercising both spiritual and temporal rights of a corporate character.[89]

Then the juristic conception of the parish grew, with the

[83] Pollock and Maitland, *o. c.*, I, 477.

[84] Reeves' *History of English Law,* II, 359—Finlason.

[85] *Institutes*, 2, 1, 6.

[86] Pollock and Maitland, *o. c.*, I, 479.

[87] *Ibid* 481.

[88] *Ibid.*, referring to D. B. i, 121; D. B. ii, 416b.

[89] Thus the Bishop of Exeter held property as a representative of his See, and the Episcopal Church of Worcester is recorded to have held property, D. B. i, 164b.

rector merely an administrator. As far back as 1307, the principle was stated in the following judgment: "The Church is always under age and is to be treated as an infant and it is not according to law that infants should be disinherited by the negligence of their guardians or be barred of an action in case they would complain of things wrongfully done by their guardians while they are under age."[90] The Church in the above passage is referred to as a legal personality. The right of *restitutio in integrum* conceded the Church was a distinctive and important characteristic of such personality.

The Canonical Sources deal with the question of alienation of Church property by Bishops in England,[91] and the principles therein enunciated are given full force in the temporal courts of the time.[92] The juristic personality of the Episcopal Sees was extended to apply in the case of Abbeys, convents and the like.[93]

Later on, the ecclesiastical groups in England became less and less powerful, and Common law began to overshadow Canon law. This change was beginning in England, long before the so-called Reformation. Yet Common law jurists still kept in mind the vital distinction between the civil and canonical corporation, in that the latter might be created by the Church without reference to the State. Mortmain statutes were springing up as early as 1217 with the promulgation of a charter[94] to prevent the enjoyment of certain immunities by those dealing with religious houses.[95] The resolutions of the Oxford Parliament of 1258 and the Provisions of Winchester in 1259, the latter being

[90] Pollock and Maitland, *o. c.*, I, 484.

[91] Cc. 1, 2, 3, X, *de his, quae fiunt a praelato sine consensu capituli,* III, 10.

[92] Pollock and Maitland, *o. c.*, I, 485.

[93] *Ibid.* 486.

[94] Charter 1217, c. 43.

[95] "Mortmain statutes of medieval England were intended to keep lands from accumulating in the possession of the Church. The great nobles lost certain services and charges when a landed estate became the property of a religious order or corporation" . . . . Desmond, *The Church and The* Law, 36.

incorporated into the Statute of Marlborough in 1267 and thereby given legal authority, were the forerunners of the more important Statute 7 of Edward I, "De Viris Religiosis" which ended alienations in mortmain.[96] In 1279, Edward III followed this statute with further penalties against ecclesiastical liberty in England by the Statute 40 Edward III.[97] Severe restrictions were imposed upon ecclesiastical corporations in England by Richard II by *praemunire* statutes. About the time of Henry V, the persecutions resulted in the escheating of all lands held by ecclesiastical corporations of foreign monks.[98] Wholesale confiscations of Church property belonging to ecclesiastical corporations and subsequent suppression followed from the break of Henry VIII with Rome.[99] With the separation of England from the Church, it became necessary for religious legal personalities to obtain the Crown's consent: "They might build churches without the king's license, yet they could not erect a spiritual body politic to continue in succession and capable of endowment without the King's consent."[100]

IV. American Law. The conception of corporation law in the United States is traceable to the English common law. And just as the legal personality in English jurisprudence was designated a "corporation,"[101] so likewise in the United States. But there is a difference of opinion as to whether there exists in this country a counterpart of the English ecclesiastical corporation in reference to the organizations incorporated in the different states for religious purposes.[102] The status of the canonical juristic personality in the United States will be taken up later.[103] Suffice it to say here that the canonical legal personality is

[96] Pollock and Maitland, *o. c.*, 1, 315.
[97] Blackstone, *Commentaries,* IV, 108.
[98] Blackstone, *Commentaries,* IV, 112, 113.
[99] *Ibid.* 435.
[100] Coke, *Institutes of the Laws of England,* III, 202.
[101] Blackstone, *Commentaries,* I, 468; Kent, *Commentaries,* II, 267.
[102] *Pro:* Kent, *Commentaries,* II, 274; *contra:* Augustine, *o. c.,* II, 2.
[103] *Infra* chapters VII, VIII, IX.

not recognized as such in the United States; that is, unless it is incorporated like non-religious corporations by recourse to the proper statutes.[104] The history of the canonical legal personality in the United States is the record of the attempts of the Church to reconcile its juridical scheme of corporate law with the regulations of the State in this matter, and to secure ecclesiastical holdings and properties in the most effective and efficient manner, by incorporating differently in the different states. Catholics in this country have established Church corporations in different ways at different times and depending upon the particular jurisdiction involved. This will be considered in a subsequent chapter.[105]

[104] Taunton, *The Law of The Church,* 310.
[105] *Infra* Chapter IX.

CHAPTER IV.

THE METAPHYSICAL CONCEPTION OF THE CANONICAL JURISTIC PERSONALITY.

Some human societies exercise certain transcendent legal rights. These organizations are generally called juridical persons or corporations, although during the past century the expression "moral person" was usual to indicate this transcendent element i. e., lying beyond the material world.[1] A juridical person is one that is not composed of flesh and blood but elevated in some way above the material and physical; yet it is a *capax* before the law, a subject of legal rights and duties. But the sharpest difference of opinion prevails among the authorities as to just what constitutes the basis of this juridical entity, a subject not identical with either the incorporated members in the case of a corporation, or the accumulation of property in the instance of an institution. Whether there is a fiction merely, or something else has been and still is a controversy among jurists.[2] They may be classified according to their theories on this subject into three great camps, the Fictionalists or Nominalists, Realists and Canonists, although there are various intermediate positions, so that the gradation is almost as imperceptible as that of the colors of a spectrum.

I. The Fiction Theory. The philosophical controversy with regard to the metaphysical basis of the juridical personality was precipitated by Savigny[3] and Brinz[4] in Germany, in the first part of the nineteenth century. They brought forward the fiction theory, which was championed

[1] Dernburg, *o. c.*, I, 95.

[2] Wernz-Vidal, *o. c.*, II, n. 27.

[3] Savigny, *System des heutigen römischen Rechts*, II, 235, seqq.

[4] Brinz, *Die juristischen Personen*, 1052 seqq. Cf. *Lehrbuch der Pandecten.*

by Josef Unger[5] in Austria, and generally accepted in France, England and the United States.[6] This form of legal philosophy was widely discussed during the last century by jurists in their effort to come to a better understanding of the nature of the legal personality.[7] Indeed, the theory continues to have its defenders up to the present time. The arguments included reasoning which involved the whole gamut of *universals,*[8] though according to Hohenlohe[9] the philosophical struggle between the Nominalists and Realists in the general field of metaphysics had nothing to do with the question of juridical personality.

What is the fiction theory of Savigny?[10] He would require for the existence of the juristic person a *fundamentum* (*universitas personarum vel bonorum*) upon which the Legislator might construct a fictitious subject of rights and duties.[11] From the observation that it was possible in law for a corporation to possess property which did not belong to the individual members, he concluded that such property could only belong to a fictitious being and not to a reality.[12] For he reasoned that a will was necessary for ownership, but since a non-rational being like a corporation was actually without a will, the law simply presumed one by a legal fiction.

[5] Unger, *System* I, §44 seqq.

[6] Machen, Jr., 24 *Harvard Law Review* 255.

[7] Dernburg, *o. c.*, I, 95. The controversy has been so protracted that the bibliography is immense; to quote a few of the more modern works: Binder, *Das Problem des juristischen Persönlichkeit* (Leipzig, 1907); Hölder, *Natürliche und juristische Personen* (Leipzig, 1905); Meurer, *Die juristische Personen* (Stuttgart, 1901); Mayer, *Die juristische Personen und ihre Verwertbarkeit im öffentlichen Recht* (Tübingen, 1908); Schwabe, *Die juristische Person und das Mitgliedshaftsrecht* (Basel, 1900); *Rechtssubject und Nutzbefugnis* (Basel. 1901); *Die Körpershaft mit und ohne Persönlichkeit* (Basel, 1904); De Vareilles-Sommières, *Les Personnes Morales* (Paris, 1902); Michoud, *La Théorie de la Personnalité Morale* (Two volumes, Paris, 1906, and 1909): Pic, *Sociétés Commerciales,* Vol. I, title II, ch. 1 (Paris, 1908); Ferrara, *Le Persone Giuridiche* (Naples, 1907–1910); Barillari, *Sul Concetto della Persona Giuridica* (Rome, 1910).

[8] Hohenlohe, *o. c.*, 24.

[9] *Ibid.*

[10] Savigny, *l. c.*

[11] Wernz-Vidal, *o. c.*, II, 27, note 11.

[12] Machen, *l. c.*

It was not long after Savigny had given to the world his fiction theory of the legal person that another school arose in Germany headed by Brinz[13] who claimed that such an entity was indeed a fiction, but his conclusion was reached by a different process of reasoning. Accepting the hypothesis of Savigny that the legal person was a mere name or fiction, Brinz taught that the distinction between a physical and a moral person was fictitious intrinsically, for it was unreasonable to think of rights and duties existing in something which does not exist. He therefore rejected the notion of a juridical personality. He asserted that a person was not necessary for the exercise of rights which are always referable to something, *ad aliquid.* Hence the property in a corporation was not owned by any person.[14] In place of a legal person, he would substitute a *patrimonium ad aliquem scopum,* a *Zweckvermögen,* in which situation there would be debt without debtor, credit without a creditor, ownership without an owner. The arguments from the Canonical Sources, however, by which Savigny endeavors to sustain his theory may be rebutted. The Savigny hypothesis, moreover, seems to be unsound in theory and undesirable in practice. The fiction theory of Brinz is contradicted by legal experience.

A. THE CANONICAL ARGUMENTS OF SAVIGNY MAY BE REBUTTED. The development of the notion of legal personality has been largely the work of Canonists. The Canonical Sources with respect to the juristic person eclipse all that civil jurisprudence can offer in depth and comprehension. The metaphysical basis of legal personality, therefore, may be discussed most effectively from the viewpoint of Canon law, which contains a strongly theological and philosophical element by virtue of which it surpasses even Roman law in metaphysical depth, though perhaps inferior to the latter in point of form.

Savigny recognized this when he endeavored to show that

[13] Brinz, *l. c.*

[14] *Ibid.*

his fiction theory was in conformity with the teachings of Canon law. Savigny claimed that Innocent IV, before his elevation to the Papacy Sinnabaldus Fieschi, was the father of the fiction theory.[15] While the exponents of this form of juridical philosophy declare that it is derivable from the Sources of Canon law, the opponents of the school insist that the theory can not be justified thereby. Innocent IV formulated his doctrine of the moral person in his *Apparatus in quinque libros Decretalium.*[16] In that production, he stated the following legal doctrine: "Cum collegium in causa universitatis fingatur una persona, universitas, sicut et capitulum populus, gens et hujusmodi, nomina sunt juris et non personarum."[17]

It is this passage that is used by Savigny and the Fiction School to prove that the fiction theory is of Canonical origin. But the anti-Nominalists deny that this passage is evidence that Innocent IV intended to go on record as presenting the fiction theory. The commentary in question related to c. *Praesentium* 57, X, *de testibus et attestationibus,* II, 20. But in the *Corpus Juris Canonici* there are only 56 chapters under II, 20 of the *Decretals of Gregory IX,* and number 57 discussed by Innocent IV is to be found in *Corpus Juris Canonici,* c. 2, *de testibus et attestationibus,* II, 10 in VI, Joannes Andreae stating that the Decretal was changed from its original place.[18] From this latter passage, it appears that a dispute had arisen between two convents and Gregory IX had written to the Archbishop of Rouen asking for an oath with reference to the truth of the affair from both Superiors: "in nomine suo et in animas conventuum eorundem vel majoris et sanioris partis ipsorum," and requesting further evidence, such as mutual views upon the matter and the like. But there is nothing in the passage to show that there was a *verum et distinctum juris sub-*

[15] Hohenlohe, *o. c.,* 24.

[16] This epoch-making commentary on the *Decretals of Gregory IX* first appeared in 1477, Strassburg, and later in 1570, Venice.

[17] Vermeersch, *Periodica,* t. 5, (21).

[18] *Ibid.*

jectum which must be shown by the Nominalists, for the anti-Nominalists may admit that a *universitas* (*collegium*) is a society of individuals so bound together that from many persons there arises as it were one person or one *corpus;* and the statement of Kahl in his *Lexicon, voce* "collegium": "We imagine a *collegium* to be a certain person produced from many persons" may be admitted by the anti-Nominalists; also that what pertains to the *collegium* pertains not to the members as individuals but as a collectivity.[19] But this does not prevent the anti-Nominalists from opposing the idea that there was ever recognized either in Canon or Roman laws a society of individuals forged by law into a person entirely distinct even from the collectivity or totality of the members. Vermeersch insists that Innocent IV did not intend to describe the *universitas* as a fiction, since the above passage emphasized the idea of unity (*UNA*), and not the quality of *persona*.[20] Innocent IV declared that abbeys and convents can swear through one procurator because the *collegium* is one person, adding: "Cum collegium in causa universitatis fingatur UNA persona, dignum est quod per unum jurent." Again: "licet per se jurare possint," so that the procurator represents not the *subjectum* as though it were a fiction, but the persons constituting the *collegium*. If the *persona* to which Innocent refers were actually fictitious, then, there would be no need of his using the adjective *una*, for unity would then be unescapable. Innocent IV states that the abbot and prior are distinguishable from the rest of the members not because they are the *domini* of the property, but because they are its representatives. But at the end of the passage, he leaves it to the convent whether it shall act through a procurator or through itself, either in the collective or in the individual names of the monks, thereby indicating that the totality of the monks constitutes the *universitas*.[22]

[19] *Ibid.*
[20] *Ibid.*
[21] *Ibid.*
[22] Vermeersch, *o. c.*, t. 5, (22).

The above is the reasoning of Vermeersch. Ruffini[23] also takes exception to the validity of the interpretation which Savigny placed upon the commentary of Innocent IV and upon which Savigny endeavored to ground his contribution to legal thought in the domain of the corporate theory. Gierke[24] also maintains that Savigny's theory is not in accord with the true intent of Innocent IV.[25] But Hohenlohe in attacking the fiction theory of Savigny suggests[26] that neither Ruffini nor Gierke actually considered the principal fallacy of Savigny, namely, that Canon Law never regarded the juridical person as a mere shadow. Hohenlohe[27] supports the opinion of Vermeersch[28] that the juridical personality is an unfortunate invention of Savigny which has no foundation in the Canonical Sources.

B. The Fiction Theory of Savigny Seems To Be Unsound In Theory. Opponents of Savigny's theory, as Hohenlohe, declare that he was a reactionary adopting a type of legal philosophy which was based on his dislike for the great corporate bodies of medieval development and which sought to reconcile the work of the French Revolution with severe absolutism, a form of thought tinctured with Kantian individualism, grazing the ideals of Rousseau and the Revolution by emphasizing the freedom and sacredness of ethical personality but at the same time tearing down one of the chief bulwarks of freedom, i. e., the right of free association which was placed under the arbitrary dominion of the State.[29] Ruffini shows that it was Savigny who narrows the juridical person so as to have it possess merely property rights, as distinguished from its capacity to exercise wide, public rights; these were to belong exclusively to the State.[30]

[23] Ruffini, *La classificazione delle persone giuridiche in Sinnibaldo dei Fieschi* (*Innocenzo IV*), II, 313 seqq.

[24] Gierke, *Das deutsche Genossenschastsrecht,* III, 521 seqq.

[25] Hohenlohe, *o. c.,* 29.

[26] *Ibid.*

[27] *Ibid.* 25.

[28] *o. c.,* t. 5, (22); *Supplementa et Monumenta,* VI, (99).

[29] Dernburg, *o. c.,* I, 95; Hohenlohe, *o. c.,* 30, 31.

[30] Hohenlohe, *o. c.,* 30, 31.

Julius Binder[31] also takes the position that Savigny was in no small measure influenced by the philosophy of Kant; thus, Savigny, like Kant, maintains that the end of right lies in the protection of the ethical personality of man and that the end of right is realized by protecting the freedom of the citizen. Both Kant and Savigny consider right as the means by which the will of one individual harmonizes with the will of another also free. This is the basis of Savigny's doctrine that "right is only for man, indeed only for the single man."[32] But he observed large corporate bodies, as convents and monasteries, which also enjoyed rights. The existence of these he could explain, therefore, only by supposing a creative act of the State,[33] which formed artificial men out of nothing. Hence, the whole right of corporate association is put under the power of the State. Educational, charitable, and even ecclesiastical institutions thus become State institutions, a situation tantamount to State Absolutism, which is an undesirable form of State tyranny.

Savigny's conception of the purpose of law was too restricted; for the protection of the ethical personality of man is only one of the many functions and purposes of law. There are many other aims and among these is the promotion of the welfare of society, a natural unit, by fostering the natural rights of free association, and hence corporate association, since the organization can best achieve its end by this superior type of union. Law has a triple mission, i. e., the effecting of legal, distributive, and commutative justice.[34]

C. THE FICTION THEORY OF SAVIGNY APPEARS TO BE UNWISE IN PRACTICE. It is not practical. Its application produces unjust consequences and focuses too much power in the State. The reason in general is that if the corporate entity is admitted to be a mere

[31] Binder, *Das Problem der juristischen Persönlichkeit,* 9 seqq.
[32] Hohenlohe, *o. c.,* 31.
[33] Dernburg, *o. c.,* 1, 95.
[34] Hohenlohe, *o. c.,* 31.

"fiction" or shadow, it must be the creature of the State, and if the State has the power to create, it likewise has the power to destroy. The door is thereby opened to arbitrary and wanton confiscation of Church property by the State, through an escheating process, and there may be a repetition of what was done during the French Revolution, and at various other times.[35] Hence, Vermeersch in his work, *"Le Belge et la personne civile,"* opposes the fiction theory of the legal personality in Belgium on the ground that such a theory denies existence to religious orders and societies. Both Hohenlohe and Vermeersch maintain that it was this erroneous legal philosophy which produced the anomalous juridical situation in Belgium, Italy and France whereby certain ecclesiastical corporate bodies have been *de jure* abolished, and yet exist *de facto*. The fiction theory was used as the basis of the arguments of the three great leaders of Masonic Liberalism in Belgium, namely, Laurent,[36] Frère Orban [37] and Orts,[38] who claim [39] that these orders have absolutely no right to existence since the State has *de jure* destroyed the corporate "fiction"; that the property thereby become *res nullius,* or common property which must escheat to the State; that re-organization is impossible since the law has forbidden trustees (*persone interposte*)[40]; and finally, that juridical personality is necessary for the functioning of all organizations created for ideal ends, necessary for the capacity to inherit, make contracts and the like. The anomaly is produced by the position of those other jurists who admit the *de facto* existence of these suppressed ecclesiastical organizations by virtue of a *contractus innomminatus.*[41]

[35] Hohenlohe, *o. c.,* 26.

[36] Laurent, *L'Église et l'État en Belgique,* t. III; *Principes de droit civil,* 298; XI, 161, 180, 189, 279; XXVI, 186a, 207.

[37] Frère Orban, *La main morte et la charité.*

[38] Orts, *De l'incapacité civile des Congrégations religieuses.*

[39] *Ibid.*

[40] Hohenlohe, *o. c.,* 27.

[41] *Ibid.* 28.

THE FICTION THEORY OF BRINZ IS CONTRADICTED BY LEGAL EXPERIENCE. The theory of Brinz may be attacked by bringing forward the objection that there are certain juridical persons which do not even possess a *patrimonium,* (such as the *universitas personarum*) at times. But these could not be explained by the *Zweckvermögen* theory of Brinz. Yet the *universitas personarum* may enjoy all the rights and privileges of a person, even the capacity of subsequently acquiring a *patrimonium,* in direct refutation of the principle that it is the *patrimonium ad aliquem scopum,* that is incorporated.[42] True, the property of all legal personalities is dedicated to a specific purpose but his conclusion is too broad, for this dedication necessarily implies also a peculiar trust relationship, conferring, as it does, upon physical persons the power of exercising certain rights. It may be suggested that the enduring character of the purpose to which the donor, though now deceased, has dedicated property and which is personified in the case of the non-collegiate type of juristic person arises, as it were, from the legal fictional extension of the physical personality of the deceased; this thought is ultimately referable to the innate belief in the immortality of the soul.

II. The Theory of the Realists. Gierke,[43] as the leader of the diametrically opposite type of reasoning, asserted that the juridical entity is a Reality. It may be mentioned that Gierke views Innocent IV as a Nominalist, thus sustaining the view of Savigny, and considers the Canonists of medieval times in their speculations over the character of the *universitas* also as Nominalists. But Gierke takes a position in direct contrast with the Nominalists and Savigny. "Whatever the Roman '*universitas*' may have been * * * and Dr. Gierke is for pinning the Roman jurists to Savignianism * * * our German Fellowship is no fiction, no symbol, no piece of the State's machinery, no collective name for individuals, but a living organism and

[42] Wernz-Vidal, *o. c.,* II, 27, note 11.

[43] Gierke, *l. c.*

a real person, with body and members and a will of its own. Itself can will, itself can act; it wills and acts by the men who are its organs as a man wills and acts by brain, mouth and hand. It is not a fictitious person; it is a '*Gesamme-person*' and its will is a '*Gesammtwille*'; it is a group person and its will is a group will."[44] Gierke considers the State, for instance, a living thing.[45] Thus, the corporate personality is, as it were, analogous to that of an oriental idol.

The principal objection to the realistic theory is that it tends to a *reductio ad absurdum.* This very thing happened among Gierke's disciples who carried the theory far beyond what Gierke had intended, and made the entity almost an actuality, a corporate organism like an animal or human being. It is true that these various anthropomorphic conceits were not the original intention of Gierke, but they were logical consequences. Moreover, if the juridical personality is a living thing and has a will, it would be possible to hold a corporation liable for murder and various other crimes which is evidently contrary to the general conception of jurists. Zitelmann[46] went so far as to attribute such a will to the legal person.

III. The Modern Canonical Theory of the Juridical Person. The proponents of this school[47] incline to the theory of social necessity calling into existence certain groups of a social character, which exist by virtue of the natural law. These organizations, such as the corporation, alone can adequately administer property toward the realization of ends which transcend the scope of the individual man. Such juridical persons are not actual, not apparent to the senses, but neither are they mere fictions, unreal entities, but rather representations of real things. The fiction in the mind is referable to the actual fact. Such is the opinion of Wernz.[48] Dernburg also

[44] Gierke, *Political Theories of the Middle Ages, Translator's Introduction,* xxvi.

[45] Hohenlohe, *o. c.,* 36.

[46] Machen, *l. c.*

[47] Cf. such authors as Wernz, Dernburg, Hohenlohe, Schulte, etc., etc.

[48] Wernz-Vidal, *o. c.,* II, 27, note 11.

reasons that certain organizations and undertakings must have the right of acting as units with the right to possess property, to sue and be sued, to enjoy rights and to be subject to duties in order to bring about the fullest development of human society. Evidently legal persons are not physical, but that does not mean that they are unrealities. They are rather representations, since fiction and actuality unite by a process of reasoning to form the concept known as the juridical personality. The reality arises by virtue of the representative character of the juridical entity.[49]

Hohenlohe argues that the legal person is an amorphous body deriving its existence through the *rei rationabilis substantia,* as Johannes Andrea defines a person, through its ability to exercise rational powers, and not through any creative act of the State. Only the individual man and men considered as a group can be the subject of law and right; the animal is only the object of law. Hence, the metaphysical basis of the juridical personality springs from the natural right of man to form associations and lies in the philosophical concept of the relations of the individuals to the union, and since these relations are real, the moral person must be a reality, and not a mere fiction.[50]

Legal personalities are, therefore, *entia rationis cum fundamento in re.* Hohenlohe maintains that it is in this sense that the *mere nomen juris* of Innocent IV is to be understood when he refers to the *universitas.* By way of example, "forest" designates trees which in varying sizes and kinds cover a certain area of lands. "State" refers to human beings who dwell in a fixed territory, with certain definite relations to each other, and under a sovereign power. "Paternity" indicates the relation of a father to his children. All these concepts are neither fictitious nor yet actualities, i. e., tangible things. The concepts of State, forest, paternity are actualized in the individual State, forest, father, but the concepts are generalized to express

[49] Dernburg, *o. c.*, I, 96.

[50] Hohenlohe, *o. c.*, 33.

mental relationships, and in that process become realities, but never fictions.[51] Hence, it is incorrect to say that the great medieval societies, cities, guilds and corporations received their corporate life by civil creative acts, without reference to a *fundamentum in re,* and the word "creative" necessitates the exclusion of such a *fundamentum.* It was not in the sense of Savigny that Church officers exercised power in the erection and control of convents and the like. The action of Rome in such foundations is analogous to the act whereby a donee receives a *donatio sub modo.* The former theory in this respect, now a part of the New Code of Canon Law[52] was that various Church institutions were independent subjects of rights and duties, so that if one of these bodies was dissolved the property went to the immediately higher ecclesiastical moral person. The thought that what is in the Church is all ecclesiastical property simply meant that it is all included under the same general administration. But at no time was the property of a dissolved ecclesiastical legal personality considered as *bona vacantia* with reference to the whole Church, a situation which contradicts the theory of Savigny; thus, the Holy See did not claim the property of the French society Sillon upon its dissolution by Rome.[53]

The basic contention of the modern Canonical school, and it seems most reasonable, is that the creative act of the State is not necessary for the establishment of the juridical entity. Hence, this entity is something more than a mere fiction. St. Thomas writes that right is the moral claim to one's own, and that one's own is "*quod ad utilitatem cujusvis dirigitur.*"[54] The scholastic conception has always been that natural rights are not the result of civil legislation, and that man's legitimate development in society is not exclusively produced thereby, since natural rights precede positive civil laws. But if this is true of the

[51] *Ibid.* 34.

[52] Canon 1501.

[53] Hohenlohe, *o. c.,* 53.

[54] *Ibid.* 32.

single individual, *a fortiori,* it must be true of a group of individuals. Schulte maintains that it was not the view of the Romans that the juridical entity was a mere fiction.[55] For there was no positive law in Roman jurisprudence which conferred personality; hence, its silence indicated that the metaphysical basis of the juridical entity existed in something other than the positive act of the State. The presumption that the creative act of the State was necessary is not only of modern origin but seems to be illogical and in keeping with the tendency of the modern State to assume more and more power. Of course, the modern State may so enact its law that today so far as the State is concerned there will exist no corporate entity except by the State's positive act. But that does not change the fact that in Roman law as soon as the State's approval was given expressly or impliedly, there arose immediately an independent personality. The only limitation was that the undertaking must be licit.[56]

Savigny's idea of legal personality must be sharply distinguished from the theory that the State has the right to protect itself against those corporate undertakings which threaten her existence and tend to impair it. The State has the right to suppress, if need be, such types of corporations, and even to prevent their formation. This concession theory differs, however, from the State-Creation view of Savigny, for the right of suppression presupposes a previous existence. The principle was enunciated in Justinian law: "Non omnibus licet corpus habere, sicut militibus in castris."[57]

Canon law may also be referred to in support of the proposition that the legal personality is not to be considered a mere fiction, for under the old law of censures which has been taken unchanged into the New Code, the *universitas* is subject to suspensions and the like, for example a

[55] Schulte, *o. c.,* 26.

[56] *Ibid.* 25.

[57] Hohenlohe, *o. c.,* 35.

cathedral chapter.[58] It is actually the legal personality which is punished for the individual members are under no censure; yet, this would be impossible if the legal person were a mere fiction, since how could a mere "fiction" be subject to punishment?[59] A compelling argument to show that Innocent IV did not consider the juridical personality a mere fiction, as subsequent jurists have endeavored to make out, but sought to distinguish it from a physical person may be presented by indicating that Innocent in his *Apparatus* declares that the *universitas* probably can not be excommunicated and can not be baptized, since it has no soul—indicative of the distinction between legal and physical personality—but admits that a suspension or interdict is possible—indicative of the foundation of the juridical personality in fact, i. e., in the individuals constituting it.[60] The reality of the *universitas,* namely, the moral union by which the members are forged together for the attainment of a definite end is affected by a suspension or interdict. Rational men are grouped in fixed relations toward each other, pursuing common ends with common means, organizing themselves by virtue of a natural right. The union springs not from nothing but from the men themselves, and from the fact that the corporation is a social necessity, not from the creative act of the State.[61] For the right of association for common purposes is a natural prerogative, and this organization then is entitled to those means which will best aid it to attain the desired end, usually legal personality. The escheating of Church property to the State is one of the practical consequences of the fiction theory which can not be grounded upon Canon law.[62] Perhaps, a fiction could be admitted in the case of a benefice since there is conceived, as it were, an immortal possessor, yet

[58] Canon 2285.
[59] Hohenlohe, *o. c.,* 35.
[60] *Ibid.*
[61] *Ibid.* 36.
[62] *Ibid.*

it is impossible even there to dissociate the benefice from the physical persons who are connected with it.

Other legal theories with regard to the metaphysical basis of the juridical entity were proposed by such jurists as Ihering, Meurer, and Vareilles-Sommières. Thus, Meurer[63] considered the metaphysical basis as lying in the crystalized will of the founder; Ihering[64] made those for whom the undertaking was organized the subject of right; Schwabe[65] in Switzerland, and M. de Vareilles-Sommières[66] in France maintained that legal personality is identical with the natural members who constitute the organization, and that the personification is a fiction, but not a legal fiction, for they reason that it is illogical to talk of "creating" nothing (a fiction). The fiction thus becomes a mere matter of convenience for the incorporators.[67]

What is the Canonical view of the basis of the public ecclesiastical legal personality? What is its *fundamentum in re?* Since the Church Universal is of divine foundation, it is impossible to reduce the character of the personality of the Church, as such, or even of its inferior moral persons to a merely natural, metaphysical plane. The discussion must assume theological aspects. The right of the Church to enjoy moral personality may be substantiated from various arguments. Generally, the right is adduced by showing its divine ordination: "Tu es Petrus et super hanc petram aedificabo ecclesiam meam. Quodcunque ligaveris super terram erit legatum in coelis etc."[68] And: "Ego rogavi pro te, ut non deficiat fides tua; et tu * * * * confirma fratres tuos."[69] And: "Pasce agnos meos, pasce oves meas."[70] And: "Quaecumque alligaveris super terram, erunt ligata et in coelo etc."[71] And: "Euntes in mundum

[63] Meurer, *Die juristische Personen,* §4 seqq.
[64] Ihering, *Geist des römischen Rechts,* III, 356.
[65] Schwabe, *Die juristische Person und das Mitgliedshaftsrecht.*
[66] De Vareilles-Sommières, *Les Personnes Morales,* ch. II seqq.
[67] Machen, *l. c.*
[68] Matth. XIV, 18 and 19.
[69] Luc. XXII, 32.
[70] Jo. XI, 15, 17.
[71] Matth. XXIII, 18.

universum, praedicate evangelium omni creaturae."[72] And: "Docete omnes gentes, baptizantes eos; docentes eos servare quaecumque mandavi vobis, et ecce ego vobiscum sum omnibus diebus, usque ad consummationem saeculi."[73] It was then the intention of Christ to constitute the Church and the Holy See a moral person, perpetual and transcendent.[74] Christ created a truly perfect society, sovereign and independent, for the purpose of realizing a definite end, with all the means necessary for its achievement, including therefore legal personality. The Apostolic See is the office itself of the Primacy, the Pontifical See, the Roman episcopacy, with its necessary *corpora* by which it realizes actual existence and functions. It is to endure and constitutes the *fundamentum in re* for the whole Church.[75] But it is a disputed question whether the basis of the moral personality of the Church Universal lies in the See itself in which the divine office of the Pope inheres or whether it is in the series of the persons beginning with Peter and continuing down to the present time in unbroken succession and continuity. In other words, whether the Holy See as referred to in Canon 100 is an institution or a corporation sole is a mooted question: "Utrum autem sustinens denominationem personae moralis sit ipsum officium supremum regendi, ipsa sedes cui tale officium cohaeret, an persona moralis sit consideranda in series personarum, ut eadem perseverat in quolibet membro succedente, est res disputabilis."[76] Thus Cocchi maintains that it is a corporation sole.[77]

In the strict sense, ecclesiastical juridical persons can exist only by authority of that power which was directly received from Christ. The right to form an ecclesiastical corporation is not a merely natural right, but a privilege

[72] Marc. XVI, 15.
[73] Matth. XXVIII, 19, 20.
[74] Toso, *Jus Pontificium,* I, 38.
[75] Wernz-Vidal, *o. c.,* II, 29.
[76] *Ibid.*
[77] Cocchi, *Commentarium in Codicem Juris Canonici,* lib. II, pars 1, sec. I, p. 31.

which transcends the natural. The creation of an ecclesiastical corporation can not be reduced to the same plane as the formation of lay legal personalities,[78] for one is supernatural, the other only natural. Neither can the ecclesiastical moral person be approached from the viewpoint that it owes its existence merely to cultural and social needs, the ground upon which many jurists place the right to establish lay corporation.[79]

But even apart from revelation, the right of corporate personality in the instance of the Church might be based upon reasoning from the natural law. This would eliminate the necessity of a creative act on the part of the State.[80] For the outward worship of God is a social necessity, arising from the fact that God is the Creator both of the individual man and of society, placing in man as He did the natural impulse to form society.[81] Man both individually and collectively, therefore, must acknowledge God by public acts of worship.[82] From this it follows that men have the natural right to form religious organizations, and to claim the rights and privileges which spring from legal personality, necessarily recognized by the State, or even to attach such personality to one of their members. Hence, the scheme of organization of the Catholic Church, with the Pope as its Head, might be justified on the basis of the natural law.

The discussion would not be complete without some reference to the corporate philosophy adopted in the United States. American law has followed the English common law in accepting the Savigny fiction theory. This is not surprising, for from the historical point of view the English common law is the foundation of our own jurisprudence.[83] The metaphysical basis of the legal person, however, has

[78] Wernz-Vidal, *o. c.*, II, 27.
[79] Cavagnis, *o. c.*, I, 234.
[80] Moulart, *L'Église et l'État,* 555.
[81] Cathrein, *Philosophia Moralis,* 337.
[82] Tanquerey, *Synopsis Theologiae Dogmaticae,* I, 102; Leo XIII, ep. encycl. *"Immortale Dei,"* Nov. 1, 1885. *Fontes* n. 592.
[83] Kent, *Commentaries,* I, 473.

not been debated by the common law jurists. Thus Coke[84] and Blackstone[85] refer to the nature of the juridical person only incidentally. Both these accept the Savigny theory without any attempt to justify its philosophical soundness, though, as a matter of reason, brief reflection would serve to indicate the inconsistency of that position, for Savigny calls the legal person a fiction, yet, in the same breath speaks about a "creative" act of the State.[86] But it is impossible for the corporate entity at the same time to be both an artificial person and yet a fiction. "What we may call the Bracket Theory or Expansible Symbol Theory of the Corporation really stands in sharp contrast with the Fiction Theory as Savigny conceived it * * *. In America, where law schools flourish, where supreme courts are many and the need for theory is more urgent than it is in England, highly interesting attempts have been made to dispel the Fiction, or rather to open the Bracket and find therein nothing but contract-bound men."[87] Indeed, it is encouraging to find that in recent years in the United States there are authors who are beginning to accept the Canonical viewpoint of the metaphysical basis of the legal personality.[88] At times, courts will pierce the veil of the fiction and look, as it were, at the collectivity of the incorporators, but notwithstanding, the Fiction Theory continues to be an integral part of American corporation law.

[84] Sutton's Hospital Case, 10 Co. 32.

[85] Blackstone, *Commentaries*, I, 476.

[86] De Vareilles-Sommières, *Les Personnes Morales, l. c.*

[87] Gierke, *o. c.*, *Translator's Introduction*, xxiv.

[88] Machen, *l. c.*, *cf. Conflict of Laws*, No. 3, American Law Institute, (Beale), May 1927, 41.

CHAPTER V.

THE LEGAL BASIS OF THE CANONICAL JURISTIC PERSONALITY BEFORE THE CODE.

In law the terms person and individual are not identical. An individual is a *homo,* but personality is the result of a legal status and signifies the recognition by law of capacity to enjoy certain legal privileges. Every individual or *homo* is by nature the subject of rights and duties, but to be a person in the juridical sense one must besides be recognized by law as *capax jurium.*

According to the natural law, every human being is a person with capacity to enjoy rights which flow directly from human personality. But before the time of Christ, the positive law did not confer legal personality on all human beings.[1] Thus, rights were often denied to slaves in Pagan times.[2] *"Homo est vocabulum naturae, persona est vocabulum juris"* was a legal axiom. A person was defined as, *"homo statu civili praeditus."*[3] After Christ through the influence of Christian teachings the juridical personality of men gradually came to be recognized in so far as those rights were natural.[4] But even in Church law natural personality and ecclesiastical personality are not co-extensive. It is only upon baptism that a human being acquires the right to the Christian privileges with the corresponding duties.[5]

Legal persons are not necessarily rational beings. Persons in the Church may be either physical or moral. Just as there are certain legal requisites for the existence of

[1] Sherman, *o. c.,* II, 23-26.
[2] Wernz, *Jus Decretalium,* I, 103.
[3] Lilla, *Manuale di Filosofia del Diritto,* 72.
[4] Maroto, *Institutiones Juris Canonici,* I, 456.
[5] Ayrinhac, *General Legislation in the New Code,* 188.

canonical personality with respect to a natural person, so in like manner are there definite characteristics which identify an ecclesiastical moral person. And just as all human beings under ecclesiastical law have not legal personality, so also all organizations of persons under that law are not juridical persons possessing legal personality. The moral person has a legal capacity under the law of the Church as distinct and actual as that which attaches to physical persons.

The external aspects of the Canonical legal personality, i. e., its outward form and operation, are in last analysis referable to the Roman law under which the Church first developed. It will, therefore, be profitable, in fact necessary, to consider the legal notions which the Romans had with respect to corporate law.

The etymology of the word *persona* may be traced to the Etruscan. *Personare* was an Etruscan verb which meant to mask, and hence the noun form conveyed the idea of a masked figure or character.[6] To the Romans, *persona* also meant a theatrical character; later on, they applied it to the dramatic part which the actor took, differentiating between the role and the individual, or more exactly, between the mask and the individual. The dramatic connotative force of the word was gradually lost, and it finally became applicable to the part which an individual played in society, and ultimately to the individual himself. The histrionic analogy was still retained, however, in the sense that just as a single actor might take various parts, so likewise the individual might assume various legal relationships, as *dominus, tutor,* creditor and the like.[7]

Roman law drew a distinction between individual and person. Personality was equivalent to the capacity to exercise rights and to be subject to duties. It understood that all rights ultimately are grounded upon human, rational

[6] Walde, *Lateinisches etymologisches Wörterbuch,* 578.

[7] Smith, *o. c.,* II, 374, *persona*; Bernard-Sherman, *First Year of Roman Law,* 102

creatures, but that it was expedient for the attainment of certain transcendent ends, which are of far-reaching importance, to form a juridical personality, thus escaping the limitations otherwise involved. Hence, the fundamental characteristics of a juridical personality viewed from the civil, legal angle are first, perpetuity of existence without regard to the lives of the natural individuals who may temporarily constitute it, and secondly, its status as an entity over and above them, capable of rights and subject to duties.[8] According to the legal theory which the late Romanists presumed had been worked out by the Romans, the personality of the Roman corporate entity was not identical with the personality of the individual members or with the totality of the *corporati*. This of course does not mean there was an absolute disassociation.[9] A manumitted slave was not allowed to give testimony against a corporation which had given him his liberty, in accordance with the law that a manumitted slave could not testify against a natural *manumittor;* yet the rule did not apply against the individual corporate members.[10] It therefore follows: *"Servus nec enim plurium esse videtur sed corporis,"* i. e., the slave of a corporation is not the common property of the individual incorporators, but the property of another person, an invisible, juristic person, namely, the *corpus.*

This sharp line of demarcation between the collective person and the individual members represents the fundamental idea developed by Roman jurisprudence. *"Si quid universitati debetur, singulis non debetur, nec quod debet universitas, singuli debent."*[11] The rights and liabilities of the corporation are not the rights and liabilities of the members taken individually. That the incorporators were separate from the juridical entity may be shown from the Sources: *"Universitatis sunt, non singulorum veluti quae in civitatibus sunt theatra et stadia et similia et si qua alia*

[8] Girard, *Droit Romain,* 250.
[9] *Supra* chapters II, IV.
[10] *Dig.* 2, 4, 4.
[11] *Dig,* 34, 7, 1.

sunt communia civitatium. Ideoque nec servus communis civitatis singulorum pro parte intellegitur, sed universitatis et ideo tam contra civem quam pro eo posse servum civitatis torqueri divi fratres rescripserunt."[12] This shows that the *universitas* as such owned property. The situation may be such that members of the corporation may sue the corporate entity: "*Si autem collegium vel corpus sit, quod rogatum est restituere decreto eorum cui, qui sunt in collegio vel corpore, in singulis inspecta eorum persona restitutionem valere.*"[13]

But not all organizations under the Roman law had legal personality. The expressions *fraternitas, societas, universitas, collegium, institutum, persona moralis* are not identical in meaning. The *societas* was substantially the resultant of a collection of property, skill, labor or a combination of these. The essence was "joint-exploitation." The relation involved *affectio societatis* and these confidential relationships were called *fraternitates.*[14] Sohm declares that a *societas* was merely a legal relationship as between the members themselves and was not referable to outsiders.[15] There were different types of *societates;* as *societas vectigalis,* for tax-farming; and *societates publicanorum,* those which contracted with the State.[16]

Under Roman law, it seems that two requisites must be present for the existence of a corporation, namely, first a plurality of members and secondly, a licit scope. In order that a corporation may come into being there must be a number of physical persons, not merely a fund or a sum of money, which, it will be seen later, was sufficient in the instance of a foundation. Besides, there must be some lawful purpose for which the corporation has been instituted.

To say that there must be a plurality of members for the

[12] *Dig.* 1, 8, 6, 1.
[13] *Dig.* 36, 1, 1, 15.
[14] *Dig.* 17, 2, 31; *Dig.* 17, 2, 63 pr.
[15] Sohm-Ledlie, *o. c.,* 202.
[16] *Dig.* 3, 4, 1 pr.

formation of a corporation under the Roman law is to declare that as a condition precedent for corporate existence there must be at the outset at least three incorporators: "*Neratius Priscus tres facere existimat collegium, et hoc magis sequendum est.*"[17] The persons who formed a *collegium* were called *collegae* or *sodales* and when they had duly and legally constituted a *collegium* were said *corpus habere.* If one of the three incorporators thereafter died, there would still be a corporation and such would be true even though but one of the members survived. Membership changes did not affect its existence; thus its perpetuity was assured. A *corpus* once validly constituted could continue to exist without a quorum of three members, viz., with only one member: "*In decurionibus vel aliis universitatibus nihil refert, utrum omnes idem maneant an pars maneat vel omnes immutati sint. Sed si universitas ad unum redit, magis admittitur posse eum convenire et conveniri, cum jus omnium in unum reciderit et stet nomen universitatis.*"[18] This single remaining member, however, need not be one of the original incorporators.

Secondly, the purpose or scope of the corporation must not be prohibited by law. A *collegium* which had a licit scope was termed *legitimum,* while associations attempting to act as *collegia* when their scope was not legitimate were called *collegia illicita.* Corporations hostile to the interests of the State were not tolerated.[19] In general the right of association was not limited. But proof of a manifestly criminal purpose would constitute it a *collegium illicitum.*

It is interesting to note the attitude taken by the Roman State toward these legal personalities. Before 64 B. C., during the Republic, there was no governmental supervision; individuals were allowed a free hand in the formation of such organizations.[20] In 64 B. C., a decree of the senate (*senatusconsult*) dissolved many *collegia,* those which were

[17] *Dig.* 50, 16, 85.
[18] *Dig.* 3, 4, 7, 2.
[19] Smith, *o. c.,* II, 979, *universitas.*
[20] Smith, *o. c.,* I, 471, *collegium.*

threatening the existence of the State by virtue of their having become weapons of political conspiracy.[21] The tendency toward State control existed also during the Empire. A number of juristic persons were suppressed and in general during the period of the Empire, *collegia* were to be formed only with the sanction of the Senate: *"Sed permittitur tenuioribus stipem menstruam conferre, dum tamen semel in mense coeant, ne sub praetextu hujusmodi illicitum collegium coeat. Sed religionis causa coire non prohibentur, dum tamen per hoc non fiat contra senatus consultum, quo illicita collegia arcentur. Non licet autem amplius quam unum collegium licitum habere, ut est constitutum et a divis fratribus; et si quis in duobus fuerit, rescriptum est eligere eum oportere, in quo magis esse velit, accepturum ex eo collegio, a quo recedit, id quod ei competit ex ratione quae communis fuit. Quisquis illicitum collegium usurpaverit, ea poena tenetur, quae tenentur, qui hominibus armatis loca publica vel templa occupasse judicati sunt. Collegia si qua fuerint illicita, mandatis & constitutionibus & senatusconsultis dissolvuntur."*[22] An authorized society was one: *"quibus senatus c. c. c. (coire, convenire, collegium habere) permissit e lege Julia ex auctioritate Augusti."* Augustus sought to improve the corporate system by constructive legislation.[23] In the first part of the Empire, the Senate gave the authorization after consultation with the Emperor, but later on with the increasing strength of the Emperor he acted alone in the matter: *"Collegia Romae certa sunt, quorum corpus senatus consultis atque constitutionibus principalibus confirmatum est, veluti pistorum * * * et naviculorum."*[24]

Whether the State's permission under the Roman law constituted the creative act without which the corporation could not exist is one of the most controverted problems in the entire discussion of the Roman conception of the juris-

[21] *Ibid.*
[22] *Dig.* 47, 22, 1 to 3.
[23] Waltzing, *o. c.*, I, 115, 116.
[24] *Dig.* 3, 4, 1.

tic personality. Romanists agree that corporations may not exist against the will of the State, that corporations not in harmony with the State may be disbanded, but a sharp difference of opinion prevails among them as to the question of whether or not the State's sanction actually gave life to the corporation. Some Romanists hold that an association might be vested with the corporate character under general law or custom but that this was not necessary. This latter is regarded by Smith[25] as the better view. He asserts that while certain types of corporations were the creatures of the State, yet others arose by the mere banding together of individuals for the achievement of common purposes, which of course must neither be illicit nor immoral. In like manner, Ferrini maintains that the State did not create the legal personality under Roman law but only recognized it, either expressly or impliedly. The State has the right of intervention only when the corporation becomes a source of danger, but this presumes that the corporation actually existed before it was ousted by the State.[26] Some *collegia* might exist even though illicit up to the time the State dissolved them. Willis tends to this same view, namely, that there was no Roman law which prescribed the State's creative act as a condition precedent for corporate existence.[27] Blackstone[28] contends that corporations under the civil law were formed merely by the association of the members for some legitimate purpose. But many authorities seem to hold that the grant of corporate capacity under the Roman law came from the State. This is the opinion of Buckland[29] and Morey.[30] Sherman states that no corporation under the Empire could exist unless it was expressly authorized by the State.[31] The State does more, then, according to him, than simply give per-

[25] Smith, *o.c.*, II, 979, *universitas*.
[26] Ferrini, *Pandette*, 73.
[27] Willis, *Catholic Encyclopedia*, IV, 38, *corporation*.
[28] Blackstone, *Commentaries*, I, 468-473.
[29] Buckland, *A Text Book of Roman Law*, 178.
[30] Morey, *o. c.*, 265.
[31] Sherman, *o. c.*, II, 547.

mission or recognition of corporate existence. It alone created corporations. It is the opinion of Sohm[32] that a lawful society was the creature of the State. Whether a special recognition of associated persons as a corporation by the State was essential under Roman law, so that without it a corporation could have no existence as such, can not be regarded as settled.

Of course, the corporate entity could not perform all the acts of a human being, since its personality was only legal and not natural. Thus, it could not marry, vote, and the like. Its outward acts were performed by a *magister* through whom the corporation acted as a minor through his guardian.[33] Yet the *persona moralis* of the Romans was classed with physical persons in many instances: *"Animadvertendum autem, quod praetor hoc edicto generaliter et in rem loquitur nec adicit a quo gestum: et ideo sive singularis sit persona, quae metum intulit, vel populus vel curia vel collegium vel corpus huic edicto locus erit."*[34] And it enjoyed such fundamental rights as the capacity to acquire, hold and dispose of property in its own name and under its own seal.[35] It had the right of *dominium,* that is, the propriety of property as distinguished from mere possession, which may imply only the custody of the thing: *"Quibus autem permissum est corups habere collegii societatis sive cujusque alterius eorum nomine, proprium est ad exemplum rei publicae habere res communes."*[36] It had the capacity of being a *patronus* and of manumitting slaves: *"Divus Marcus omnibus collegiis, quibus coeundi jus est, manumittendi potestatem dedit."*[37] Manumission was the giving of freedom to a slave by a master.[38] And the right of manumission necessarily implied the capacity of buying, holding and selling slaves. Roman corporations had ca-

[32] Sohm-Ledlie, *o. c.,* 199.
[33] Wernz-Vidal, *o. c.,* II, 26; *Dig.* 46, 8, 9.
[34] *Dig.* 4, 2, 9, 1.
[35] Savigny, *o. c.,* II, 91.
[36] *Dig.* 3, 4, 1, 1.
[37] *Dig.* 40, 3, 1.
[38] *Institutes* 1, 5 pr.

pacity to acquire easements in the land of another: "*Non dubito quin fundo municipium per servum recte servitus adquiratur.*"[39] They had the right of usufruct.[40] They could acquire property by adverse possession: "*Item municipes ad exhibendum conveniri possunt: quin facultas est restituendi. Nam & possidere & usucapere eos posse constat.*"[41] They could alienate property.[42] They could assume contractual obligations[43] and sue in tribunals of justice: "*Sicut municipum nomine actionem praetor dedit, ita et adversus eos justissime edicendum putavit. Sed et legato, qui in negotium publicum sumptum fecit, puto dandam actionem in municipes.*"[44]

But a corporation could not have a will, a capacity which belonged to the *corporati:* "*Municipes per se nihil possidere possunt, qui universi consentire non possunt.*"[45] And under the older law it could be neither heir nor legatee,[46] but this was changed under the later law. Municipalities received the right to take legacies by an enactment of Nerva, and further concessions in this respect were made by Hadrian.[47] Private corporations received this capacity during the reign of Marcus Aurelius: "*Cum senatus temporibus divi Marci permiserit collegiis legare.*"[48] At that period the corporation was no longer a *persona incerta:* "*Et de iis quae perpetuo petuntur relicta ecclesiis xenonibus vel ptochiis vel venerabilibus domibus vel universitati totius cleri vel ad redemptionem captivorum vel ipsis pauperibus vel captivis* (*valet defuncti voluntas*)."[49] Corporations could become heirs: "*Quare hi quoque legitimam*

[39] *Dig*. 8, 1, 12.
[40] *Dig*. 7, 1, 56.
[41] *Dig*. 10, 4, 7, 3.
[42] *Dig*. 3, 4, 1, 1.
[43] *Dig*. 3, 4, 7, 1.
[44] *Dig*. 3, 4, 7, pr.
[45] *Dig*. 41, 2, 1.
[46] *Ulp. Reg*. 22, 5; *Ulp. Reg*. 24, 18.
[47] *Ulp. Reg*. 24, 28.
[48] *Dig*. 34, 5, 20.
[49] *Code* 6, 48, 26.

hereditatem liberti vindicabunt."[50] And: *"Habeat unusquisque licentiam sanctissimo catholicae venerabilique concilio decedens bonorum quod optavit relinquere. Non sint cassa judicia. Nihil est quod magnis hominibus debetur, quam ut supremae voluntatis, post quam jam aliud velle non possunt, liber sit stilus et licitum quod iterum non redit arbitrium."*[51] And: *"Cum senatus temporibus divi Marci permiserit collegiis legare, nulla dubitatio est, quod, si corpori cui licet coire legatum sit, debeatur: cui autem non licet si legetur, non valebit, nisi singulis legetur; hi enim non quasi collegium, sed quasi certi homines admittentur ad legatum."*[52] It appears, though, that a limitation was imposed upon this right of a private corporation to accept legacies at the time of the Emperor Diocletian, unless the organization had received authority to take property by will: *"Collegium, si nullo speciali privilegio subnixum sit, hereditatem capere non posse dubium non est."*[53] But no limitations were imposed upon the acquisition of property by juridical persons in ways other than by legacy or inheritance.[54]

Corporations could not be held responsible for crimes under Roman law, for they had no capacity for the *mens rea.* Nor as a distinct entity could a corporation commit a tort.[55] But when the representatives of the corporation, acting within the scope of their authority, were guilty of tortious conduct by virtue of which the corporation receives a benefit, the corporation was liable under Roman law and an action would sound in tort.[56] For what the agents of the corporation decided upon and did within the scope of their authority was considered the act of the corporation

[50] *Dig.* 40, 3, 2.
[51] *Code* 1, 2, 1.
[52] *Dig.* 35, 5, 20.
[53] *Code* 6, 24, 8.
[54] *Dig.* 41, 2, 1, 22.
[55] *Dig.* 4, 3, 15, 1.
[56] *Dig.* 43, 16, 2.

itself: "*Quemadmodum ergo pareri potest per eos? Itaque jurabunt, per quos municipii res geruntur.*"[57]

The *corporati* were not restricted in the formulation of laws for the government of the organization as long as such rules were not a menace to the State: "*Sodales sunt qui ejusdem collegii sunt; quam Graeci 'etaireian' vocant, his autem potestatem facit lex pactionem quam velint sibi ferre, dum ne quid ex publica lege corrumpant.*"[58] The incorporators might have an internal organization similar to that of a public corporation, though this was not at all compulsory: "*Quibus autem permissum est corpus habere collegii societatis sive cujusque alterius eorum nomine, proprium est ad exemplum reipublicae habere res communes, arcam communem et actorem sive syndicum per quem tanquam in re publica, quod communiter agi fierique oporteat, agatur fiat.*"[59] But it was usually necessary that the corporation have an *actor:* "*Actor a tutore datus omnimodo cavet: actor civitatis nec ipse cavet, nec magister universitatis, nec curator bonis consensu creditorum datus.*"[60]

The intentions of the incorporators were carried out by the duly appointed representatives: "*Sed hoc jure utimur, ut et possidere et usucapere municipes possint idque eis et per servum et per liberam personam adquiratur.*"[61] These intentions were made known by official meetings, but the validity of resolutions adopted at such sessions necessitated the presence of at least two thirds of all the *corporati:* "*Nulli permittitur nomine civitatis vel curiae experiri nisi ei, cui lex permittit, aut lege cessante ordo dedit, cum duae partes adessent aut amplius quam duae.*"[62] This quorum of two thirds of the incorporators, in order to pass resolutions which were binding upon the corporation as expressive of its will must record a majority vote; a majority of

[57] *Dig.* 35, 1, 97; *Dig.* 50, 1, 14.
[58] *Dig.* 47, 22, 4.
[59] *Dig.* 3, 4, 1, 1.
[60] *Dig.* 46, 8, 9.
[61] *Dig.* 41, 2, 2.
[62] *Dig.* 3, 4, 3.

the *corporati* present must concur: *"Quod major pars curiae effecit, pro eo habetur ac si omnes agerint."*[63]

Under Roman law, corporations might be extinguished in various ways. Thus, the State might dissolve those organizations whose scope was unlawful: *"Collegia si qua fuerint illicita, mandatis et constitutionibus et sensatusconsultis dissolvuntur * * *. In summa, autem, nisi ex senatus consulti auctoritate vel Caesaris collegium vel quodcumque tale corpus coierit, contra senatus consultum et mandata et constitutiones collegium celebrat."*[64] This ouster by the State might arise in either one of two ways, first, the corporation might be suppressed by reason of its object having become illicit, as where the State prohibits associations of certain types which at first were legal, by retroactive legislation; or, secondly, the corporation might be specifically ousted by a State declaration that a certain, single corporation was in the future extinct on grounds of public policy: *"Si usus fructus civitati legetur et aratrum in ea inducatur, civitas esse desinit, ut passa est Carthago."*[65] The Roman corporation was also dissolved by death of all its members if the undertaking was merely private. But this was not a universal rule,[66] according to Savigny. The Sources nowhere declare directly that a corporation may cease by death or withdrawal of all the members, yet Romanists arrive at this conclusion from the fact that the Sources do expressly declare that one member must survive. This they regard as a condition subsequent, so that there is no corporation if there are no members.[67] When *collegia licita* were dissolved, the members could divide the assets among themselves: *"Sed permittitur eis, cum dissolvuntur, pecunias communes si quas habent dividere pecuniamque inter se partiri."*[68] But upon dissolution of an illicit corpo-

[63] *Dig.* 50, 1, 19.
[64] *Dig.* 47, 22, 3.
[65] *Dig.* 7, 4, 21.
[66] *Dig.* 3, 4, 7, 2.
[67] *Dig.* 3, 4, 7, 2.
[68] *Dig.* 47, 22, 3 pr.

ration, the assets were disposed of according to the imperial will.[69]

The *universitas personarum* outlined above was one of the two grand divisions of corporate existence under Roman law; the other was the *universitas bonorum* or institution. What was the legal character of this latter type? Its origin was the result of a dedication of goods or valuables to a definite end of a religious or charitable character.[70] Like the *universitas personarum,* it had capacity to inherit property and to receive legacies.[71] Technically, in Roman law two acts were necessary for the erection of the institution; first, the dedication of property by the founder, and secondly, the "assent" of the State.[72] The two elements, therefore, of a *fundus* (usually money), and scope were essential.

The Sources always refer to some definite purpose, usually religious or charitable, when speaking of the formation of institutions. They were usually *piae causae,* indicative of the predominant scope: *"Sancimus si quis moriens piam dispositionem faciat vel institutionis modo vel per legatum vel per fideicommissum vel per mortis causa donationem vel per quemlibet alium legitimum modum, sive pro tempore episcopo curam injunxerit, quo ea quae disposuerit impleantur, sive de hoc tacuerit, sive e contrario eum prohibuerit, necesse esse heredibus facere et implere omnimodo quae ordinata sunt: quod si sponte non faciunt, tum religiosissimi locorum episcopi de iis anquirant atque eos conveniant, ut omnia secundum defuncti voluntatem impleantur."*[73] And: *"Ac si quidem ecclesiam aedificari defunctus jussit, infra triennium omnino eam extruendam curent, sin xenonem, infra unum annum eum facere cogantur, cum hoc tempus ad defunctorum voluntatem implendam sufficiat: possunt enim et domum conduci ibique aegroti deponi pos-*

[69] *Theod. Code* 16, 10, 20.
[70] Smith, *o. c.,* II, 979, *universitas.*
[71] *Code* 1, 2, 23; *Code* 1, 3, 24, 49.
[72] Sohm-Ledlie, *o. c.,* 200.
[73] *Code* 1, 3, 45.

*sunt, dum xenonis extructio perficiatur. Si quid vero semel dare in pias causas jussi sunt, statim id facere cogantur, id est postquam testamentum apertum est hereditatemque vel legatum ii quibus ea relicta sunt adquisierunt. Quod si memoratum tempus praeteriit neque ecclesia vel xenon aedificatum est neque xenodochi officio fungitur, cui hoc commissum est, tum episcopi ipsi exigant, * * * et procurent aedificationem sacrosanctarum ecclesiarum et xenonum vel gerontocomiorum vel orphanotrophiorum institutionem vel * * * ptochotrophiorum vel nosocomiorum extructionem vel captivorum redemptionem vel alium quemcumque pium actum qui defuncto placuerit, ac praeficiant eorum administrationi xenodochos vel orphanotrophos vel brephotrophos vel gerontocomos vel denique piarum causarum administratores curatoresque, ut ex supra dicti temporis lapsu memorataque contumacia qui id non fecerint non amplius se memoratae rerum administrationi immiscere vel religiosissimos episcopos ab earum administratione excludere possint."*[74] But the institutional scope was not identical with the purposes for which the *universitas personarum* was created, for a corporation may be either of private or public interest, but an institution is almost always of public interest; for this reason its scope was presumed to be licit.

Not only must there be a scope for the Roman institution, but there must also exist a *fundus*. This was not essential for the *universitas personarum;* its basis was the aggregation of the members. But without money or its equivalent there could be no institution under Roman law; it did not require *corporati.*[75] The dissipation of the *fundus* was required to cause the extinction of the institution; for example, an institution erected for the care of orphans would be destroyed if all the funds were spent, even though there still existed orphans in the asylum.[76]

[74] *Code* 1, 3, 45, 1.
[75] *Code* 1, 3, 45.
[76] *Ibid.*

The State exercised a policy of "*laissez faire*" toward institutions, but in last analysis the government had the power of dissolution over them on the grounds that private property had been dedicated to a public purpose.[77] The appointment of administrators if not outlined by the founder and thereafter specified in the constitution was within episcopal discretion.[78] The Church exercised general control over institutions and foundations in the matter of administration: "*Ea enim, quae ad beatissimae ecclesiae jura pertinent vel posthac forte pervenerint, tamquam ipsam sacrosanctam et religiosam ecclesiam intacta, convenit venerabiliter custodiri, ut, sicut ipsa religionis et fidei mater perpetua est, ita ejus patrimonium jugiter servetur illaesum.*"[79] The administrative power still existed in the absence of the appointment of managers by the founder, even though the Bishop had been excluded.[80]

The work of the institutional manager was under the scrutiny of both Church and State.[81] This was particularly so with regard to the use and alienation of the institution's property.[82] Retention of the managers was within the discretion of the Bishop who might discharge representatives not faithfully fulfilling their obligations and take personal control.[83]

The question of the termination of the institution or foundation is not covered by the Sources, but Romanists have constructed a very reasonable theory, basing their opinion upon the necessity of the continued existence of those two elements which are conditions *sine qua non* for institutional existence. They agree that the institution may end either by dissipation of the assets (*fundus*), or by termination of the object or *scope* for which the institution was formed. The object of the institution may no longer

[77] *Code* 1, 9, 1.
[78] *Nov.* 131, 11; *Code* 1, 3, 46, 3.
[79] *Code* 1, 2, 14, 2.
[80] *Code* 1, 3, 45 pr.
[81] *Nov.* 131, 11.
[82] *Code* 1, 2, 12, 2.
[83] *Nov.* 120.

be possible, or it may no longer be licit as when property is left to a monastery which becomes heretical. Extinction of the institution by force of law would then follow. Romanists argue that upon dissolution of the institution its assets went to the Church, since the property was originally left for charitable ends, and under Roman law, the Church was the representative of all charities.[84]

This in brief was the Roman law conception of the juristic personality. How did the principles of pre-Code Canon law coincide with this juridical conception? Before the present Code of Canon law, legal personality in ecclesiastical jurisprudence had reached an advanced legal development. As in Roman law, so likewise in Canon law, the *persona juridica* was a "*subjectum capax jurium.*" The law relative to canonical legal personality so precisely and compactly formulated in the New Code was abstracted, however, from a Source authority which is vague and couched in a language nowise resembling the terminology employed in the Code, although the thought now concisely expressed reflects substantially the viewpoint of the canonists before the Code. Thus, the early Sources may be searched in vain in an effort to find the words *persona moralis,* yet there existed in the old law the equivalent of the idea which this expression conveys.

I.

NATURE OF THE ECCLESIASTICAL MORAL PERSON.

A. The Church Universal. The Catholic Church occupies a position analogous to that of a sovereign State, being perfect, supreme, and possessing the right to have inferior corporate bodies for the accomplishment of her end. The position of the Church Universal had been outlined very definitely before the Code by a series of Papal Documents which emphasized the divinity, perfection, unity, perpetuity and mystical character of the Church.

[84] Ferrini, *o. c.*, 116.

The Divine Institution of the Church. Christ founded His Church upon Peter, and his successors are to have complete power in carrying forward the divine commission of teaching all nations, etc.[85] The divine mission was not to be executed through an intangible organization, but the Church was to be something visible and possess such outward characteristics as the power to make laws, to enforce them and the like.[86] God Himself, therefore, founded the Church. Christ divinely commissioned the Apostles. The Bishops are the successors of the Apostles. *"Apostoli nobis Evangelii praedicatores facti sunt a Domino Jesu Christo, Jesus Christus missus est a Deo, etc."*[87] All contrary views on the subject have been condemned.[88]

The Catholic Church, a Perfect Society. It was an unvarying principle of pre-Code law that the Catholic Church was constituted a perfect society by Christ, circumscribed by no regional limitations and untrammeled by the civil authority.[89] Perfection is an essential characteristic of the Church.[90] This was necessarily intended by God;[91] indeed, such was His express command.[92]

The Unity of the Catholic Church. There are many members in the Church, but the Church is one; similarly, there are many bishops but one episcopacy.[93] Jesus Christ, the Author of the Church, instituted a true unity among Christians *"in fidei et regiminis unitate consistens."*[94] This unity is stressed in the *Corpus Juris Canonici.*[95]

[85] Ep. Encycl., *"Quanta Cura,"* 8 dec. 1864, *Fontes* n. 542.

[86] Ep. Encycl., *"Vix dum a nobis,"* 7 mart. 1874, *Fontes* n. 567.

[87] Cf. Ep. Encycl., *"Satis cognitum,"* 29 jun. 1896, *Fontes* n. 630, referring to St. Clemens, Rom. ep. I *ad Corinth.,* cc. 42, 44, and S. Pacianus *ad Sempronium,* ep. III, n. 11.

[88] S. C. Off., decr. *"Lamentabli,"* 4 jul. 1907, prop. 52, damn., *Fontes* n. 1283.

[89] Allocut., *"Multis gravibusque,"* 17 dec. 1860, *Fontes* n. 529.

[90] Ep. *"Officio sanctissimo,"* 22 dec. 1887, *Fontes* n. 596.

[91] Allocut., *"Mirandum sane,"* 1 jun. 1888, *Fontes* n. 599.

[92] Ep. Ap. *"Praeclara,"* 20 jun. 1894, *Fontes* n. 625.

[93] Ep. Encycl., *"Etsi multa,"* 21 nov. 1873, *Fontes* n. 566, quoting St. Cyprian *contra* Novatien, *ep.* 52, *ad Antonian.*

[94] Ep. Ap., *"Praeclara,"* 20 jun. 1894, *Fontes* n. 625.

[95] Thus, in c. un., *de majoritate et obedientia,* I, 8, in Extrav. Com.

The Perpetuity of the Catholic Church. The Church was not founded for one generation but for the all humanity; Peter lives, as it were, in his successors.[96] The eternal character of the Church has been emphasized by the Sources.[97] To hold that the Church is not organically perpetual has been declared error.[98]

The Mystical Character of the Church. Christ has been termed the Head of the Church, and the faithful its members.[99] *"Vos autem estis corpus Christi."*[100] This *corpus* is a living body.[101] Scripture and tradition both declare that the Catholic Church is the mystical body of Christ.[102]

B. Inferior Ecclesiastical Persons. Now all these attributes which the Church possesses as outlined above establish the moral personality of the Church Universal, a body which is therefore transcendent, perpetual, perfect. The remainder of the discussion will deal with the inferior ecclesiastical moral persons by means of which the Church Universal functions.

The juridical conception of these inferior canonical persons is in ultimate analysis the result of the adaptation to Church affairs of legal notions borrowed from Roman law. The similarity becomes evident upon noting the parallel which prevails between the two systems in the realm of the legal personality, with reference to its formation, status, mode of acting, duration and degree of subjection to the proper authority.

Before the Code, the ecclesiastical corporation was de-

[96] Pius IX, allocut., *"Singulari quadam,"* 9 dec. 1854, *Fontes,* n. 518; Litt. ap. *"Cum Catholica Ecclesia,"* 26 mart. 1860, *Fontes,* n. 528.

[97] Thus, cf. Ep. Encycl., *"Immortale Dei,"* 1 nov. 1885, *Fontes,* n. 592; Ep. Encycl., *"Satis cognitum,"* 29 jun. 1895, *Fontes* n. 630.

[98] S. C. S. Off. decr. *"Lamentabili,"* 4 jul. 1907, prop. 52, damn., *Fontes* n. 1283.

[99] Allocut., *"Maxima quidem,"* 9 jun. 1862, *Fontes* n. 534.

[100] Ep. Encycl., *"Satis cognitum,"* 29 jun. 1896, *Fontes* 630, referring to I. Cor. XII. 27.

[101] *Ibid.,* referring to Eph. I, 22, 23.

[102] Pius X, ep. encycl., *"Vehementer nos,"* 11 febr. 1906, *Fontes* 671, referring to Ephes. 11, seqq. and Matth. XXVIII, 18-20.

scribed by such words as *collegium, universitas, fraternitas, ecclesia.* The terminology of Roman law was therefore borrowed. Thus, with respect to the word *collegium*: "Collegii *appellatione veniunt etiam monasteria & conventus religiosorum.*"[103] Again: "Collegii, *aut capituli appellatione venit etiam illius caput, sive Praelatus, in favorabilibus.*"[104] But: "Collegiatorum *appellatione in privilegiis non veniunt famuli.*"[105] The corporate character of the idea expressed by the word *universitas* is thus suggested: "*Universitatem non comprehendit dictio* ALIQUIS *cum ad personas singula res referatur.*"[106] And: "*Et cum ejus natura fit, quod opponatur ad singulares personas, ideo non continere universitatem docet Gemin, etc.*"[107]

II.

CONDITIONS PRECEDENT FOR THE EXISTENCE OF INFERIOR ECCLESIASTICAL MORAL PERSONS.

A. Authority. It was disputed in Roman law whether the Roman corporation was always the result of a creative act by the State. But in Canon law, it was settled that an ecclesiastical legal personality required a creative act by the proper Church authority. For it is impossible to speak of natural rights, the basis of the contention of those who argue that civil corporations are not creatures of the State. with reference to spiritual privileges. This is evident from the Sources,[108] and from the Doctors.[109] Santi writes: "*Erectio seu fundatio aut aedificatio locorum religiosorum fieri debet cum interventu auctoritatis Episcopi.*"[110] The Coun-

[103] Barbosa, *Tractatus Varii,* 176.
[104] *Ibid.*
[105] *Ibid.*
[106] Barbosa, *o. c.,* 648, n. 3.
[107] *Ibid.,* n. 9.
[108] Cf. c. 4, X, *de religiosis domibus, ut episcopo sint subjectae,* III, 36.
[109] As Santi, *o. c.,* III, 321, and Devoti, *Institutionum Canonicarum,* Tom. I, lib. ii, tit. X, n. 2.
[110] Santi, *o. c.,* III, 321, n. 2.

cil of Trent declared that new monasteries could not be established without the consent of the Bishop.[111] Of course this regulation did not derogate from the former rule.[112] The permission of the Holy See was required for the erection of monasteries, even though they were outside Italy: *"Si quaeratur utrum necessaria sit licentia etiam S. Sedis dicendum est eam certe requiri pro Italia et insulis adjacentibus. Ex. Constitut. Instaurandae docet communem sententiam esse et a tribunalibus adoptatam, requiri hanc licentiam etiam extra Italiam et adjacentes insulas."*[113] Even those ecclesiastical legal persons which are administered by the laity should be erected by episcopal authority: *"Quod de hospitalibus dico, id etiam dictum volo de ceteris piis locis, uti sunt confraternitates quas vocant, collegia, cetera similia, quae cuncta Episcopi subsunt, quamquam a laicis administrentur. Ac de confraternitatibus praesertim decet animadvertere, eas erigendas esse auctoritate Episcopi; qui earumdem etiam statuta cognoscere atque approbari debet.*[114] Papal or episcopal authority was therefore required for the erection of ecclesiastical moral persons depending upon the precise nature of the juridical entity.

B. **The Decree of Erection**: The decree of erection from the proper ecclesiastical authority was necessary for the establishment of a canonical juristic personality. Thus, a new monastery required a decree from the Bishop and the Apostolic See.[115] It was to be formal, in writing, and it was to specify the nature, purpose etc. of the moral person: *"An ad institutionem opus sit scriptura? Resp. Ad ejus substantiam, et valorem actus scriptura opus non esse, cum id*

[111] Conc. Trident., sess. XXV, *de ref.*, c. 2.

[112] This has been stated as follows by Devoti, *o. c.*, Tom. I lib. ii, tit. X, n. 2, "in cap. unic § confirmatos de relig. domib. in 6, et in cap. unic. de Exces. praelat. in 6 *qua de re edita est ab Innoc. X Const.* Instaurandae 157 Bull. t. 6, par. 3, p. 233, *qua sancitum est, ut sine venia Sedis Apost. novum monasterium excitari nequeat * * * . Quare in novo monasterio erigendo et Episcopi et Sedis Apost. venia necessaria est; confer Benedict XIV* de Syn. dioec. 19b, 9, c. 1, num. 9."

[113] Santi, *o. c.*, III, 322, n. 2.

[114] Devoti *o. c.*, Tom. 1, lib. ii, tit. XII, n. 4.

[115] Devoti, *o. c.*, Tom. 1, lib. ii, tit. X, n. 2.

nullo jure expressum sit. Consuetudine tamen receptum est, ut fiat per scripturam, sicut et praesentatio: expeditque ita fieri ad faciliorem probationem."[116]

C. Scope. The scope of the canonical moral personality must be religious or charitable, relating to the love of God. Ante-Code Sources are agreed upon this point.[117] It must be more than a merely humanitarian undertaking.

D. Plurality of Members. The pre-Code Canon law followed the Roman law in requiring three persons for the establishment of the *collegium.* It is true that certain canonical authorities required but two persons, but the weight of authority was to the contrary. The argument has been concisely presented by Schmalzgrueber: "*Alii volunt duos sufficere, alii tres requirunt. Utrique sententiae aliquid tribuendum existimo, et dico, ad congregationem, seu collegium, initio constituendum tres ut minimum personas requiri; si tamen illud semel sit constitutum, conservari posse collegium ejusque jura etiam in duobus, imo in uno.*"[118] He continues: "*Pars I. responsionis de jure civili patet ex l. Neratius 85 ss. de V. S. et l. detestatio 40 in fin. ss eod ubi dicitur quod duo non faciant familiam; sed saltem tres requirantur: igitur idem dicendum etiam est de jure canonico; nam ut c. intelleximus* I, *de nov. oper. nunt. habetur, ss. canones non dedignantur imitari leges, ubi istae ab illis non sunt immutatae; non autem constat de immutatione; nam quod c. nullus, 1. h. tit. pontifex dicat, nullus in ecclesia, ubi duo, vel tres fuerint in congregatione, nisi eorum electione canonica, presbyter eligatur, solum probat, quod jus eligendi conservetur in duobus, si hi soli superstites sint, non vero, quod duae tantum personae sufficiant ad collegium in principio suo constituendum.*"

"*Pars. 2: ex eo videtur ostendi; quod plus plerumque requiratur ad primam rei constitutionem, quam ad ejusdem conservationem; igitur etsi ad constitutionem collegii pri-*

[116] Schmalzgrueber, *o. c.,* Tom. III, pars I, tit. VII, n. 39.

[117] Cf. c. 4, X, *de religiosis domibus, ut episcopo sint subjectae,* III, 36; Santi, *o. c.,* III, 321.

[118] Schmalzgrueber, *o. c.,* Tom. I, pars II, tit. VI, n. 8.

mam necessariae sint personae saltem tres, ad conservationem illius tamen sufficient duo, vel unus."[119]

E. **Fundus.** This was required for the existence of the non-collegiate type of canonical moral personality. Thus, *titulus VII* in *Book III* of the *Decretals of Gregory IX* specifies the need of a *fundus.* Pre-Code canonists were agreed upon the necessity of this element in the non-collegiate form of moral person.[120]

III.

STATUS OF THE ECCLESIASTICAL MORAL PERSONALITY.

Pre-Code canon law was similar to Roman jurisprudence in assimilating the legal person to the status of a minor. Thus, the legal person enjoyed the right of *"restitutio in integrum."* Santi commenting on c. 1, X, *de in integrum restitutione,* I, 41, defines *"restitutio in integrum"* as follows: *"Hince aequitate praetoria invectum est remedium extraordinarium restitutionis in integrum, quo qui laesionem passus est,*[121] *restituitur in eum statum in quo versabatur ante laisionem.* The Sources indicate that the ecclesiastical legal person, like the Roman, possessed the right of *"restitutio in integrum,"* a protective right arising from the nature of the corporate entity. Thus, in c. I, X, *de in intgrum restitutione,* I, 41: *"Requisivit a nobis tua fraternitas quid agendum sit de possessione laicis sub modo censu concessis."* Alexander III answered: *"Noveris itaque, quod, si ecclesia laesa est, et manifeste apparet detrimentum ipsius, quam episcopo ejusdem ecclesiae conditionem facere deteriorem non liceat, et ecclesia jure minoris debeat semper illaesa servari, quae in damnum ejus data constiterit ad ipsius convenit jus proprietatemque redire."*[122] This principle is

[119] *Ibid.*

[120] Santi, *o. c.,* III, 113.

[121] Santi, *o. c.,* I, 399.

[122] C. 1, X, *de in integrum restitutione,* I, 41.

shown by the headnote referring to c. 3, X, *de integrum, restitutione,* I, 41, a passage formulated by Innocent III: *"Ecclesia laesa in probatione necessaria omissa potest petere restitutionem in integrum, non obstante termino juris probationis exclusivo. Et restitutionem petere potest non solum contra privatum sed etiam contra ecclesiam."* Santi declares that the privilege was extended to pious institutions and the like: *"Sub nomine Ecclesiarum intelliguntur, non solum ecclesiae proprie dictae et beneficia, sed etiam, quaelibet pia loca seu pia institutio, ex. gr. claustra religiosa, confraternitates, hospitalia auctoritate Episcopi fundata."*[123] The right applied even *"in negotiis extra judicium gestis."*[124] But a time limit was fixed: *"Ab ecclesia adversus lapsum temporis, in quo se laesam affirmat, in integrum restitutio peti potest, et causa restitutionis hujusmodi finiri debet infra quadriennium continuum a tempore laesionis, etiamsi minus quadriennio tempus laesionis exsistat. Sed non fiet restitutio, nisi ad tantum tempus, quantum se laesam fore probabit."*[125]

IV.

MODE OF ACTING OF THE ECCLESIASTICAL COLLEGIATE MORAL PERSONALITY.

A similarity prevailed between the Roman law and the pre-Code Canon law in the matter of the corporation's method of acting, and in a later chapter it will be seen that the New Code of Canon law has substantially followed these principles. The pre-Code Canon law made a distinction between matters affecting all the members, and corporate policies which were proper to the ecclesiastical moral personality as such.

As to the latter, the corporate policies were to be determined by the major and saner part of the convention. What

[123] Santi, *o. c.,* I, 400.
[124] *Ibid.,* 399.
[125] C. 1. *de restitutione in integrum,* I, 11, in Clem.

the major and saner part of the voters, therefore, agreed upon was expressive of the will of the corporation.[126] A resolution thus passed was not to be affected by the will of the opposing side.[127] But the two elements, major and saner, must concur; thus, the major part must be the saner part.[128] Notice of the meeting must be given to all those who had the right to vote. If less than two thirds of such voters had not been notified, the convention would not possess the authority to pass binding resolutions.[129] Of course if one who has been called to the session leaves without reason, he loses the right of balloting.[130]

These rules applied to all deliberations of the corporate entity, as such; thus, in regard to elections, Schmalzgrueber declares: "*Vocandi autem ad electionem sunt omnes non tantum in loco praesentes, sed etiam absentes, qui interesse debent, volunt, et commode possunt, ut dicitur c. quia propter 42. in princ. h. tit. * * * Si ex 12 contempti sint quinque electio ipso jure est nulla * * * ob defectum potestatis eligendi, quae residet in duabus partibus capitularium, qui debent, volunt, et commode possunt interesse: Abb. in c. 30 h. tit. n. 9 et in c. 42. in princ. eod. n. 12. * * * Si et tantum unus, vel pauciores contempti sint, reliqui autem convenerint ad electionem, tunc electio ab his facta de jure est valida, si tamen in electum convenerit major pars omnium suffragii jus habentium. Addidi, si tamen in electum convenerit major pars eorum omnium, qui jus suffragii habent (c. auditis 29, h. tit.).*"[131] He continues: "*Quis a majore, et saniore parte capitularium electus sit? (1) Numeri ad*

[126] C. 22, X, *de electione et electi potestate,* I, 6.

[127] Cc. 42, 48, X, *de electione et electi potestate,* I, 6.

[128] C. 57, X, *de electione et electi potestate,* I, 6; cf. c. 2, X, *de renunciatione,* I, 9; c. 6, X, *de his, quae fiunt a praelato sine consensu capituli,* III, 10; c. 1, X, *de his quae fiunt a majori parte capituli,* III, 11; c. 16, C. Lat., III, 1179, Mansi, *o. c.,* I, 408; c. 4, X, *de his quae fiunt a praelato sine consensu capituli,* III, 11; c. 23, *de electione et electi potestate,* I, 6 in VI.°

[129] C. 1, X, *de electione et electi potestate,* I, 6; cc. 42, 50, 55, X, *de electione et electi potestate,* I, 6.

[130] S. C. C. in *Eugub. Mansionariae,* 5 aprilis, 1794.

[131] Schmalzgrueber, *o. c.,* Tom. 1, pars II, tit. VI, n. 22 seqq.

numerum;" (but only absolute votes are to be counted; thus, if 8 out of 12 are absolute, and 5 are for Titius, he is elected). "(*2*) *Zeli ad zelum;*" (the prudence of the electors themselves, their intentions, etc.). "(*3*) *Meriti ad meritum;*" (by considering the science, prudence, etc. of the electors to find the *sanior pars*). * * * *Quoties duae partes capitularium in unum consentiunt c. si quando 9, h. tit. in 6. ubi dicitur, quod contra electores, qui partem reliquam sic excedunt, vel contra eum, qui ab his electus est, a reliqua parte nihil opponi possit quod, etc.* * * * *Facta collatione, si vota ita reperiantur dispersa, ut vel duo aequalem numerum suffragiorum habeant, vel nullus a majore, et saniore capituli parte electus sit, scrutinio illo cassato, ad novum est procedendum. Si vero appareat, quod vel omnes, vel major, et sanior pars in unum, eumque dignum consenserit, mox decretum electionis formari debet, et omnium nomine ab eo, qui capitulo praeest, vel ab alio, per capitulum deputato, publice promulgari c. quia propter. 42. c. cum post petitam 46 h. tit. A majori autem parte electus tunc censebitur, quando in ipsum convenerint non tantum suffragia respective plura, sed quando pars absolute, et respectu omnium ceterarum major, ut constat ex c. ecclesia 48. h. tit.*"[132]

Matters that affected all the members must be approved by all.[133] "*Quod omnes tangit debet ab omnibus approbari.*"[134]

V.

DURATION OF THE CANONICAL MORAL PERSONALITY.

The Canonical moral person was perpetual of its nature, but corporate death was possible. Pre-Code Canon law was similar to Roman jurisprudence in the methods by which the legal personality might be terminated. Thus, the cor-

[132] Schmalzgrueber, *o. c.*, Tom. I, pars, II, tit. VI, n. 48, 49.

[133] c. 7, X, *de officio archidiaconi,* I, 23.

[134] Reg. 29, R. J. in VI.°

poration might be dissolved by the power which created it, for "*omnis res per quascumque causas nascitur, per easdem dissolvitur.*"[135] It might also end by the absence of an essential element for a long period of time, as incorporators. "*Ante Codicem unicus casus, quo ex solo facto deficientiae seu cessationis actualis, juridice quoque persona moralis extinguebatur erat iste, quando scilicet omnis spes et possibilitas resurrectionis amissa fuerat.*[136]

But if a single member survived, all the rights and duties of the corporation vested in this survivor. Pre-Code Canon law borrowed from the Roman juridical scheme the idea that all rights were to vest in the surviving incorporators, even though the membership be reduced to but one individual. To quote from Barbosa: "*Si collegium esse desinat per mortem canonicorum debent substitui alii & quod jus collegii remanet etiam in* UNO *donec fuerit auctoritate Superioris destructum.*"[137] Says Schmalzgrueber: "*Si duo, manet collegium actu, sed velut imperfectum; ac si unus solummodo manet, non erit collegium actu, erit tamen quodammodo habitu: quia jura collegii in illo unico perseverant: Laym. 3 cit.*"[138] The principle that the canonical corporation followed the Roman law to the extent that if the organization was reduced to one member, all rights and duties centered in him may be illustrated by specific cases. Thus, the Congregation for the Propagation of the Faith was asked the question: "*An redacto Capitulo ad unum tantum membrum (in Hibernia) possit, sede vacante, per se solum eligere Vicarium, de quo in cap. 16, sess. 24, Conc. Trid.*" The reply was: "*R. Affirmative dummodo non eligat seipsum.*"[139] Substantially, therefore, all rights centered in the survivor. The Sacred Congregation of the Council was asked: "*Dubitum, 'An ecclesia Carmelitarum*

[135] c. 1, X, *de regularis juris*, V, 41.

[136] Bondini, *Jus Pontificium*, III, 190.

[137] Barbosa, *De Officio et Potestate Parochi*, 20, 28.

[138] Schmalzgrueber, *o. c.*, Tom. I, pars II, tit. VI, n. 8.

[139] S. C. C. Armacana, 12 mart. 1672, "*Collectanea S. Congreg. de Prop. Fide*," n. 203; cf. Waterworth, *o. c.*, 223.

adhuc gaudeat jure sepeliendi seu funerandi, ita ut ad ejus rectorem spectet officium funebre peragere super cadaveribus defunctorum in eadem sepulorum gentilitium habentium.' R. ad I; Affirmative, salvo jure parochi domicilii defuncti pro quota funerum juxta consuetudinem loci."[140] The Carmelites in Forolivien Italy, had been suppressed, but the right of burial was still centered upon the rector (Passinari) who remained.

VI.

ECCLESIASTICAL JURISDICTION OVER THE CANONICAL MORAL PERSON.

The ecclesiastical moral person was usually under the authority of the Bishop of the place in which it was located, unless an exemption from such authority was shown.[141] In the latter event, the moral personality was directly subject to the Pope, as in the case of religious Orders.[142] The rights of the Bishop with respect to those legal persons which came under his jurisdiction included that of visitation, to see, for instance, whether its affairs were being properly administered.[143] This right extended to both collegiate and non-collegiate persons.[144] Roman law recognized this episcopal jurisdiction over canonical moral persons.[145]

The parellel between Roman and pre-Code law with regard to legal personality has been pointed out. In the following chapter, it will be found that the pre-Code law on this subject and hence the conceptions of the Roman law have been generally made a part of the New Code of Canon Law.

[140] *Forolivien,* 16 sept. 1871, ad 1; cf. *Thesaurus Resolutionum Sacrae Congregationis Concilii,* vol. 130, p. 657, 1871, sess. 25, cap. 13, *de ref;* and on p. 669, ad 1.

[141] Cc. 1, 4, 6, X, *de religiosis domibus, ut episcopo sint subjectae,* III, 36.

[142] C. 8, X, *de religiosis domibus, ut episcopo sint subjectae,* III, 36; Conc. Trident., sess. XXV, *de ref.,* c. 8.

[143] Conc. Trident., sess. XXV, *de ref.* c. 8, 9; Santi, *o. c.,* III, 332.

[144] C. 1 to 20, X, *de officio judicis ordinarii,* I, 31; c. 1 to 20, X, *de foro competenti,* II, 2; c. 1 to 27, X, *de censibus, exactionibus et procurationibus,* III, 39.

[145] *Supre* pp. 34, 35.

CHAPTER VI.

THE LEGAL BASIS OF THE CANONICAL JURISTIC PERSONALITY AFTER THE CODE.

I. ITS NATURE.

Canon 99.

"In Ecclesia, praeter personas physicas, sunt etiam personae morales, publicae auctoritate constitutae, quae distinguuntur in personas morales collegiales et non collegiales, ut ecclesiae, Seminaria, beneficia, etc."

Although there is no definition of a *persona moralis* in the *Codex Juris Canonici,* it may be said to be *"quidquid praeter personas physicas in Ecclesia juris possidendi et exercendi capax in ss. canonibus habetur."*[1] It is one that receives its existence from the Church, while a *persona moralis* from the civil viewpoint is one that is at least recognized by the State. Canon 99, then, is authority for the proposition that the Church at the present time recognizes moral persons, as distinguished from physical persons. The nature of the *persona physica* is suggested in the following canon: **"Baptismate homo constituitur in Ecclesia Christi persona cum omnibus christianorum juribus et officiis, nisi, ad jura quod attinet, obstet obex, ecclesiasticae communionis vinculum impediens, vel lata ab Ecclesia censura."**[2] It is therefore manifest from the Code that ecclesiastical personality, that is the power or capacity to acquire and exercise rights in the Church, which arises from the reception of baptism in the case of human beings, may also be conferred upon corporate bodies and institutions by public ecclesiastical authority. These latter are called

[1] Blat, *Commentarium Textus Codicis Juris Canonici,* II, 36.
[2] Canon 87.

moral or legal as contrasted with physical or individual persons.[3] That ecclesiastical moral persons may be constituted *legal* persons by the authority of the Church, with the power of acquiring, retaining and administering temporal goods is also evident from the Code.[4]

Canon 99 does not distinguish the canonical juridical personality according to its activity into public, as the Church bodies in European countries where certain ecclesiastical corporations are agencies of the State, and into private, as the present day American Church corporation. Nor does it divide the ecclesiastical legal person into those with a divine and those with an ecclesiastical origin;[5] the Apostolic See would be an example of the former, while the incorporation of a religious order would be an instance of the latter. Nor does it divide the ecclesiastical juristic personality into lay and clerical. But it emphasizes the *structural* division of the juristic person, according to which the canonical moral person is divided into, first, the collegiate or corporate body, and secondly, the non-collegiate or non corporate, as a benefice.[6] And in emphasizing such a division the New Code is following the Roman and pre-Code law. At the outset, therefore, it is seen that a fundamental conception of the legal personality in Roman and pre-Code has been "canonized" by the New Code. Further similarities will become apparent upon a more specific examination of the Code law.

[3] Ayrinhac, *o. c.*, 213.

[4] Canon 687: *"Ad normam can. 100, tunc tantum fidelium associationes* juridicam *in Ecclesia personam acquirunt, cum a legitimo Superiore ecclesiastico formale obtinuerunt erectionis decretum. Canon 1489 § 1: Hospitalia, orphanotrophia aliaque similia instituta, ad opera religionis vel caritatis sive spiritualis sive temporalis destinata possunt ab Ordinario loci erigi et per ejus decretum* persona juridica *in Ecclesia constitui. Canon 1495 § 2; Etiam ecclesiis singularibus aliisque personis moralibus quae ab ecclesiastica auctoritate in* juridicam personam *erectae sint, jus est, ad normam sacrorum canonum, bona temporalia acquirendi, retinendi et administrandi.*

[5] This is done in Canon 100.

[6] Ayrinhac, *o. c.*, 214.

Canon 100.

"§ 1. Catholica Ecclesia et Apostolica Sedes moralis personae rationem habent ex ipsa ordinatione divina; ceterae inferiores personae morales in Ecclesia eam sortiuntur sive ex ipso juris praescripto sive ex speciali competentis Superioris ecclesiastici concessione data per formale decretum ad finem religiosum vel caritativum."

This part of the canon expresses the thought that it is only from God immediately or through the Church that canonical personality may arise.[7] With respect to the creation of juristic persons or bodies, it must be borne in mind that there are two distinct types in the Church; reference is made to the Holy See and inferior ecclesiastical moral persons respectively.

The Catholic Church and the Holy See have the nature or character of a legal person by direct, divine ordinance. They are not created by public authority and hence are not moral persons in the strict sense.[8] But Apostolic See does not here include Roman Congregations, Tribunals or Offices.[9] *Ratio* means character or nature, i. e., the Catholic Church and Holy See have their own proper rights. They are, therefore, not called "moral persons" by the Code, but are said to have only the *ratio* of such persons. Hence, the Church and the Apostolic See must not have been included among the moral persons mentioned in canon 99 since there churches, benefices and seminaries are directly called (*sunt*) moral persons in the strictly legal acceptation of the word. The *personae morales* of canon 99 would be referable to the *ceterae inferiores personae* of canon 100. They share, however, in the divine *ratio* of the Church and the Holy See.[10] The Church and Holy See are not dependent upon human authority in regard to their foundation, creation or existence or capacity to exercise

[7] *Ibid.*
[8] *Ibid.*
[9] *Ibid.*
[10] Canon § 1.

rights. They transcend the range of civil rights conferred by any particular system of jurisprudence. The Code intended to bring out this fact by the distinctive terminology of *sunt* and *rationem habent.* The Church would, therefore, enjoy corporate rights even in countries and among peoples that had no judicial system. This quasi-juridical personality is God-given, a principle of public law based upon the fact that the Church is a perfect, moral person, divinely commissioned by Christ to teach all peoples,[11] with the two essential elements of corporate personality, i. e., a plurality of members and a definite scope, in union with the Pontifical Primacy.[12] All this is a re-statement of the law which existed before the Code.[13]

II.

CONDITIONS PRECEDENT FOR THE EXISTENCE OF INFERIOR ECCLESIASTICAL MORAL PERSONS.

A. Authority. The creation of inferior moral persons in the Church is the result of ecclesiastical authority. **"Ceterae inferiores personae morales in Ecclesia eam sortiuntur"**[14] . . . is indicative that these minor juridical persons are dependent upon the Church and must be supported by her in the fulfilment of their ends and in the choice of means. They have a share in the divine commission, though they themselves were not divinely founded. There is thus implied the incompetency of civil power in the creation of any ecclesiastical moral person. According to the law of the Code, it is certain that competent authority, namely, the authority of the Church is needed. No canonical moral personality can exist which does not derive its authority from the Church.[15] This is a confirmation of the

[11] Bachofen, *Summa Juris Ecclessiastici,* 44 seqq.
[12] Augustine, *o. c.,* II, 4.
[13] *Supra* pp. 76, 77, 78.
[14] Canon 99.
[15] Cappello, *Summa Juris Publici Ecclesiastici,* 50.

ante-Code ecclesiastical law,[16] and it is in accord with the principles of Roman public law, with regard to municipalities and other inferior State corporations, but differs from Roman private law where State *recognition* was alone necessary to constitute the civil legal personality.[17] Ecclesiastical authority is therefore always needed for the establishment of canonical moral persons,[18] and this even though the undertaking is intended to promote spiritual purposes.

But what ecclesiastical superiores may erect such personalities? An act of public authority is required; hence, only those superiors who possess jurisdiction *"in foro externo,"* i. e., episcopal or at least quasi-episcopal authority. Pontifical moral persons can be erected only by the Apostolic See. According to the Code, Papal authority is required for the establishment of ecclesiastical provinces, dioceses, abbeys or *prelatures nullius,* vicariates Apostolic, perfectures Apostolic.[19] And it is the same in reference to Cathedral or collegiate chapters.[20] The Papal *beneplacitum* is necessary, together with the written consent of the local Ordinary, for the constitution of a house of an exempt Order or congregation, whether it be a *domus formata* or *non formata,*[21] for a monastery of nuns with solemn vows, and for any religious house in countries subject to the Propaganda.[22] Similarly, the Holy See can alone constitute consistorial benefices, and canonically erect Catholic Universities or Catholic faculties.[23]

But the Bishop has the right to erect certain moral persons in his diocese. Thus, he can establish religious congregations, but the Holy See must first be consulted,[24] before the Bishop establishes such moral persons or allows

[16] *Supra* pp. 79, 80, 81.
[17] *Supra* pp. 11, 66, 67.
[18] Augustine, *o. c.,* VI, 546.
[19] Canon 215.
[20] Canon 392.
[21] Canon 488 § 5.
[22] Canon 497, § 1.
[23] Canons 1376, 1414.
[24] Canon 492, § 1.

their foundation. In his diocese, the Bishop has the right to erect confraternities,[25] Seminaries,[26] parishes, hospitals and orphanages.[27] To erect and approve societies is the privilege of the Roman Pontiff and of the Bishop; some are by Papal indult reserved to others.[28] A Vicar General, however, by a merely general commission and a Vicar Capitular can not erect societies nor give consent for their erection.[29] They are similarly limited with reference to the establishment of religious congregations of diocesan right.[30] And a Vicar General can not erect benefices or other forms of the non-collegiate person without a special mandate of the Ordinary.[31] Besides the Pope, the Ordinaries may erect in their respective territory non-consistorial benefices, with the exception of canon 394 § 2, which reserves to the Holy See the erection of dignities in the Cathedral Chapter.[32] Cardinals may erect in the Church of their title benefices which have not the care of souls attached, unless the Church belongs to a clerical exempt community of religious.[33] Religious are able to erect *pia opera,* hospitals, schools and the like with the consent of the local bishop.[34]

B. The Decree of Erection. Societies and charitable undertakings do only then acquire the right of a legal person in the Church when they have obtained from the competent ecclesiastical superior the decree of erection.[35] This decree must constitute a positive conference of legal personality upon the organization either by express statement or by implication, for it would not be enough if the document was only an approval such as is given to Church organizations which amount to nothing more than collective

[25] Canon 708.
[26] Canon 1354.
[27] Canon 1489, § 1.
[28] Canon 686, § 2.
[29] Canon 686, § 4.
[30] Canon 492, § 1.
[31] Canon 1414, § 3.
[32] Canon 1414, § 2.
[33] Canon 1414, § 4.
[34] Canon 497, § 3.
[35] Canon 687.

persons.[36] The decree should be formal, stating that this moral personality is for this particular end, specifying its character, etc. It is to be in writing. It is not the same as the constitution of the body; the constitution rather contains the complete specific law of the moral personality. It is in the above sense that the words "ex speciali competentis Superioris ecclesiastici concessione data per formale decretum" of canon 100 are to be understood. This canon indicates that not only may the inferior moral persons of the Church be erected *ab homine* as indicated above, but also *a jure,* i. e. automotically, as it were, by compliance with specified conditions.[37]

C. Scope. "Ad finem religosum vel caritativum" indicates that the purpose or scope of the canonical moral person must be of a particular kind, after the fashion of the pre-Code law. Roman law, however, was satisfied with any legitimate scope. These inferior moral persons are subordinate to the Church whose mission is supernatural. Hence, the end of such legal entities must be in accord with this general aim. They must exist for religious or charitable purposes.[38] This end is necessarily different from that of merely civil corporations since Church and State were created for different ends.[39] The scope of the ecclesiastical corporation must pertain directly to the love of God, otherwise it would not be different from a humanitarian undertaking based simply on natural motives of philanthropy.[40] If the proper scope does not exist there can be no ecclesiastical moral person. There is no *subjectum* of canonical rights and duties. There may exist a *persona collectiva,* as in the case of certain pious associations, and these may enjoy special ecclesiastical privileges, but these are not moral persons. The moral person acts *per se;* a *persona collectiva* is simply the agent of the members.

[36] Ayrinhac, *o. c.,* 215.
[37] Toso, *Jus Pontificium,* I, 100.
[38] Canon 100, § 1; Ayrinhac, *o. c.,* 215.
[39] Augustine, *o. c.,* II, 191.
[40] Wernz, *o. c.,* III, 95.

D. Plurality of Members. In order that an ecclesiastical collegiate moral person may come into being the Code stipulates that there must be a number of physical persons. This element has been directly taken from the Roman and ante-Code law.[41]

Canon 100 § 2.

"Persona moralis collegialis constitui non potest nisi ex tribus saltem personis physicis."

There must be at least three incorporators for the establishment of the corporation. Various reasons have been given to explain the psychology of this numerical requirement. Thus, it has been suggested that it enables the corporation to act as such, and it makes it possible for the incorporators to be of such numbers as to permit a majority in votes which determine corporate policy.[42]

E. Fundus. Not only may an ecclesiastical *persona moralis* be a plurality of members pursuing a particular end,[43] but it may assume the form of a non-collegiate body which may be an institution or a collection of property destined for a certain end, by virtue of which the *fundus* becomes the subject of rights and duties, as *pia causa,* benefice and the like. The distinction between collegiate and non-collegiate, called in Roman law, *universitas personarum* and *universitas bonorum* respectively, and between the pre-Code *collegium* and *institutio,* is clearly drawn in canon 99. The non-collegiate canonical body is not supported by natural persons, although this support is essential for the *de facto* existence of the corporation. Hospitals, orphan asylums, benefices, etc., are instances of non-collegiate bodies. The subject of non-corporate ecclesiastical persons is dealt with in the fifth part of the Third Book of the New Code. Ecclesiastical institutions may be looked upon either as juridical entities in the strict sense, or in the

41 *Supra* pp. 64, 81.
42 Ayrinhac, *o. c.*, 215.
43 Cavagnis, *Institutiones Juris Publici Ecclesiastici,* III, 363.

broader connotation which would include a corporate character, as when the institution is under the administration of a religious corporation. The Code has substantially followed the principles of Roman and pre-Code Canon law with respect to the non-collegiate moral personality by requiring the *fundus,* a specific scope, and the authority of the proper Superior.

The benefice is an important example of the ecclesiastical non-collegiate moral person. It may be used to illustrate in a general way the essential character of such personalities. The term *benefice* has been defined as a juridiical entity permanently established or erected by a competent authority and consisting of a sacred office and the right of receiving the revenues from the endowment attached thereto.[44] In canon 1409 it will be noticed that the term *ens juridicum* is used instead of *persona moralis. Ens juridicum* is the generic phrase which includes all types of persons recognized by law, and it here indicates the basic element of the non-collegiate juristic person. There is a personification of the benefice, which is thus looked upon as a new distinct subject of rights and duties. A spiritual and a material element, as it were, combine to form a benefice. The sacred office is the spiritual principle, the capacity of receiving revenues for services rendered is the material constituent.[45]

Benefices may be traced to Germanic law, where the term indicated a "grant" or more particularly the property given to vassals as a reward for services performed.[46] It was not until later, however, that the canonical benefice reached a high degree of development. It dated from the 6th century and was universally adopted about the beginning of the 11th.[47] The system of benefices was one of the methods by which the clergy was sustained, and this finan-

[44] Canon 1409.
[45] Augustine, *o. c.,* VI, 493.
[46] *Ibid.*
[47] Cf. Creagh, *Catholic Encyclopedia,* II, 473, *benefice.*

cial arrangement was endorsed by both ecclesiastical and civil law. The Bishop at first administered these revenues in the support of the clergy, but eventually the rural clergy were permitted to keep a certain part of the gifts of realty which they received, together with the money derived from the usufruct of lands. But these proceeds were called *precaria* because of the short tenure of the property, since each parochial vacancy necessitated a new petition asking for the privileges. The *fundus* including the lands and the revenues derived therefrom became a benefice as soon as the need for successive petitions was done away with; the *fundus* became a permanent juridical personality. The final step was the giving of permanency to the incumbent's office[48] Nor did subsequent secularization radically change the nature of the benefice. The clergy simply received their revenues in annual installments and were called "beneficed clerics."[49]

The conception of benefices was not the product of ecclesiastical law so far as their origin was concerned. But ecclesiastical sanction is essential for their formation, since their purpose or end is spiritual and there is involved the combination of a spiritual and a material element for the realization of this end. Ecclesiastical jurisdiction always exists in spiritual matters.

The revenues which are connected with a benefice are used in the support of a spiritual undertaking. But this indicates that there exists a financial source or treasury. Such a source is called a *dos* or *dowry*. Each benefice must have its *dos*. To be adequate, the *dos* must have certain elements. It must be stable and of a size sufficient for the maintenance of the ministers and the accomplishment of the spiritual undertaking.

In the case of an endowment of a benefice, the founder may recommend certain conditions for the administration of the benefice provided they are acceptable to the ecclesi-

[48] *Ibid.* 475.
[49] Augustine, *o. c.*, VI, 492.

astical authorities.[50] This implies that the stipulations must be reasonable and in keeping with the end to be attained by the endowment. These conditions must be complied with when once accepted since they are contractual, unless their change is for the best interests of the Church and the founder consents to their modification.[51] Regardless of whether it is the Church, *dos,* or benefice or combination of them which is the non-collegiate moral personality, in any event this legal person is ecclesiastical and participates in the divinely conferred rights of the Church. Moreover, the administrators of the legal personality would be the same in each case.

III.

STATUS OF THE ECCLESIASTICAL MORAL PERSONALITY.

Canon 100 § 3.

"Personae morales sive collegiales sive non-collegiales minoribus aequiparantur."

The *status* of a moral person has reference to its position as a distinct personality, involving its legal capacity to exercise certain rights and to be subject to certain duties, which are not the rights and duties of the members who constitute it. The ecclesiastical moral person may do all those things which by law a physical person can do, except what is peculiar to the physical person as such. In a word, it can perform those acts which are proper to its end.[52] All moral persons are assimilated to the *status* of minors.[53] The law extends to them the same protection as to persons un-

[50] Canon 1417, § 1.

[51] Canon 1417, § 2; Reiffenstuel, *Jus Canonicum Universum,* Tom. III, lib. iii, tit. V, § IV, n. 112.

[52] Canon 691; Maroto, *Institutiones Juris Canonici,* I, 544.

[53] Blat, *Commentarium,* 29.

der age because no doubt the interests of the body are not cared for with the same attention as they would be in the event that the individuals were directly affected.[54] The Roman and pre-Code law are followed in this matter The corporation, like a child, has the right of *restitutio in integrum,*[55] and like a minor it is represented by agents who correspond to a tutor in relation to his minor.[56]

IV.

MODE OF ACTING OF THE ECCLESIASTICAL COLLEGIATE MORAL PERSON.

Canon 101.

§ 1. Circa actus personarum moralium collegialium:

1.° Nisi aliud expresse jure communi aut particulari statutum fuerit, id vim juris habet, quod, demptis suffragiis nullis, placuerit parti absolute majori eorum qui suffragium ferunt, aut, post duo inefficacia scrutinia, parti relative majori in tertio scrutinio; quod si suffragia aequalia fuerint, post tertium scrutinium praeses suo voto paritatem dirimat aut, si agatur de electionibus et praeses suo voto paritatem dirimere nolit, electus habeatur senior ordine vel prima professione vel aetate.

2.° Quod autem omnes, uti singulos, tangit, ab omnibus probari debet."

Since the collegiate body is not a physical but only a moral person, it can not act without *corporati,* who are evidently necessary for the transaction and management of corporate affairs. The corporation can perform legal acts only through agents or administrators. In some matters these collegiate persons may be represented by administrators authorized to act in their own name and according to their own discretion.[57] And what these representatives de-

[54] *Ibid.*
[55] Canon 1688, § 1.
[56] Canon 1647, § 2; Canon 1649.
[57] Ayrinhac, *o. c.*, 216.

cide upon and do within the scope of their authority is looked upon as the act of the corporation itself. But the corporation may also act in a collegiate manner. Two types of questions may come before the meeting, namely, those which affect each one individually, and those which do not. The collegiate procedure will vary according to the type of question, as suggested above.

With regard to the actions of collegiate legal bodies in the Church not affecting each individually, it is the rule, unless either the common law or particular statutes prescribe a different course of action, that the absolute majority of votes of all those who have a right to vote and actually do vote, decides a question, and if in the first two votings no majority is obtained the relative majority of votes in the third voting decides; if in the third voting, the votes are even, the president of the election can end the tie; if the president does not want to do this, and there is question of an election, the senior in ordination, in first profession or in age is to be considered elected. This canon, then, establishes certain norms to be followed at meetings which are convened to determine matters proposed to the vote of the members of the corporate body. The law speaks only of such acts as are voted on by valid ballot of the members present. By the common law, members who absent themselves thereby forfeit their ballot and can not later be heard to object to the decision arrived at by the majority. But if the corporation has a constitution or is subject to a statute containing a clause that the votes are to be counted with reference to the whole number of members, present or absent, then this rule is to be respected.[58] Particular law may prescribe a special mode in certain cases, thus, the Code stipulates certain norms in regard to elections in general,[59] and the *Vacante Sede Apostolica*[60] formulates specific rules for the conduct of Papal elections. Particular

[58] Augustine, *o. c.*, II, 25.
[59] Canons 160 to 178.
[60] Pius X, dec. 25, 1904, n. 57, *Fontes* n. 663.

statutes, therefore, may indicate those who have the right of participating in elections directing corporate policies, and those who must be summoned, but there are certain rules applicable to all corporate procedure by ecclesiastical authorities.[61] With reference to the number required for a quorum, it may be said that provided at least two thirds of the voters had been notified the right of electing vests in those who appear on the appointed day.[62]

If there is no special legislation to the contrary, there must be an absolute majority of the valid votes cast in the first and second ballotings for a valid decision. Votes which are null and void are not included. But what constitutes an absolute majority? How does it differ from a relative majority? An absolute majority is at least more than half of the votes cast. Thus, if out of 49 voters upon the issue of the purchase of property, 25 are affirmative and 24 negative, there would be an absolute majority of one. A relative majority will be sufficient in the third balloting if an absolute majority can not be obtained either in the first or second voting.[63] But a relative majority presupposes that there are at least 3 resolutions, or 3 candidates before the consideration of the convention. Thus, if 14 out of 40 voters would decide for candidate A, while 11 would vote for candidate B, and 15 would favor candidate C, the last vote would carry. A relative majority, therefore, corresponds to a plurality, i. e., more votes than any other candidate. But for the first two ballots, an absolute majority is required; hence, in this case, 21 out of 40 votes would be essential for the election of candidate C.[64]

In every collegiate body there are not only rights which are proper to the corporate entity as such, for instance corporate property, but also rights which radically and vitally affect each member as such. It is to this second type that the words "**quod autem omnes, uti singulos, tangit, ab om-**

[61] Maroto, *Institutiones Juris Canonici*, I, 467; Canon 162.
[62] Canon 162, § 3; Canon 163.
[63] Ayrinhac, *o. c.*, 216.
[64] Augustine, *o. c.*, II, 26.

nibus probari debet" refer. Compromise of an election would be an instance of this second type.[65] It would have to be agreed upon by all: *"Electio, nisi aliud jure caveatur, fieri et jam potest per compromissum, si nempe electores unanimi et scripto consensu, in unum vel plures idoneos, sive de gremio sive extraneos jus eligendi pro ea vice transferant, qui nomine omnium ex recepta facultate eligant."*[66] Unanimous consent would also be required where an additional personal obligation is imposed, as a personal assessment.[67]

Canon 101.

"§ 2. Si de actibus personarum moralium non collegialium agatur, serventur particularia statuta ac normae juris communis, quae easdem personas respiciunt."

Non-collegiate moral persons are governed by the law which is specified at the time of the establishment of such a person. The founder of such an institution, i. e., the one through whose generosity the institution is possible, has the privilege of attaching certain conditions at the time of the foundation.[68] These are to be followed; afterwards, the common law.[69] In general, therefore, if there is question of the actions of non-collegiate legal persons, the particular statutes and the norms of the common law regarding such persons are to be followed.

What does a comparative study of Roman, pre-Code and Code laws with respect to elections indicate? The principles of the Roman and pre-Code laws have been "canonized" by the New Code in that all those of the *collegium* who have the right to vote should be summoned.[70] Roman

[65] Blat, *o. c.*, II, 40.
[66] Canon 172, § 1.
[67] Blat, *o. c.*, II, 40.
[68] Cf. Canons 1417, § 1; 1450, § 2; 1492, § 2.
[69] *Toso Jus Pontificium* II, 46.
[70] *Supra* pp. 71, 84.

law demanded that for the validity of a resolution's adoption that at least two thirds of all *corporati* should be present, the *Digest* declaring: *"Nulli permittitur nomine civitatis vel curiae experiri nisi ei, cui lex permittit, aut lege cessante ordo dedit cum duae partes adessent aut amplius quam duae."*[71] But pre-Code Canon law and the New Code insist that at least two thirds of the electors should be notified and that if more than a third part did not receive such notice the election is invalid.[72] Those who then assembled constitute a quorum. According to Roman law, the quorum of two thirds of the *corporati,* in order to pass resolutions which are binding upon the corporation as expressive of its will must record an absolute majority vote.[73] To quote from the Roman Sources: *"Quod major pars curiae effecit pro eo habetur ac si omnes egerint."*[74] This principle was followed by the pre-Code Canon law with the limitation that this major part must also be the saner.[75] The Code, however, requires this absolute majority, i. e., at least more than half[76] only on the first two ballots, a relative majority or plurality is sufficient on the third ballot.[77] The Code has not "canonized" the pre-Code conception of the *sanior pars.* But the Code and ante-Code law are identical in that the unanimous consent of the members is required in the disposition of matters affecting all.

V.

DURATION OF THE CANONICAL MORAL PERSON.

Canon 102.

"§ 1. Persona moralis, natura sua, perpetua est; extinguitur tamen si a legitima auctoritate supprimatur, vel si per centum annorum spatium esse desierit."

[71] *Dig.* 3, 4, 3.
[72] Canon 162, § 3.
[73] Ayrinhac, *o. c.,* 217.
[74] *Dig.* 50, 1, 19.
[75] *Supra* pp. 83, 84.
[76] Canon 101, § 1, n. 1.
[77] *Ibid.*

After the fashion of the Roman and pre-Code laws, the Code regards the moral person as perpetual of its very nature. There is a perpetual succession in a collegiate body, i. e., old members can be replaced by new ones and in a non-collegiate body, the scope is immortalized as it were. But according to the Code, extinction may result in either one of two ways, first, by suppression through legitimate authority, and secondly, by the personality's having ceased to exist, there being no members for the period of one hundred years.

First, legitimate authority would be that authority by which it was established or some higher authority; if there is no particular law to the contrary, the competent Superior.[78] Of course in certain cases Superiors who erected the moral person can not extinguish it.[79] Non-ecclesiastical power would always be ineffectual,[80] thus lay or civil authority.[81] Any religious body, even a diocesan congregation, which has been legally established can not be dissolved, even though it should consist of only one house, except by authority of the Holy See, to which is also reserved the disposition of the goods of the congregation, saving the legitimate will and intention of the donors.[82] A religious house belonging to an exempt religious organization can be suppressed only by permission of the Holy See; if it belongs to a non-exempt congregation of papal law it can be suppressed by the General with the consent of the local Ordinary; if it is a house of a diocesan congregation, it can be suppressed by the sole authority of the Bishop after having given hearing to the head of the congregation, and then the congregation has the right of appeal to the Holy See *in suspensivo*, i. e., the community or house can not be disturbed before Rome has decided.[83] For serious reason the

[78] Maroto, *o. c.*, I, 463.
[79] Canons 493, 498.
[80] Canon 493; Cappello, *Summa Juris Publici Ecclesiastici*, 64.
[81] Canon 498.
[82] Canon 493.
[83] Canon 498.

Bishop of the diocese can suppress societies which were erected either by himself or by his predecessor, and also societies erected by religious in virtue of apostolic indult with consent of the Ordinary. Recourse to the Holy See is permitted to those concerned. Societies erected by the Holy See itself can be suppressed only by the Holy See.[84] With reference to non-collegiate moral persons, the suppression and dismembration of such bodies are reserved to the Holy See.[85]

Secondly, an ecclesiastical moral person may *de jure* die by complete cessation for a period of one hundred years. If at any time there is a total absence of members, the moral person can not function and it may be said to be *de facto* dead, i. e., it does not act because there exist no individuals through whom it can function. But such *de facto* death does not destroy *de jure* existence. For this latter, the complete lack of membership must continue for at least one hundred years.[86] Any time during this period it may be revived and a new decree is not necessary. But after one hundred years have elapsed, this is not the case. It can not be revived by its own power.[87]

Canon 102.

"§ 2. Si vel unum ex personae moralis collegialis membris supersit, jus omnium in illud recidit"

A collegiate canonical moral person once duly constituted can continue to exist without the full quorum of three members. The corporation would still remain if one of the incorporators subsequently died, and this would be true even though but one of the *corporati* survived. The rights of all vest in this survivor. Of course, this does not generally happen. This surviving member need not be one of the original incorporators, as the corporation is an entity

[84] Canon 699.
[85] Canon 1422; Canon 1494.
[86] Ayrinhac, *o. c.,* 219.
[87] Bouix, *De Capitulis,* 601.

distinct from the personality of the members. This vesting of all rights in a single survivor is a re-statement of the pre-Code law and Roman jurisprudence upon this subject. Indeed the phraseology of this part of the canon is taken almost verbatim from the Justinian Sources, *Digest* 3, 4, 7, 2.

VI.

ECCLESIASTICAL JURISDICTION OVER THE CANONICAL MORAL PERSON.

Generally speaking all ecclesiastical moral persons are subject to the Bishop, but some are placed under the jurisdiction of the Holy See. Such persons are always under ecclesiastical authority and all which that implies. According to the law of the Church there are different degrees of ecclesiastical authority depending upon the conditions involved in the establishment of the moral person. Moral persons may be directly subject to the Pope, or to the Bishop of the place where they exist. Or they may occupy, as it were, an intermediate position with regard to these two authorities. Thus, religious orders are withdrawn from the jurisdiction of the Bishop and are immediately subject to the Pope;[88] there the Bishop has only limited rights. Or it may be an exempted religious congregation of papal approval enjoying episcopal exemption by way of privilege, not by law, as would be the case in the instance of an order.[89] While certain religious congregations are exempted, non-exempt religious congregations are subject to the Bishop except in certain things in which the Pope has authority.[90] Or the moral person may be a diocesan institute entirely subject to the Bishop. Hence, it may be said that there are three different degrees of authority, illus-

[88] Canon 613, § 1 and 2; Canon 500; Canon 488, § 2.
[89] Canon 488, § 2.
[90] Canon 394.

trated by religious orders, congregations, and diocesan institutes.

The jurisdiction of the Bishop over ecclesiastical moral persons is extensive. Thus, he has the power of visitation. To the visitation of the Bishop are subject the persons, goods and pious institutions, even though exempt, within the limits of his diocese, unless special exemption is proved to have been granted them by the Holy See. The Bishop can visit the exempt religious only in the cases stated in law.[91] The episcopal right of visitation extends to diocesan seminaries and the like.[92]

According to the Code, the local Ordinary must either himself or through another every five years visit, first, each monastery of nuns with solemn vows which is subject to him or immediately subject to the Holy See, and secondly, each house of diocesan congregations of both men and women; and within the same time, he must visit monasteries of nuns with solemn vows subject to the regulars, to inquire about the observance of the law of enclosure and also concerning the rest of the religious life if the regular Superior did not hold any visitation within the last five years; each house of clerical congregations of papal law, even those enjoying exemptions, the visitation to extend only to the Church, sacristy, public oratory and places where the confessions are heard; each house of laical congregations of papal law, the visitation to embrace not only those points above mentioned but also all other affairs concerning internal discipline.[93] All societies of faithful even those erected by the Holy See are under the jurisdiction and vigilance of the Ordinary of the diocese unless there is a special privilege of exemption.[94] Ordinaries of dioceses have the right, either in person or through others, to visit

[91] Canon 344, § 1.
[92] Canon 1357, § 2.
[93] Canon 512.
[94] Canon 690.

in reference to religion and moral instruction any schools, oratories, and the like, and from this visitation the schools conducted by a religious community are not excepted, unless it is a school exclusively for the professed members of an exempt order.[95] And the diocesan Ordinary has the right to visit all non-collegiate bodies though they have been made legal persons and given in charge of exempt persons.[96]

In general, such visitations are made for the purpose of assertaining whether the moral person is carrying out its obligations in view of its charter, and whether it is observing the obligations of canon and general law, etc. The visitor has the right and duty to ask, for instance, any of the religious whom he thinks according to his own judgment that he should ask, to obtain knowledge of those things that are within the scope of the visitation. But he must act with respect for everybody's rights. Thus, the visitor should proceed in a paternal manner concerning the object and purpose of the visitation, in accordance with the rules of law,[97] and should not unduly prolong the visit.[98] The act is rescindable if his conduct is contrary to the rights of all those concerned.

The Ordinary is to be given an accounting. In every monastery of nuns with solemn vows, even exempt ones, the Superioress shall once a year or more frequently if the constitutions so demand give an account to the Ordinary of her administration.[99] If the Ordinary does not approve of the administration he may employ proper means to remedy the defect even removing if necessary the *Oeconomus* and other administrators. If the house is subject to the regular superior, the Ordinary shall admonish the Superior to remedy the deficiency and if he does not attend to it, the Ordinary has the right to take the matter in hand. In all

[95] Canon 1382.
[96] Canon 1491.
[97] Canon 345.
[98] Canon 346.
[99] Canon 535.

other houses of religious women, an account must be given to the Ordinary of the administration of goods that constitute the dowry of the sisters. The Ordinary shall have the right to inquire into the financial standing of the religious houses of diocesan sisterhoods and to demand an account of the administration of real estate and legacies given to parishes or for works of religion and charity.[100] Though pious institutes should be exempt from the jurisdiction and visitation of the Ordinary, either by foundation or prescription, or Apostolic Indult, he has the right to demand a financial statement; every contrary custom is disapproved.[101] Delegated executors of institutions administering pious donations must also give an account to the Ordinary of the exercise of their office,[102] and each year all diocesan administrators are bound to give a financial inventory to the Bishop.[103]

In conclusion, the Code has substantially followed the principles of Roman and pre-Code Canon law with respect to the moral personality by requiring a plurality of members or a *fundus,* depending upon the character of the personality, a specific scope and the authority of the proper Superior; and it has formulated the same general plan of administration and similar rules for the termination of this type of legal personality. It now remains to shift the point of view and to consider the canonical juristic personality with reference to its *status* in the United States. This will be the purpose of the remaining chapters.

[100] Canon 535.
[101] Canon 1492.
[102] Canon 1515.
[103] Canon 1525.

CHAPTER VII.

THE CHURCH IN THE UNITED STATES UNDER FEDERAL AND STATE CONSTITUTIONAL LAW.

Constitutional law is the organic or basic law of the land whether it be federal or state. The federal constitution is the written formulation of the fundamental legal principles which are to govern the people of the United States as citizens of the national government; the constitutions of the respective states are the basic law which has been chosen by the people as citizens of an individual state to be the foundation of their rights and duties. It is proposed to examine the *status* of the Catholic Church under the federal constitution and under the constitutions of the respective states. But as an approach to this juridical question, it will be useful to suggest briefly the background under which the American view toward religion generally was developed.

"Religious enthusiasm, human affection, the pursuit of gain—these three motives account for the peopling of America by men of European stock and Christian faith."[1] Though there were many other influences at work, the birth of this government was in no small measure the result of the religious impulse. Early migrations, such as those of the colonists of Plymouth,[2] Massachusetts Bay,[3] New Haven,[4] Maryland[5] and the like; the brilliant Spanish expeditions into the unchartered Southeast and Southwest; the spirit that sent the Jesuits and Franciscans into the wilderness of the Middle-West . . . are manifestations of the religious motive that permeated the early history of the American continent.

[1] Channing, *A History of the United States*, I, 1.
[2] *Ibid.*, 293 seqq.
[3] *Ibid.*, 322 seqq.
[4] *Ibid.*, 407 seqq.
[5] *Ibid.*, 241 seqq.

Though the religious urge was a vital factor in the discovery, exploration and colonization of America, by a strange anomaly, intolerance was an accompaniment. This was true of the thirteen original colonies. There discriminations were aimed at sects which were at variance with the faith of the particular commonwealth, but most particularly at Roman Catholics.[6] Massachusetts limited the full exercise of civil rights to Church members of the "Bible Commonwealth."[7] Statutes there against Protestant dissenters, however, were repealed in 1691.[8] The colonists of the New Haven Colony passed laws for the enforcement of one religious system to the exclusion of all others and allowed only Church members to hold public office.[9] Maryland by legislative enactment limited religious liberty to Protestants who professed the Trinity.[10] New York in its Charter of Liberties of 1683 extended full civil liberty only to Christians, and Pennsylvania by its Code of Laws of 1701 took a somewhat similar position.[11] In Connecticut, certain sects as Quakers were excluded.[12] Religious tolerance was the rule only in Rhode Island, by Charter in 1663,[13] and for a time in Carolina; in the latter instance to attract immigrants.[14]

What was the status of the Catholic Church and Catholics in these pre-Revolutionary days? In Massachusetts, the Charter of William and Mary of 1691 provided that there should be "a liberty of conscience allowed in the worship of God to all Christians except Papists."[15] East Jersey by the Declaratory Act of 1698 extended religious tol-

[6] Channing, *o. c.*, II, 423 seqq.

[7] General Court of Massachusetts, 1631, Tyler, *o. c.*, § 80; Channing, *o. c.*, I, 342 seqq.

[8] Landon, *The Constitutional History and Government of the United States*, 29.

[9] Channing, *o. c.*, I, 409 seqq.

[10] *Ibid.*, 430.

[11] Tyler, *o. c.*, § 82.

[12] Landon, *o. c.*, 29.

[13] Landon, *o. c.*, 30.

[14] Tyler, *o. c.*, § 85.

[15] Landon, *o. c.*, 29.

erance only to Protestant denominations; West Jersey by the Legislative Act of 1693 allowed only those to hold office who made the prescribed profession of faith.[16] North Carolina as late as 1776 by constitutional provision permitted only Protestants to hold public office.[17] From 1704 to the Revolution anti-Catholic laws prevailed in Maryland.[18] In 1704 Governor Seymour of Maryland forbade public Catholic services but Queen Anne abrogated this rule by permission to hold services in individual houses.[19] It was not until 1783 that Catholics received full political rights in Rhode Island.[20] Pennsylvania had discriminatory statutes, but the act of 1730 was not put into effect so that the anti-Catholic enactments were in practice non-operative. These statutes forbade all but Protestants the right of tenure of lands and real estate for asylums, schools, and churches.[21] Laws directed against Catholics were passed in New York and Massachusetts in conformity with the English Parliamentary Act of 1699.[22]

This in brief was the religious situation among the early Colonists until political trouble arose with England. Religious differences to a large extent yielded to governmental necessity. Of course there still existed union of Church and State in many of the Colonies even after the Revolution. But New England Congregationalists, New Jersey Presbyterians, Southern Episcopalians and Maryland Catholics, all comrades in the War of the Revolution, had learned the need of religious tolerance if all were to share in the benefits of a united government. The representatives of the states in the memorable Constitutional Convention of 1787 did not forget to dispose of the question of religious liberty. They inserted Art. VI, cl. 3 into the first draft of the

[16] Tyler, *o. c.*, § 80; Landon, *o. c.*, 32.
[17] Tyler, *o. c.*, § 83.
[18] Channing, *o. c.*, II, 424.
[19] Baart, *o. c.*, 8.
[20] Channing, *o. c.*, II, 427.
[21] Baart, *o. c.*, 7.
[22] Channing, *o. c.*, II, 426.

Constitution: "No religious test shall ever be required as a qualification to any office or public trust under the United States." But even this did not satisfy the different states when the document was submitted to them for approval. They wished to end once and for all every possibility of a national church, first, because they realized that as between the states, soon to be united in a more perfect union, differences over religion would prove a disturbing issue, and secondly, many of the states maintained religious establishments with which they did not wish the federal government to interfere.[23] Accordingly, the first Congress meeting under the Constitution proposed the following amendment, which was approved by the necessary number of states: "Congress shall make no law respecting an establishment of religion or prohibiting the free exercise thereof."[24]

This integral part of the organic law of the land is not, however, to be construed as binding the states to assume an attitude of religious liberty. The contents of the Constitution are binding only upon the federal government.[25] Nor does the clause: "Citizens of each state shall be entitled to all the privileges and immunities of citizens in the several states,"[26] alter the situation, for the section has been interpreted by the United States Supreme Court as not applying to the question of religious tolerance.[27] Our national government is one of delegated powers, for by the tenth amendment: "The powers not delegated to the United States by the Constitution, nor prohibited by it to the states, are reserved to the states respectively or to the people." Hence, the Constitution of the United States does not limit the action of the states in the matter of religious liberty, but only Congress.[28] In theory, then, a state might

[23] Baart, *o. c.*, 13.
[24] First Amendment.
[25] Desmond, *o. c.*, 17.
[26] Art. IV, Sec. 2.
[27] Slaughter House Cases, 16 Wallace 36 (U. S.).
[28] Permoli *v.* Municipality No. 1 of New Orleans, 3 Howard 589 (U. S.).

now establish a state religion and restrict the activities of other religious professions,[29] but in practice it seems that the fourteenth amendment offers a constitutional guarantee against extreme methods of state religious intolerance, such as laws of a confiscatory character,[30] although this opinion is denied by certain authorities.[31]

The religious situation in the United States today, then, is this: that the federal and state constitutional law aims to confer complete religious liberty within reasonable bounds. Just as liberty in general is to be tempered with reason, so too religious freedom is not allowed as a guise to shield acts and practices contrary to public policy, morality and good citizenship.[32] For a religious belief can not be accepted as a justification of an overt act made criminal by the positive law.[33] Thus, the first constitutional amendment could not be used as a defense against action by Congress in enacting a law making polyamy a crime.[34] In a general way, the fundamental moral principles and ethical tenets of Christianity which is the predominant religion of the American people are accepted by the federal and state governments as the norm by which good citizenship is to be measured.[35] Indeed, the stupendous march of our civilization is in no small measure due to the establishment and maintenance of Christianity.[36] But in so far as legislative enactment is concerned there is sanctioned a governmental policy of *laissez faire* toward all religions,[37] although the civil government has frequently intervened in the prevention of practices purported to be the result of religious motive, which have offended against public welfare.[38]

[29] People *v.* Board of Education, 245 Ill. 334; 92 N. E. 251.

[30] Cooley, *Principles of Constitutional Law*, 224.

[31] Desmond, *o. c.*, 17.

[32] Opinion of the Justices, *In re*, 214 Mass. 599; Zollmann, *American Civil Church Law*, 12.

[33] Reynolds *v.* U. S., 98 U. S. 145.

[34] Zollmann, *o. c.*, 9.

[35] D. C. *v.* Robinson, 30 App. D. C. 283.

[36] Hunt, *Laws relating to Religious Corporations*, xviii of Introduction by E. L. Fancher.

[37] Cooley, *o. c.*, 225.

[38] Zollmann, *o. c.*, 36.

There is no religious establishment in the United States, either under the organic law of the federal or the state governments. Religious qualifications for the exercise of the electoral franchise or as a condition precedent for tenure of civil office and the like have never been known in the domain of the national law. They have never been prescribed by Congress. Its legislation in the field of religion has been restricted to the inconsequential practice of providing chaplains for purposes of prayer in the two Houses of Congress, and for the military and naval forces of the government.[39] All denominations enjoy equality of *status* under the constitution of the United States.

That document, however, does not recognize the divine institution of the Catholic Church nor its legal authority to create corporations which can exercise civil rights irrespective of the government.[40] Hence, in the United States proper, the Catholic Church is looked upon merely as a hierarchy,[41] not as a corporate entity. This same view is shared by the states. The Church as such can acquire temporal rights only by treaty with the government in Washington, after the fashion of a foreign power.[42] But the corporate personality of the Church is expressly recognized in certain of our territorial possessions.

It was the acknowledgment by the United States of the Papal sovereignty in international law that influenced this country to recognize by the Treaty of Paris in 1898 the legal personality of the Church in those territorial acquisitions which were originally under Spanish dominion.[43] European countries, including Spain, since the fourth century or the time of Constantine the Great,[44] had given certain lands to the Church which was universally recognized as a corporate entity.[45] Roman Catholicism was the state

[39] Cooley, *o. c.*, 225.

[40] Pawlett *v.* Clark, 9 Cranch 292 (U. S.).

[41] Baart, *o. c.*, 14.

[42] Bonacum *v.* Murphy, 71 Neb. 463.

[43] Santos *v.* Holy Roman Catholic Church, 212 U. S. 463; *Treaty,* Art. VIII, cited in Ponce *v.* Roman Catholic Church, 210 U. S. 296.

[44] Milman, *History of Latin Christianity,* I, 507.

[45] Baart, *o. c.*, 15.

religion of Spain from the time of the Visigoths. The Spanish Monarchs were patrons of the Church in the West Indies and Spanish America generally. Alexander VI (1492-1503) and Julius II (1503-1513) had agreed with Spain to accept from her financial assistance in consideration of Spain's receipt of the tithes of the Indies.[46] From the very beginning of Spanish colonization in America, the legal personality of the Church with unrestricted corporate rights, including ownership, had been acknowledged by a number of concordats entered into between Spain and the Papacy.[47] There was, therefore, an international obligation on the part of the United States, when she took over these territories to allow the continuance of the *status quo*. Nor was this *status* affected even though some of the money for the support of the churches had been given by the State.[48]

In Cuba, Porto Rico and the Philippines, the United States by treaty guaranteed the Church the enjoyment of her corporate rights, extending the constitutional principle of the sanctity of contract to international dealings.[49] But the recognition thus extended in the Treaty of Paris should not be considered in the nature of a concession, but rather as a written guarantee. The highest tribunal of the United States has always insisted upon the binding character of contracts made between states and corporate bodies; for example, in the celebrated Dartmouth College case[50] where the United States sustained a corporate grant by the English government to Dartmouth College; and also in the field of international relations between two sovereign powers.

Though the Pope is without territorial dominion, he is recognized as a sovereign power in international law, with

[46] Lincoln, The Civil Law and The Church, 685.

[47] *Ibid.* 678.

[48] Ponce *v.* Roman Catholic Church, 210 U. S. 296.

[49] For status of Church in the Philippines, cf. Barline *v.* Ramirex, 7 Philippines 41.

[50] Dartmouth College *v.* Woodward, 4 Wheaton 518; Kent, *Commentaries,* I, 413-419.

the capacity to make international contracts, called concordats.[51] Indeed, the corporate existence of the Roman Catholic Church and the *status* of sovereignty occupied by the Papacy were specifically recognized by the fact that the United States had diplomatic relations with the Papal States.[52]

If our insular possessions were to be admitted into the union, the property rights of the Church would doubtless be safeguarded. The federal government after such admission would not permit the indefinite continuance of the ecclesiastical legal personality since to do so would be contrary to the Constitution, but when new territory is obtained, the federal government may by treaty agree with the country surrendering dominion to recognize the corporate personality of the Church and its corporate title to property. The federal government controls such acquisitions and organizes an adequate government, as long as they are not incorporated as states of the union.[53] This principle may be illustrated by reference to the purchase of Louisiana from France, the cession of California from Mexico and the acquisition of Florida from Spain. "The property rights of the Church were confirmed by Congress in what are now the states of Washington, Oregon and by special act after the Texan Revolution of 1848 the Congress of Texas restored certain properties of the Church."[54]

The spirit of the national constitution in regard to liberty of conscience and religious equality permeates the constitutions of the respective states, though strictly speaking, they are not bound to accept this view in virtue of federal constitutional law.[55] As a matter of fact, they did not al-

[51] I *Moore's Digest* 39, and 130-131; Ponce *v.* Roman Catholic Church, 210 U. S. 296.

[52] Lincoln, *o. c.*, 669.

[53] Baart, *o. c.*, 14.

[54] *Ibid.*, 15; Blair *v.* Odin, 3 Tex. 288.

[55] The following are the sections of the various state constitutions covering the question of religious liberty: Alabama, Art. 1, Sec. 3; Arizona, Art. II, Sec. 12, 13; Arkansas, Art. II, Sec. 24; California, Art. I, Sec. 4; Colorado, Art. II, Sec. 4; Connecticut, Art. I, Sec. 4; Delaware, Art. I, Sec. 1;

ways maintain this attitude, many of them supporting various Protestant sects for some time after the Constitutional Convention of 1787.

Cooley[56] has ably summarized the provisions of the state constitutions as follows:

"1—They establish a system not of toleration merely, but of religious equality. All religions are equally respected by the law; one is not to be favored at the expense of others, or to be discriminated against, nor is any distinction to be made between them, either in the laws, in their positions under the law, or in the administration of the government.

2—They exempt all persons from compulsory support of religious worship and from compulsory attendance upon the same.

3—They forbid restraints upon the free exercise of religion according to the dictates of conscience or upon the free expression of religious opinion."

But the states following the policy of the federal government will not allow the constitutional guarantee of freedom of conscience to be used as an excuse to justify acts which destroy the public peace or fall within the police power of the state in its maintenance of public morality.[57]

Florida, Preamble, Sec. 5; Georgia, Art. I, Sec. 1; Idaho, Art. I, Sec. 4; Illinois, Art. II, Sec. 3; Indiana, Art. I, Sec. 2; Iowa, Art. I, Sec. 3; Kansas, Preamble, Sec. 7; Kentucky, Bill of Rights, Sec. 1, 2, 5; Louisiana, Art I, Sec. 4; Maine, Art. I, Sec. 3; Maryland, Declaration of Rights, Art. 36; Massachusetts, Declaration of Rights, Art. 2; Michigan, Art. II, Sec. 3; Minnesota, Art. I, Sec. 16; Mississippi, Art. I, Sec. 18; Missouri, Art. II, Sec. 5, 6; Montana, Art. II, Sec. 4; Nebraska, Art. I, Sec. 4; Nevada, Art. I, Sec. 4; New Hampshire, Part I, Art. 4, 5; New Jersey, Art. II, Sec. 5; New Mexico, Art. II, Sec. 11; New York, Art. I, Sec. 3; North Carolina, Art. I, Sec. 26; North Dakota, Art. I, Sec. 4; Ohio, Art. I, Sec. 7; Oklahoma, Art. II, Sec. 5; Oregon, Art. I, Sec. 2, 3, 4, 5; Pennsylvania, Art. I, Sec. 3; Rhode Island, Art. I, Sec. 3; South Carolina, Art. I, Sec. 9, 10; South Dakota, Art. VI, Sec. 3; Tennessee, Art. I, Sec. 3; Texas, Art. I, Sec. 4; Utah, Art. I, Sec. 4; Vermont, Chapter I, Art. 3; Virginia, Art. I, Sec. 16; Washington, Art. I, Sec. 11; West Virginia, Art. III, Sec. 15; Wisconsin, Art. I, Sec. 18; Wyoming, Art. I, Sec. 18. Cf. Kettleborough, *The State Constitutions,* 12 seqq.

[56] Cooley, *o. c.*, 226.

[57] Tyler, *o. c.*, § 14.

There are a few of the state constitutions, however, which still bear traces of the old common law theory of mortmain; thus Virginia and West Virginia contain constitutional prohibitions against the incorporation of any ecclesiastical denominations.[58] Such a policy has been condemned even by non-Catholic authors as a "denial of a substantial right on academic theory."[59] But these states will allow subordinate church organizations to incorporate.

There are two unmistakable evidences of the original union of Church and State in the United States; first, the exemption of churches from taxation, and secondly, the recognition of priests and ministers as public officers in the performance of the marriage ceremony. This immunity from taxation in the majority of instances is guaranteed by constitutional provisions.[60] Thirty-eight out of the forty-eight contain such clauses.[61] In these thirty-eight states, twenty-five authorize their respective legislatures to pass exemption statutes; the other thirteen contain self executing clauses which either explicitly remove the burden of taxation from ecclesiastical holdings or deny the legislature the power to tax them.[62]

The original union of Church and State is doubtless the reason why priests and ministers are considered as public officers for the purpose of performing the marriage ceremony.[63] Declares a Massachusetts court:

[58] Virginia, Art. IV, Sec. 59: "The General Assembly shall not grant a charter of incorporation to any church or religious denomination but may secure the title to church property to an extent to be limited by law." West Virginia, Art. VI, Sec. 47: "No charter of incorporation shall be granted to any church or religious denomination. Provision may be made by general laws for securing the title to church property and for the sale and transfer thereof, so that it shall be held, used or transferred for the purpose of such church or religious denomination."

[59] Zollmann, *o. c.*, 24.

[60] Franklin St. Soc. *v.* Manchester, 60 N. H. 342, 349.

[61] The following do not contain such clauses: Massachusetts, Vermont, Maine, Rhode Island, New Jersey, Wisconsin, Iowa, Maryland, New Hampshire, Connecticut.

[62] Zollmann, *o.* c., 239.

[63] Milford *v.* Worcester, 7 Mass. 48, 53, 54; Goshen *v.* Stonington, 4 Conn. 209, 218.

> That a minister is a public officer for the performing of the marriage ceremony is an anomaly, and can not be reconciled with any consistent theory of the separation of the state and church.[64]

Nevertheless "the American clergyman in the performance of the marriage ceremony is recognized as a public officer, and in the performance of his other duties is recognized as a public man subject to public comment."[65]

[64] Baker *v.* Fales, 16 Mass. 488.
[65] Zollmann, *o. c.*, 361.

CHAPTER VIII.

THE RECOGNITION OF THE CORPORATE PERSONALITY OF THE CHURCH IN THE FEDERAL AND STATE COURTS.

Before the law, ecclesiastical organizations have a triple aspect; they may be regarded, first, as spiritual units, secondly, as human societies, and thirdly, as legal corporations. Numerous cases distinguish between the church as a spiritual body and the merely human society sustaining the former.[1] Again, adjudications bring out the distinct existence of the society and the corporation;[2] and a distinction is drawn between the corporation and the church.[3] Finally, courts have differentiated with reference to church, society and corporation.[4]

The law recognizes only those religious organizations which have been incorporated either by special charter or by compliance with the general incorporating statutes of the particular state.[5] Since unincorporated organizations of a religious character, therefore, are not involved in the question of legal personality, it follows that only the two aspects of the church as a spiritual organization and the corporation as a person before the law need be considered.

What is the general attitude of the federal and state courts toward the Church as a spiritual body, especially

[1] Downes *v.* Bowdoin Square Baptist Soc., 149 Mass. 135; 21 N. E. 294; Wilson *v.* Livingston, 99 Mich. 594; 58 N. W. 646; Anderson *v.* Brock, 3 M. E. 243.

[2] Order of St. Benedict *v.* Steinhauser, 179 Fed. 137; Feener *v.* Reiss, 90 N. Y. Supp. 586.

[3] Catholic Church *v.* Tobbein, 82 Mo. 418; Hardin *v.* Baptist Church, 51 Mich. 137; 16 N. W. 311.

[4] People *v.* German Church, 53 N. Y. 103; Zollmann, *o. c.*, 14, 52; Lincoln, *o. c.*, 109.

[5] Ref. Prot. Dutch Church, Schenectady *v.* Veeder, 4 Wend. 494; Green *v.* Cady, 9 Wend. 414; Banks *v.* Phelan, 4 Barb. 80 (N. Y.).

with respect to its nature? This has been brought out in a number of decisions. Since all ecclesiastical sects stand upon a plane of equality before the law, the attitude of the courts toward one represents the view in regard to all. "The church consists of an indefinite number of persons of one or both sexes, who have made a public profession of religion and who are associated together by a covenant of church fellowship for the purpose of celebrating the sacraments and watching over the spiritual welfare of each other."[6] Again: "There can not be a sect or denomination of religious persons without any common system of faith."[7] And: "The church is a voluntary association of its members united together by a covenant or agreement for the public worship of God, observing the ordinances of His house, the promotion of the spirituality of its membership, and the spirit of divine truth among others as they understand and teach it. It is a purely voluntary association and it is not a corporation or a quasi-corporation."[8] "Church membership implies at least two elements, first, a profession of a common faith, and secondly, a submission to its rules and regulations. Simply holding the same faith without submitting to the government and discipline of a church can not make or keep a man a member of a church."[9] "The association between a religious corporation and its incorporators is voluntary on the part of the latter and is dissolved by withdrawing from attendance on its worship, omitting to contribute to its support and uniting in the establishment of another like corporation."[10] In brief, the union of church members one with another is based upon contract.[11]

[6] Stebbins *v.* Jennings, 27 Mass. 172; First Baptist Church *v.* Witherell, 3 Paige 296 (N. Y.).

[7] State *v.* Trustees of Township, Nine, 7 Ohio St. 58.

[8] Hundly *v.* Collins, 131 Ala. 234; Baker *v.* Fales, 16 Mass. 488; Holt *v.* Downs, 58 N. H. 170; Lincoln, *o. c.*, 106; St. Andrews Church *v.* Shaunessy, 63 Neb. 792; Church & Congreg. Soc. *v.* Hatch, 48 N. H. 393.

[9] Day *v.* Bolton, 12 N. J. L. 206.

[10] Perry *v.* Tupper, 74 N. C. 722.

[11] Zollmann, *o c.*, 328.

The trend of the above decisions is to the effect that the civil courts consider the church simply as a voluntary association of religiously inclined persons for the promotion and practice of a common faith, bound together either by express or by implied contract. The basis, therefore, of church membership is held to be contractual, based on a multilateral agreement after the fashion of a benevolent society. But these adjudications with reference to the courts' theory of the basis of church membership and the nature of the church seem to be contradicted by the fact that the civil courts will not assume jurisdiction of the church in its spiritual sense, nor controversies arising therefrom. Nor does the fact of incorporation change the situation. Of course the courts are unanimous to the effect that whenever there are involved temporal or property rights growing out of ecclesiastical disputes, civil jurisdiction will always be invoked. There are numerous decisions to this effect; thus, "civil courts will control the action of churches where rights of property or individual rights are in question."[12] And: "Civil courts can not determine questions of purely ecclesiastical nature but when questions become facts on which property rights depend the civil courts will decide them."[13] Again: "An ecclesiastical court has no power to make a decision determining property rights which is binding on the civil courts."[14]

But apart from questions involving temporal rights, numerous adjudications indicate the exemption of the church as such from the jurisdiction of the civil courts. "The church being principally an ecclesiastical body, membership must be obtained as prescribed by the rules and regulations of the particular church you wish to join."[15] "Every person entering into a church membership, im-

[12] Landrith *v.* Hudgins, 121 Tenn. 556; 120 S. W. 783.

[13] Yanthis *v.* Kemp, 43 Ind. A. 203; 85 N. E. 976.

[14] Watson *v.* Garvin, 54 Mo. 353.

[15] East Norway Lake Norwegian Evangel. Lutheran Ch. *v.* Halvorson, 42 Minn. 503; American Primitive Soc. *v.* Pilling, 24 N. J. L. 653; Jackson *v.* Hopkins, 78 A. 4 (Md.); Holcomb *v.* Leavitt, 124 N. Y. Supp. 980.

pliedly if not expressly covenants to conform to its rules and submit to its authority and discipline."[16] "The rights of a member if expelled are to be determined by the laws of the church."[17] "Civil tribunals possess no authority whatever to determine ecclesiastical matters such as heresy, etc."[18] "Ecclesiastical rulings will be approved by the civil courts."[19] "The laws of an ecclesiastical body will be recognized and enforced, if not in conflict with the constitution and laws of the state."[20] "Civil courts will take ecclesiastical decisions as they find them."[21] "A decision of a lawfully constituted judicial, legislative and administrative tribunal of a church denomination, in regard to ecclesiastical matters, is, unless shown to be clearly and manifestly repugnant to the established laws of the denomination, binding and conclusive on the civil courts,"[22] "Courts will not review judgments or acts of the governing authorities of a religious organization with reference to its internal affairs, for the purpose of ascertaining their regularity or accordance with the discipline and usages of such organization. It can make no difference whether the governing authority of a religious denomination is confided to one man, or to a synod or conference or whether the mode of procedure permitted to such a person is in accord with the ordinary course of investigations or trials among laymen. Each religious organization must determine its own policy and be the judge of its own laws."[23] Thus, "the removal of a priest by the bishop can not be interfered with by the

[16] Lucas *v.* Case, 72 Ky. (9 Bush) 297; Smith *v.* Pedigo, 145 Ind. 361; Day *v.* Bolton, 12 N. J. L. 206; Clark *v.* Brown, 108 S. W. 421; Permanent Committee of Missions of the Pacific Synod of the Cumberland Presbyterion Church *v.* Pacific Synod of the Presbyterian Church, 157 Calif. 105; 106 Pac. 395.

[17] Grosvenor *v.* United Society of Believers, 118 Mass. 78.

[18] Wilson *v.* Johns Island Presbyterian Church, 2 Rich. Eq. 192, 198, 199 (S. C.).

[19] Wehmer *v.* Fokena, 57 Neb. 510; 78 N. W. 28.

[20] Kreckor *v.* Shirley, 163 Pa. 534.

[21] Harris *v.* Cosby, 173 Ala. 81; 55 So. 231.

[22] Schweiker *v.* Husser, 146 Ill. 399.

[23] Bonacum *v.* Harrington, 65 Neb. 831.

court if the action of the bishop was within the laws and authority of the Catholic Church."[24] "Where a local church congregation is a member of a general organization having general rules for the government and conduct of all its adherents, congregations and officers, the orders and judgments of the general organization through its governing authorities as far as they relate to church affairs and church government are binding on the local congregation and will not be re-examined by the courts."[25] "There is no limit to the time of inquiry by a church as to offenses against church discipline."[26] "The judicial eye of the civil authority of this land of religious liberty can not penetrate the veil of the church."[27]

The civil courts holding that the church or spiritual element of a religious association is a mere pious union of the faithful based on contract assume a contradictory and inconsistent position by saying that they will not assume jurisdiction of those controversies which are in the strict sense church disputes; for to be consistent the courts should take cognizance of all alleged breaches of contract and if the church as a spiritual unit is founded on a contractual basis, there is no reason why they should be exempted from civil jurisdiction with regard to their disputes any more than other types. A line of cases has eliminated this evident inconsistency by holding that the church rests on some thing other than mere contract. This is the consistent holding of the federal courts and the view of many of the state courts. Does this judicial interpretation serve to show that there is an implied recognition of the moral personality of the Church? It is to be remembered that of the two elements, the church and its accompanying corporation, in other words, the spiritual organization and the legal personality which is the medium for the carrying out

[24] Stack *v.* O'Hara, 98 Pa. 213.
[25] Bonacum *v.* Harrington, 65 Neb. 831.
[26] Chase *v.* Cheney, 58 Ill. 509.
[27] Shannon *v.* Frost, 42 Ky. 253, 259.

of temporal transactions,[28] only the former is here referred to, since it would plainly be incorrect to speak of an implied recognition of the legal personality of that organization which functions in reference to civil affairs.[29] Indeed, the cases are agreed that the society is not a corporation unless it has complied with the incorporating statutes of the state in which it wishes to operate and exist. But at the same time it must be understood that these same cases do not include in their decisions reference to the church spiritually considered. The fact that the courts will not assume jurisdiction over this element is evidence that the church spiritually is not a corporation; otherwise it would be the creature of the state.

What then is the attitude of the federal courts and many of the state courts toward the character of the union of church members associated together and does this attitude imply a tacit recognition of the *moral* personality of the Church in public law, as distinguished from its *legal* personality, i. e., recognition as a civil corporation? The federal courts accept the "higher plane" theory, which, first formulated in Watson *v.* Jones, 13 Wallace 679, (U. S.), considers the relationship of members to a church as something more than a mere contract. This opinion acknowledges a spiritual basis as the foundation of church association. Certain state courts also adhere to this "higher plane" theory: "Church membership stands upon an altogether higher plane, and church membership is not to be compared to that resulting from connection with mere business associations for profit, pleasure or culture. The Church undertakes to deal with spiritual interests. Admission to its fold is prescribed alone by the Church professing to act upon the word of God."[30]

The case of Watson *v.* Jones is epoch-making. It grew out of the Civil War Controversy over the issue of slavery.

[28] Gray *v.* Good, 44 Ind. A. 476; 89 N. E. 498.
[29] Hardin *v.* Baptist Church, 51 Mich. 137.
[30] Nance *v.* Busby, 91 Tenn. 303.

The General Assembly of the Presbyterian Church in the United States had expressed sympathy with the cause of the Union, condemning the institution of slavery. The Supreme Court of Kentucky in 1867 declared that the General Assembly had exceeded its jurisdiction.[31] Some of the parties to the action lived in Indiana. Hence the case was properly brought to the federal courts; the act of the General Assembly was upheld by the United States Supreme Court.[32] Justice Miller declared:

> The rule of action which should govern the civil courts, founded in a broad and sound view of the relations of Church and State under our system of laws and supported by a preponderating weight of judicial authority is that, whenever the question of discipline or of faith or ecclesiastical rule, custom and law has been decided by the highest of these church judicatories to which the matter has been carried, the legal tribunals must accept such decisions as final, and as binding on them, in their application to the case before them. * * * The law knows no heresy and is committed to the support of no dogma, the establishment of no sect. * * * If the civil courts are to inquire into all these matters, the whole subject of the doctrinal theology, the usages and customs, the written laws, and fundamental organization of every religious denomination may, and must be examined into with minuteness and care, for they would become, in almost every case, the criteria by which the validity of the ecclesiastical decree would be determined in the civil court.[33]

The decision of this case has a duel effect, first, it upholds the conference of jurisdiction upon church organizations where there is involved a strictly ecclesiastical question, rendering conclusive the judgments of church tribunals, and secondly, by this refusal to intervene in the instance of ecclesiastical associations, the federal govern-

[31] Watson *v.* Avery, 2 Bush. 332 (Ky.).
[32] Watson *v.* Jones, 13 Wallace 679 (U. S.).
[33] *Ibid.* 727, 728.

ment seems committed to a policy of recognition of church authority, evidently conceded to spring from a supernatural source, which is in keeping with the theory that in the field of public law the Church is impliedly a *persona moralis*.

Neither the federal nor the state courts have been eager to over-rule Watson *v.* Jones.[34] But there are those who bitterly attack the soundness of the decision. Thus, Zollmann[35] criticizes the case on the grounds that it violates the principle that civil courts should always be allowed to decide upon the jurisdiction of ecclesiastical courts and further that the decision "soars into the higher regions of mystic theology."[36] But actually neither of these two objections is valid. First, the case ultimately rested upon a moral issue and hence arose out of a Church controversy in the strictly ecclesiastical sense. The United States Supreme Court as a matter of fact reviewed the case and in effect declared: We have no jurisdiction since no civil right is involved. This was equivalent to saying that the ecclesiastical tribunal had power to act, but since the Supreme Court had no jurisdiction, it was not competent to say whether the ecclesiastical decision was correct. Upon what ground then can it be said that the court abdicated its judicial functions? Secondly, it is true that the jurisdiction thus conceded "must rest on a higher plane, must flow from a supernatural source, must be conferred from on high."[37] It is this very point which, it has been contended, brings out the implied recognition in the United States of the moral personality of the Church. But any other position would be tantamount to a forfeiture of the principle of religious liberty and the substitution of State Absolutism, in place of the present policy of separation of Church and State, and religious tolerance.

The implied recognition of the moral personality of the Church in American public law can not be negatived by

[34] *Supra* pp. 126, 127.
[35] Zollmann, *o. c.*, 211.
[36] *Ibid.*
[37] *Ibid.*

the contention that ecclesiastical judgments do not fall within the constitutional provision which specifies that "full faith and credit shall be given in each state to the acts, records, and judicial proceedings of every state."[38] It is to be admitted that the juridical *status* of a church organization can not be said to be *identical* to that of a state in the present system of American public law, nor can a strict parallel be carried out with reference to their respective adjudications, the findings of the latter to be taken in the sense of strictly ecclesiastical judgments where no civil right is at issue. But it would be incorrect to maintain that these ecclesiastical decisions are removed completely from the domain of American public law, even from the *unwritten constitution.* In fact, the contrary may be assumed from the consistent tendency to maintain a *laissez faire* policy toward ecclesiastical adjudications. Attempts by jurists to reduce spiritual associations to the mere level of *contractual relations* and to construct *compact-theories*[39] are actually contradicted by the sounder conclusions of the American Judiciary. Nor is it to the point to propose that "church tribunals are proverbially influenced by passion and prejudice more than any other species of judicial tribunal."[40]

The attitude assumed by the federal courts is most favorable toward the right of religious organizations, (after such bodies have complied with the proper incorporating statutes) to function without interference by the State. The federal government by the decisions of its courts has indicated its disapproval of the mortmain practices which are followed in certain states, declaring that at best "the reason for such a policy is certainly not as apparent now as it was at the time it was enacted."[41]

The federal courts have decided that it was not against the public policy of a state for one of its citizens to convey

[38] *Constitution of the United States,* Art. 4, Sec. 1.
[39] Zollmann, *o. c.,* 227.
[40] *Ibid.* 206.
[41] Miller *v.* Ahrens, 150 Fed. 644, 652, no. 583.

real property to a religious corporation located in another state, provided the second state permitted religious corporations to hold real estate, and this, even though the said property was located in the first state. Thus, in the case of Christian Union *v.* Yount,[42] the children and heirs at law of a grantor endeavored to set aside a conveyance of land located in Illinois made by him, a citizen of Illinois, to a corporation incorporated under the New York law under the sections covering the incorporation of benevolent, charitable, scientific and missionary societies in New York. The plaintiffs in the original suit based their claim on the ground that the property was not necessary for the convenience or transaction of the business of the religious corporation since it was not authorized by its charter to hold such a large amount of real estate. This contention was upheld by the Supreme Court of Illinois. But it was reversed by the United States Supreme Court. The Syllabus declared:

> Where land in Illinois was conveyed to a New York corporation, the children and heirs at law of the grantor, who file their bill to set aside the conveyance upon the ground that it was against the public policy of Illinois, can not raise the question that the grantee acquired a larger quantity of lands than its charter allowed.[43]

The decision has the effect of showing the federal policy of fostering the corporate rights of the Church in controversies involving interstate elements.

There are certain types of religious corporations peculiarly Catholic, the religious character of which includes the making of contracts involving temporal rights as a condition of membership. Reference is here made to incorporated monastic communities, which have been transplanted from the old world into the soil of American jurisprudence. Here again, the federal government upholds a canonical principle

[42] Christian Union *v.* Yount, 101 U. S. 352.
[43] *Ibid.*

by endorsing the system of monastic life with reference to its corporate activity. It sanctions the validity of contracts made by such religious bodies, after incorporation, with individuals becoming members of these communal societies, whereby the applicant agrees to forfeit certain property rights as a condition precedent to membership. This of course implies the indefinite continuance of the right of withdrawal at any time. It has been held that this type of contract neither violated any constitutional provision nor ran counter to the public policy of the particular state which chartered the society.[44] This principle may be illustrated by the case of St. Benedict *v.* Steinhauser, 234 U. S. 640. The suit in question was brought by The Order of St. Benedict of New Jersey, an organization incorporated under the laws of that state, to determine its title with respect to personal property left by Augustin Wirth, deceased, a member of the Order who died at Springfield, Minnesota, in December, 1901. The defendant, Albert Steinhauser, as administrator of the estate of the decedent, holding letters from the Probate court of Brown county, Minnesota, filed a cross-bill asserting ownership in his representative capacity and praying discovery and account with reference to whatever part of the estate had come into the complainant's possession. The United States Supreme Court decided in favor of the religious order.[45] The case, then, reflects the federal recognition of the right of monasteries and other Catholic communal organizations to function as corporations under the law of the land, although their activity is canonical, and the endorsement of such corporation's right to accept members, surrendering property rights, which is held not to be an interference with public policy.[46]

[44] Order of St. Benedict *v.* Steinhauser, 234 U. S. 640.
[45] *Ibid.*
[46] *Ibid.*

CHAPTER IX.

FORMS OF THE ECCLESIASTICAL JURIDICAL PERSONALITY UNDER STATUTORY LAW.

The conception of corporations in American civil law is based upon a philosophy and judicial temper which were developed by English jurisprudence. This is to be expected since the foundation of American juridical notions is invariably traceable back to the old common law, imported as it was by the early American colonizers. In both systems of law, "a corporation is an artificial being invisible, intangible and existing only in contemplation of law. Among the most important characteristics are immortality and if the expression may be allowed individuality, properties by which a perpetual succession of many persons are considered as the same and may act as a single individual."[1] It is looked upon as a creature of the state. This necessity for a creative act by the state as a condition of corporate existence and duration doubtless sprang from the "divine right" theories or State Absolution which magnified the power of the state and considered all rights as derivable from it. It is to be expected that corporate rights were also included. American jurists took the legal notion blindly ignoring its philosophical justification, at the same time that American legislators were loudly denouncing the corresponding principle of the Divine Right of Kings and writing into the national and various state constitutions clauses which derived political power from the people and guaranteed them certain inalienable rights. In English and American law, a franchise or its equivalent is necessary for the formation and continuance of a corporation. But a franchise has been defined as a "certain privilege conferred

[1] Chief Justice Marshall, in Dartmouth College *v.* Woodward, 4 Wheat. 518 (U. S.).

by grant from the government (or state) and vested in individuals."[2] The idea of privilege, then, is the starting point in American corporate law. The consent of the Crown in England, given either in express terms or by implication, was indispensable for the establishment of a corporation.[3] Here there is no Crown, but the equivalent power, in this instance the legislature, can alone create corporations.[4] It is true that under both systems of law, corporations may exist by virtue of a prescriptive right,[5] but this does not abrogate the rule since the justification of such a right is to be found in the theory that the association at its inception or early existence actually possessed a franchise but that it was subsequently lost.

In the United States, therefore, all corporations must be created by the authority of the state. The American civil law will not recognize the right of the Church to establish a juridical person in the sense of a corporate entity capable of exercising corporate civil rights. The Church must go through the same procedure as any business or lay association substantially to incorporate. Should this not be done, the law will recognize an organization whose rights are the aggregate rights of the totality of the members exercised by duly appointed representatives, but it will not acknowledge corporate existence. Of course, the process of incorporation allowing the church "to accomplish better its purpose of religion"[6] is not intended to alter the ecclesiastical character but to confer a more advantageous civil status.[7] It has been held that the character of persons as members of a church corporation under the statutes is entirely distinct from their character as members of the Church,[8] for an incorporated church consists of two distinct elements, to wit: the church proper and the corporation,

[2] Kent, *Commentaries,* II, 458.
[3] Blackstone, *Commentaries,* I, 472.
[4] Kent, *Commentaries,* II, 276.
[5] Kent, *Commentaries,* II, 277; Blackstone, *Commentaries,* II, 473.
[6] Beitel, *The Ecclesiastical Laws of Pennsylvania,* Int. V.
[7] Winebrenner *v.* Colder, 43 Pa. St 244, 252.
[8] First Baptist Church *v.* Witherell, 3 Paige 296 (N. Y.).

which has relation alone to the temporalities of the institution.[9] Under the American civil law, therefore, the ecclesiastical element upon incorporation is not affected, but there is simply called into being by the state a secular corporate medium, whose purpose is not to perform the spiritual duties of the church, such as the administration of the sacraments and the spread of the Gospel, but whose aim is to facilitate the management of the temporal affairs, such as business transactions, including the acquisition, tenure, and administration of property.[10] So distinct are the two elements that there is no interdependence with reference to each other.[11] The courts will adopt such view of the law as will permit religious bodies to be incorporated and yet preserve their original form of church government, instead of revolutionizing it from a hierarchical or monarchical into a congregational form.[12]

What then is an American church corporation? It has been defined as "a corporation whose charter powers are to be used in the aid of the propagation and practice of a religious belief."[13] Again: "A religious corporation is an intellectual body politic created by law composed of several individuals whose principal object is to establish and regulate the congregation of a religious denomination, acting under a common name and endowed with perpetual succession and vested with the capacity of acting in many respects, however numerous the association may be, as a single person. Like other bodies corporate, it is an artificial being, invisible, intangible and exists only in idea and has neither soul nor body."[14]

It is not a public but rather a private eleemosynary corporation, though it is created by a governmental charter.[15]

[9] Dismukes *v.* State, 83 Ala. 287; 58 So. 195

[10] Zollmann, *o. c.*, 79.

[11] *Ibid.* 75.

[12] Klix *v.* Polish Roman Catholic St. Stanislaus Parish, 137 Mo. App. 347.

[13] St Louis Institute of Christian Science, *In re*, 27 Mo. App. 633.

[14] Tyler, *o. c.*, § 103; Angel & Ames, *Corporations*, § 7.

[15] Society for the Propagation of the Gospel *v.* New Haven, 8 Wheat. 465 (U. S.).

This is true despite the fact that in its scope it includes many matters of a public character; it is not, however, similar to a municipal corporation such as a town, county or city, and hence comes under the principles of private law.[16] In this respect the American religious corporation is different from the continental.[17] It has been held that an incorporated religious society does not belong to the class of ecclesiastical corporations in the sense of the English law, but is regarded as a civil corporation governed by the ordinary rules of the common law.[18]

The American ecclesiastical corporation, however, did not always possess this private *status*. Originally, it was a public corporation. This was due to the union of Church and State in early American history. Both the territorial parish, which flourished in Massachusetts, Maine and Connecticut,[19] though separate from the town government,[20] and the corporation sole, intimately associated with and dependent upon the territorial parish in certain sections, were public corporations. In the case of the former, one became a member automatically by residence in a parish, just as today one acquires citizenship, under certain conditions, by dwelling in a specific political unit.[21] Such public prerogatives as the power of eminent domain and of taxation were enjoyed.[22] In the case of the latter type of corporation, the person constituting the legal entity was a public officer. His death did not destroy the legal entity, which was referable, as it were, to the person's chair personified by a legal fiction. The successor in office upon taking the chair continued the discharge of the corporate

[16] Tyler, *o. c.*, § 105.

[17] Zollmann, *o. c.*, 65.

[18] Robertson *v.* Bullions, 11 N. Y. 243; Calkins *v.* Cheney, 92 Ill. 463, 478. Kniskern *v.* Lutheran Church, 1 Sandf. Ch. 439 (N. Y.); Snyder, *o. c.*, 24.

[19] Alna *v.* Plummer, 3 Me. 88; Dillingham *v.* Snow, 5 Mass. 547.

[20] First Society, Waterbury *v.* Platt, 12 Conn. 181.

[21] Osgood *v.* Bradley, 7 Me. 411.

[22] Turner *v.* Burlington, 16 Mass. 208; Taylor *v.* Public Hall Co., 35 Conn. 430.

duties and the exercise of the corporate rights. The idea was borrowed from England where the King and certain public officers were corporations sole.[23] Rights and duties were suspended during the inter-regnum. Both of these public church corporations prevailed prior to the Revolution but vanished with the determination of the majority of the people to separate Church and State in the United States.[24] But while these two forms of the corporation disappeared in so far as they were public, nevertheless, they have been followed by two types of legal persons, in structure substantially similar to their predecessors, with this difference, namely, that they are private corporations only and are not characterized by municipal corporate elements. Today, then, ecclesiastical corporations in the United States are either aggregate when they are composed of a plurality of persons, or sole when constituted with reference to only one individual.[25] The trustee type of corporation is a subdivision of the aggregate form, strictly speaking.

In American civil law, therefore, there exist in the widest sense three variations of the ecclesiastical corporation, the trustee corporation, the aggregate corporation and the corporation sole. In every instance, however, the canonical juristic personality of the Catholic Church must, in order to receive express recognition before the law as a legal entity, assume one of these forms by recourse to the proper incorporating statutes. The Holy See, mindful of this legal situation in America and understanding that the question of legal personality is not confined to the field of mere theory, but is intimately bound up with the entire subject of tenure of church property, in 1911, published instructions that all church property in the United States is to be held by ecclesiastical corporations if possible, favoring a certain type of congregational corporation in preference to the cor-

[23] Brunswick *v.* Dunning, 7 Mass. 445.

[24] Zollmann, *o. c.*, 63; Austin *v.* Thomas, 14 Mass. 353; Lincoln, *o. c.*, 443; Weston *v.* Hunt, 2 Mass. 500

[25] Zollmann, *o c.*, 39 to 43.

poration sole, but accepting the latter in the event that it was the most advantageous form which could be secured in a given state. This document was issued by the Sacred Congregation of the Council, July 29, 1911, and was published in the Ecclesiastical Review for November of the same year.[26] The same issue of the Review[27] summarizes the formulation as follows:

"1. The most desirable method of holding title to and right of administering such property is that known as the Parish Corporation with the safeguards and conditions recognized at present by the State of New York. This method is to be introduced at once whenever possible.

2. In some dioceses when the civil law precludes recognition of Parish Corporations in the ownership and administration of church property, the method hitherto in use in many dioceses of constituting the bishop a corporation sole is allowed, with the understanding that the Ordinary act with the advice and in an important matter, with the consent of the diocesan consultors

3. The holding of diocesan property by ecclesiastics in fee simple is abolished."

The different forms of the ecclesiastical legal personality with their respective advantages and defects may be described by an analysis of the above document clause by clause.

I. The parish corporation is essentially an aggregate type of ecclesiastical legal personality. An aggregate corporation is a juridical person incorporating the members of a parish or congregation. All aggregate corporations, however, are not similar with reference to their management. The incorporation of a parish or of a congregation has the general effect of making each individual included in the parish or congregation a member of the corporation. This occurs regardless of the fact that only a few persons are specifically referred to by name in the charter, and that the

[26] XLV, 585.
[27] P. 591.

franchise is extended to them. *De jure,* when a parish, church or congregation becomes a corporation, consisting of the persons who compose these various units, the sovereignty of the legal personality is referable to the members themselves. But *de facto* the exercise of this sovereignty is controlled by the method by which the directors or agents or trustees are appointed. All the directors or the greater part of them may be elected by the majority of the members of the congregation or parish, or the greater number of the directors may consist of the ecclesiastical dignitaries who occupy a controlling position with regard to the management of the parish. This may occur in ecclesiastical systems of the monarchical type as the Roman Catholic Church. It is the existence of this second element in the New York law that causes it to be favored by the Sacred Congregation of the Council; for if this feature were not present, it would be possible for the lay majority of the parish or congregation, no matter whether they continued to be Catholics or not, always to dictate the management and disposition of the corporate property. They would enjoy this power even though they became heretical or recusant.[28]

The parish corporation, as evolved by New York, which is referred to in the above document as the most welcome type of ecclesiastical corporation thus far developed was of slow growth, though now it seems to be recognized as a model by numerous states.[29] In New York before the Revolutionary War, there was no general provision under which ecclesiastical organizations might become incorporated. Incorporation necessitated the grant of a special charter by a specific act of the New York legislature. The need for general incorporating statutes was soon seen, for the policy of special charters restricted the corporate privilege to only a few organizations, the vast majority of which remained with no legal existence. The result was that donors were

[28] Klix *v.* St. Stanislaus Church, 137 Mo. App. 347; 118 S. W. 1171.
[29] Desmond, *o. c.,* 73, 74.

unwilling to make contributions to churches for fear of the possible diversion of such funds ultimately.[30] The growth of religion in a large measure was thereby retarded. To obviate this difficulty a statute was passed, April 6, 1784,[31] essentially included in the statutes of 1801, and substantially re-enacted in 1813.[32] Under the 1813 Act, provision was made for the incorporation of the Protestant Episcopal Church, but the Roman Catholic Church did not seek a similar clause,[33] but preferred to allow the bishop to have a fee simple right in Church property. In 1855 the New York legislature, declaring that the Catholic Church was endeavoring to evade the law by practices contrary to the spirit of American institutions, passed an act of dubious constitutionality which provided "that no title to real property should be conveyed or descendible by an ecclesiastic to his successor in office."[34] This act seems to have been the result of religious prejudice for eight years later the law was repealed. Similar discriminatory statutes were passed in some of the states other than New York,[35] as in Ohio, but they were soon repealed.[36] In 1863 the legislature of New York passed a special law, providing for the incorporation of Catholic Churches[37] on the same plan as now obtains in New York, a plan which has received the approbation of the Holy See. In brief the statute provided that the Archbishop (or Bishop), Vicar General, Pastor of the church in question, and two lay persons chosen by these three ecclesiastics might incorporate the parish by filing an incorporating certificate with the secretary of the state. But the courts of New York have construed the statute as having the effect of incorporating not merely these five trustees,

[30] Snyder, *o. c.*, iii.
[31] Snyder, *o. c.*, iv.
[32] For discussion of 1813 Act, see Robertson *v.* Bullions, 9 Barb. 64.
[33] Desmond, *o. c.*, 69.
[34] Laws of 1855, Ch. 230; Tyler *o. c.*, § 158, 159.
[35] Desmond, *o. c.*, 70.
[36] Baart, *o. c.*, 57.
[37] Tyler, *o. c.*, § 160, 162.

but also the members of the parish; the office of the trustees consists in managing the corporation.[38] But the method provided for with respect to the appointment of the trustees insures ecclesiastical control of the incorporated parish.[39]

To quote from the Laws of the State of New York: "*Religious Corporation Law,*" § *90: INCORPORATION OF ROMAN CATHOLIC AND GREEK CHURCHES: An unincorporated Roman Catholic Church or an unincorporated Christian Orthodox Catholic Church of the Eastern confession, in this state may become incorporated as a church by executing, acknowledging and filing a certificate of incorporation, stating the corporate name by which such church shall be known, and the county, town, city or village, where its principal place of worship is, or is intended to be located.*

A certificate of incorporation of an unincorporated Roman Catholic Church shall be executed and acknowledged by the Roman Catholic Archbishop, or Bishop and the Vicar General of the diocese in which its place of worship is, and by the rector of the Church, and by two laymen, members of such church, who shall be selected by such officials, or by a majority of such officials.

On filing such certificate, such church shall be a corporation by the name stated in the certificate."[40]

The conditions thus required for incorporation, namely, the mere filing of a properly executed certificate, and the vesting of the *de facto* control of the parish in ecclesiastical hands by constituting three of the five directors clerics and the remainder ecclesiastical appointees approach the canonical theory of the legal personality of churches as far as it is possible under the present spirit of American corporate law. The plan for the selection of the two lay members is consonant with canon 1520. Further, the objectionable fea-

[38] People's Bank *v.* St. Anthony's Roman Catholic Church, 109 N. Y. 512; Lincoln, *o. c.*, 676.

[39] *Ibid.*

[40] *Consolidated Laws of New York,* Art. 5, § 90, (Cahill).

ture of vesting title and sovereignty in trustees, a system conclusively proven defective by American church history, is avoided, for the trustees with reference to the corporation have not the relation of trustee to the *cestui que trust.* They simply direct the corporate body.[41]

"§ *91: GOVERNMENT OF INCORPORATED ROMAN CATHOLIC AND GREEK CHURCHES: The Archbishop or Bishop and the Vicar-General of the diocese to which any incorporated Roman Catholic Church belongs, the Rector of such church and their successors in office, shall, by virtue of their offices, be trustees of such church. The two laymen, members of such incorporated church, selected by such officers, or a majority of them, shall also be trustees of such incorporated church and such officers and such laymen trustees shall together constitute the board of trustees thereof. The two laymen signing the certificate of incorporation of an incorporated Roman Catholic Church shall be the two laymen trustees thereof during the first year of its corporate existence. The term of office of the two laymen trustees of an incorporated Roman Catholic Church shall be one year. Whenever the office of any such layman trustee shall become vacant by expiration of term of office or otherwise, his successor shall be appointed from the members of the church, by such officers or a majority of them. No act or proceeding of the trustees of any such incorporated church shall be valid without the sanction of the Archbishop or Bishop of the diocese to which such church belongs, or in case of their absence or inability to act, without the sanction of the Vicar-General or of the administrator of such diocese.*"

These provisions controlling the operation of the parish corporation are also in accord with the spirit of Canon Law as the ecclesiastical directors have the right of appointing the two lay trustees whose tenure of office is limited to a year, and the validity of the corporate acts is dependent

[41] Cummings and Gilbert, *Membership and Religious Corporations of New York,* 315.

upon episcopal sanction.[42] The New York act by specific incorporating statutes for expressly named sects acknowledges the denominational character of the resulting corporation. The general rule is that the trustees of a corporation must act in keeping with the rules and tenets of the particular sect to which the members belong. Hence the New York courts insist that the trustees of the parish corporation, distinctly Catholic, shall not divert the property from Catholic uses, but shall act in accordance with the discipline and usages of the Catholic Church, and equity will enforce this principle.[43] Finally, provision is made for the contingency of the Bishop's death, so that there will be no cessation of operation during the inter-regnum.

In 1902 the following amendment was added to the statutes:

"§ *92. DIVISION OF ROMAN CATHOLIC PARISH: DISPOSITION OF PROPERTY: Wherever a Roman Catholic parish has been heretofore or shall hereafter be duly divided by the Roman Catholic bishop having jurisdiction over said parish and the original Roman Catholic church corporation is given one part of the old parish, and a new or second Roman Catholic church corporation is given the remaining part of the old parish, and it further appears that by reason of the said division the original Roman Catholic church corporation holds title to real property situated within the part of the old parish that was given to the new or second Roman Catholic church corporation, then the said Roman Catholic bishop or his successor shall have the right and power, of himself, independently of any action or consent on the part of the trustees of the original Roman Catholic church corporation to transfer the title of the said real property, with or without valuable consideration, to the new or second Roman Catholic church corporation. Said transfer shall be made by the said Roman Catholic bishop or his successor after having complied with*

[42] Canon 1519; 1530 § 1, 2, 3; 1532 § 2; 1521.
[43] Cummings and Gilbert, *o. c.*, 271.

the requirements of the code of civil procedure in the same manner as the trustees of any religious corporation are compelled to do before making a transfer of church property. If a valuable consideration is paid for the transfer the same shall be received by the said . . . original Roman Catholic church corporation and the new or second Roman Catholic corporation in such proportions as in the discretion of the said bishop or his successor may seem proper."

This section further stresses the power of the Bishop. Episcopal sanction is made necessary for the validity of the trustees' acts but the authority of the Bishop is here further extended by allowing him absolute power to divide Roman Catholic parish corporations. This is in complete accord with canon 1427. The authorization of the Bishop not only to divide the parish against even the will of the rector and the parishioners, but also to make whatever apportionment of the parish property that he sees fit is a confirmation by the New York law of the provisions contained in the New Code.[44]

The exact operation of the New York parish corporation may be indicated by reference to a Pastoral Letter of His Grace, Archbishop of New York addressed to his diocesans in 1910:

> The statutes of the diocese (Syn. V, Tit. XX, No. 249) make it suspension *ipso facto* to hold personally, in one's own name for three months the property of the church, unless for special reasons, permission to do so has been detained from the Ordinary.
>
> No property can be bought or sold for the church corporation without the previous consent of the archbishop. This consent is only obtained after the matter has been submitted to the consultors, and after a meeting of the trustees of the corporation has been legally called, at which at least four of the members of the corporation being

[44] Canon 1500.

> present, a resolution has been passed approving the proposed transaction. As the board of trustees in our church corporations consists of five members, namely, the Archbishop, the senior Vicar-General, the pastor of the church, and the two lay trustees, the law relating to business transactions by such board requires the presence of two thirds of this body to form a quorum; two thirds, therefore, of five calls for the presence of four members; so that a majority which would be only three does not constitute a quorum as some have been led to believe.[45]

In theory, the New York law is contrary to the canonical concept of the ecclesiastical juristic personality since it insists that its creation is the result of legislative authority, and hence distinguishes between the church as a spiritual body and the parish as an aggregate corporation. But in practice these two are identified in effect since the hierarchical structure of the church is made the groundwork of the corporation as recognized in the law of New York. The laws of the church, therefore, are just as effectively enforced as though New York state actually recognized the legal personality of the church, and their enforcement is facilitated by the favorable attitude assumed by the New York judiciary. Of course the source of the corporate power is the theoretical difference which is absolutely irreconcilable.

II. In some dioceses when the civil law precludes recognition of Parish corporations in the ownership and administration of church property, the method hitherto in use in many dioceses of constituting the Bishop a corporation sole is allowed, with the understanding that the Ordinary act with the advice and in an important matter, with the consent of the diocesan consultors.

Instances of those dioceses where the civil law precludes recognition of parish corporations would be where the incorporating laws of the given state make no special provision for the incorporation of religious organizations, but

[45] *Ecclesiastical Review,* XLV, 598.

compel them to adopt the same procedure with regard to their incorporation and assume the same general form of organization as merely lay corporations. Should the church incorporate under such statutes, the effect would be to surrender the ultimate control of the corporation to the majority of the lay members, a result which the Church can not sanction. Either such states provide for corporations sole or they do not. If they permit corporations sole, the Sacred Congregation has made it known that the ecclesiastical corporation in that locality shall assume that form. If there is no provision for corporations sole, then the Bishop, may, as a last resort, hold the property as trustee. This trustee tenure is not expressly endorsed in the Document of 1911 but it is by implication, since the only other possibility, fee simple tenure, is abolished.

The second form of ecclesiastical corporation is therefore the corporation sole. This form of corporation was particularly favored by the Third Plenary Council of Baltimore,[46] since the improvement in the way of the parish corporation might be taken advantage of in only a few places. To quote from the records of that Council:

> In the states in which a civil incorporation of parishes or ecclesiastical bodies, such as accords with Church law does not exist, the Bishop himself will be able to become a corporation sole before the law to hold and administer the property of the whole diocese.[47]

This type of corporation is not as common in the United States as the aggregate corporation. "A corporation sole consists of one person only and his successors in some particular station, who are incorporated by law, in order to give them some legal capacities and advantages, particularly that of perpetuity, which in their natural capacities they could not have had."[48] In English jurispru-

[46] *Con. Plen. Balt.* III, Tit. IX, cap. ii, n. 267.
[47] *Ibid.*
[48] Blackstone, *Commentaries,* I, 470

dence, from which the American conception of the corporation sole was taken, the King, bishops, deans, parsons and vicars possessed this right of becoming corporations sole in order that upon their death the property belonging to them as public officers might not pass to their heirs for the corporation sole was immortal. "The present incumbent and his predecessors who lived seven hundred years ago are in law one and the same person, and what was given to the one was given to the others also."[49] The same justification applies in the case of a benefice. The freehold estate possessed by the ecclesiastical beneficiaries might otherwise, should the legal fiction of the corporation sole be not invoked, be claimed by his heirs at law, and by his personal creditors. But by means of the corporation sole the full right of the benefice passes unencumbered to the successor in office.

Blackstone maintains that the English corporation sole had no counterpart in Roman law. It differed, first, from the Roman corporation; for three physical persons were always required by Roman law for the establishment of a corporation,[50] and this was true even though the corporation when once created could exist with only one member,[51] but there is never more than one member at a time in the case of the corporation sole. Secondly, it differs from the Roman institution or foundation, for the expression "successors" had to appear in a deed to a corporation sole in order to pass the fee[52] as each member of the series of persons constituting the corporation sole was in law one and the same person. Again, the Roman foundation or institution is a collection of goods, while the corporation sole is composed of but a single person. The anomalous character of the corporation sole becomes apparent when it is understood that this individual is actually the corporation, and not simply its representative or administrator. Ro-

[49] Blackstone, *Commentaries,* II, 469, 470.
[50] *Tres faciunt collegium, Dig.* 50, 18, 8.
[51] *Dig.* 3, 4, 7, 2.
[52] Kent, *Commentaries,* II, 273,

manists, however, are at variance as to whether or not there existed corporations sole under the Roman law. Some authorities believe that this would seem to be the case since a legacy to the Emperor or magistrate was valid without any further instructions or specifications.[53] But the weight of authority tends to the contrary view.[54]

The corporation sole was a common form of corporation in New England before the Revolution,[55] and also in Virginia, where the Episcopal Establishment prevailed, and the English usage of regarding the minister as a corporation sole obtained.[56] In the former place, it disappeared by virtue of the passing of the congregational system upon which it depended, and in the latter by a satutory enactment of 1802, so that there is no corporation sole in Virginia today.[57] After the pre-Revolutionary era, therefore, the corporation sole becomes rare,[58] except when the specific status of the corporation sole has been the result of the priest's or Bishop's recourse to the state's incorporating statutes. Some of the states have such statutes[59] equally applicable to all episcopal denominational systems. But in many of the states, the legislatures have refused to pass such legislation for the reason that it would be conferring special privilege upon the Catholic Church which would chiefly benefit thereby.

The character of the corporation sole is the least known of the different types of ecclesiastical corporations, since there is but a limited number of decisions construing the statutes which provide for the corporation sole.[60] It is known, however, that the power of the English corporation

[53] Smith, *o. c.*, II, 980, *universitas.*

[54] *C. J.* XIV, § 39, note 73, *Corporations.*

[55] Zollmann, *o. c.*, 39 to 43.

[56] Terrett *v.* Taylor, 9 Cranch 43 (U. S.); Lincoln, *o. c.*, 571.

[57] Zollmann, *o. c.*, 44, 45

[58] But position of a Catholic priest of a mission was analogous to that of a corporation sole in England: Illinois, Kentucky, Texas, California and Georgia; cf. Zollmann, *o. c.*, 46; *C. J.* XIV, § 39, *Corporations.*

[59] California, Connecticut, Kentucky, Illinois, Massachusetts and Maryland.

[60] Kent, *Commentaries*, II, 273.

sole to take property was restricted to real property as distinguished from personal property.[61] The single person who is constituted the corporation sole may act either for his own benefit or else may administer the property for the benefit of the *cestuis que trustent.* These, then, are the two aspects of the corporation sole.

The corporation sole has been recommended by the Holy See in the absence of a more advantageous form of corporation, with this limitation, however, that the Ordinary, the corporation sole, can act only with the advice and consent of the diocesan consultors. The advantages of this form of corporation are manifest. It insures security to ecclesiastical property holdings by making them freely descendible to each holder of the episcopal office. And it permits the Ordinary to carry on his corporate life by the application of canonical principles which will not be disturbed by the civil law. But it is not an ideal arrangement since confusion prevails as to whether such a corporation could alienate its property without the parishioners' consent, and as to whether a *cestui que trust* might have equity compel the corporation sole to surrender its legal title to diocesan property. Finally, the death of the Ordinary suspends the *de facto* corporate life of the corporation sole and thus inactivity and consequent confusion exist through the entire period of the inter-regnum.[62]

III. The holding of diocesan property by ecclesiastics in fee simple is abolished. The importance of the ecclesiastical legal personality is manifest from its necessity as a medium by which all Church property is to be acquired, held, and administered. The Catholic Church in the United States was for a time on a missionary basis. But by a decree of the S. Propaganda, June 9th, 1784, the Church here became a distinct body with the Very Rev. Dr. John Carroll as Prefect Apostolic.[63] The following year he reported

[61] *C. J.* XIV, § 39, *Corporations.*
[62] *Ibid.*
[63] Baart, *o. c.,* 18.

to the Propaganda that "the Catholic religion was cramped here by laws and no remedy has yet been found for this difficulty, though we made an earnest effort last year."[64] With the dawn of the 19th century, there was no corporate activity with respect to the Catholic Church. Its temporal affairs were administered by a system of lay trustees, sanctioned by Archbishop Carroll.[65] This was but natural, since, first, the missionary type of congregation was the rule, and the congregation was without the continued services of a priest, a situation necessitating lay tenure and control of the ecclesiastical property.[66] Secondly, Archbishop Carroll chose to adapt the Catholic method of management to suit the democratic spirit of American pioneer conditions, and to make it coincide, if possible, with the lay-trustee scheme used by Protestant denominations, by whom Catholics were surrounded in large numbers.[67] But this system proved unsatisfactory. Lay control of the temporalities of the Church often was construed as equivalent to the right to dictate ecclesiastical discipline and interfere with strictly Church affairs. Hence, Rome condemned the abuses in 1822.[68] This instruction from the Holy See was acted upon by the First Provincial Council of Baltimore in 1829.[69] In the future, all ecclesiastical property was to be assigned to the local Ordinary. Priests were forbidden to hold parish property in their own name by diocesan legislation. This was confirmed by the resolutions adopted by the Fourth Provincial Council which recognized the two alternatives of incorporation wherever possible, or else the vesting of the fee simple in the Bishop. But the

[64] This refers to a document entitled *Form of Government* in 19 Articles adopted by the Maryland and Pennsylvania chapters of priests, asking for incorporation. This chapter was incorporated by Maryland, December 23, 1792.

[65] Baart, *o. c.*, 21.

[66] MacCaffrey, *History of the Catholic Church in the Nineteenth Century*, II, 279.

[67] Baart, *o. c.*, 21.

[68] Pius VII, lit. ap. *Non sine magno*, 24 Aug. 1822, *Fontes* n. 480.

[69] Baart, *o. c.*, 53.

security of such a vesting became doubtful. The attention of the Bishops had been called to this fact in 1837 by the Third Provincial Council of Baltimore,[70] and in 1840, the Fourth Provincial Council declared "that if this security can be obtained in no other way, then the property is to be handed down by means of last wills and testaments, drawn up according to the provisions of the civil law."[71] The decree of the Propaganda of the same year[72] required a will from each Bishop passing the property upon his demise to another Bishop who was to reconvey it to the successor of the original Bishop. But upon the recommendation of the Fathers of the Fifth Provincial Council, 1843,[73] the practice was altered by having the Bishop file his will with the Archbishop within a reasonable time after his consecration.

The administration of temporal interests and the fee simple interest in diocesan realty were, therefore, taken out of the hands of the lay trustees and vested absolutely in the hands of the Bishop. But this episcopal fee simple system crumbled because of internal defects and external opposition. First, the vesting of the fee in the Bishop opened the door to its encumbrance by the personal creditors of the Bishop and left the issue in doubt upon his death should the heirs at law of the Bishop choose to contest the right of the ecclesiastical successor to take the property. These inherent weaknesses may be illustrated by two celebrated cases, namely, the Baraga Case, where it became necessary to make a private settlement with the European heirs of Bishop Baraga, who indicated their intention of endeavoring to break his will;[74] again, the Purcell Case in Cincinnati, where in 1879, Archbishop Purcell had agreed in his private capacity to guarantee the indebtedness of his brother who had undertaken to act as a banker for Cincinnati Catholics; the unpaid amount was about $2,500,-

[70] n. 43.
[71] n. 56.
[72] 15 Dec. 1840, *Collect S. Cong. de Prop. Fide*, n. 916.
[73] n. 59.
[74] Baart, *o. c.*, 68.

000, which creditors sought to recover from Archbishop Purcell, holder of the legal title of the diocesan property, by levying on said property.[75] Both cases were decided favorably to the Church, but they revealed the inherent defects of the system whereby the Bishop was allowed a fee simple interest in ecclesiastical property. Secondly, the civil law in some of the states was beginning to frown upon the system, as New York, which passed the discriminatory legislation of 1855, making it impossible for an ecclesiastic to transfer property in any way to his successor in office.

Hence, the Third Plenary Council of Baltimore in 1884 merely tolerated the system as a last resort declaring:

> Or the property of the diocese by a similar law may be committed to the Bishop in trust, that he may hold it in the name of the diocese and administer it according to the wish of the church; or as a last resource the bishop may hold the temporal goods of the diocese and administer them in his individual name, under that absolute title of law which in English is called a fee simple; in which case let the bishop be always mindful, that, although the full ownership of ecclesiastical property is given him by the civil law, nevertheless according to the admonition of the sacred canons, he is not the owner of it but only the administrator.[76]

It has been said that the vesting of the absolute ownership of property in the Bishop is "unnecessary, unsafe, unwise, expensive and detrimental to the interests of the Church in the United States."[77]

It will be noted that of the two methods thus far tried, neither was corporate. The Church was purposely avoiding the medium of the legal person for the conduct of her temporal affairs, because under the theory of American

[75] Mannix *v.* Purcell, 46 Ohio St. 102.
[76] *Con. Plen. Balt.* III, Tit. IX, cap. ii, n. 267.
[77] Baart, *o. c.*, 60.

law, these legal personalities are mere "creatures of the state," subject to its authority and liable to death and extinction should the legal umbilical cord which unites them to the state be severed; and the Church wished, first, to wait for the view of the American courts which would sooner or later be expressed by their adjudications, and secondly, the Church was uncertain as to the ultimate result which the early anti-Catholic movements in this country might have upon the stability of the corporations of the Catholic Church.[78]

But the practice of vesting the fee simple in the Bishop was specifically abolished in 1911 by the Sacred Congregation of the Council, though the Bishop was not forbidden to hold as trustee in the strict sense; and formal sanction and approval were given to the ecclesiastical corporation as the best method of taking care of the temporal needs of the Church, provided certain safeguards were insured.[79]

It is to be remembered that this sanction of the ecclesiastical corporation is not intended to exclude the practice of making the Bishop a trustee by inserting such *status* in the deed by which legal title to property is conveyed to him, nor even the episcopal holding of property by deeds which purport to confer absolute title in states which follow the practice of applying the doctrine of constructive or resulting trusts in such instances, despite the Statute of Frauds[80] and the general rule of evidence against the changing of the terms of a written instrument.[81] Of course, while there are states whose courts will declare a trust, even though the deed to the Bishop is on its face absolute, there are others which will take a diametrically opposite view. Examples of the former may be cited, as Mannix *v.* Purcell, 46 Ohio St. 102,[82] mentioned above; and Fink *v.* Umscheid,

[78] Desmond, *o. c.*, 71.
[79] *Ecclesiastical Review*, November, 1911, 591, 596.
[80] Kent, *Commentaries*, IV, 450, 452.
[81] Kent, *Commentaries*, II, 556.
[82] Cf. Desmond, *o. c.*, 103.

40 Kans. 271,[83] which declared that where property is purchased by a congregation for a special purpose, although the deed is made to the Bishop, the congregation is entitled to control the property and the Bishop holds the property in trust for the congregation. The following are adjudications tending toward the latter view: Heiss *v.* Vosburg, 59 Wisc. 532, which held that the plaintiff, the successor of a Bishop to whom the legal title of Church property had been conveyed by a deed purporting to be absolute on its face should recover in an action against the members of the Church in question who were endeavoring to erect a new building; and again, Hennessy *v.* Walsh, 55 N. H. 515,[84] which declared that the members of a local parish did not have a right of action against a Bishop to whom the legal title of the property had been given.

But does the clause of the Document issued by the Congregation of the Council in 1911 which refers to the situation in which **the civil law precludes recognition of Parish Corporations in the ownership and Administrations of Church Property,** include those jurisdictions which provide merely for the trustee type of church corporation? This can be answered only after the character of this form of corporation has been described.

The trustee corporation grew out of the trustee system. A *trust* has been defined as the right of property held by one person, called the trustee, for the benefit of another called the beneficiary or *cestui que trust*.[85] It evolved from the *use* which was based on a fiduciary relationship in which property had been given to one person for a third party's benefit. At first, before the development of equity, whose existence was largely the result of Canon and Roman laws upon the common law of England, the *cestui* had no legal redress, nor remedy of any kind should this fiduciary relationship be abused. But it could be enforced later in

[83] Cf. Lincoln, *o. c.*, 664.

[84] *Ibid.*

[85] Bouvier, *Law Dictionary,* II, 1144; *Cyclopedic Law Dictionary,* 1028.

equity.[86] The system of uses was utilized to evade the effect of the English mortmain statutes, which voided grants of land to corporate bodies. Thus the title of land was given to a natural person who held for the benefit of the Church,[87] and the use was enforcible in equity. But this method of holding property was abolished by the Statute for Transferring Uses into Possession, under Henry VIII, in 1535, by providing that the legal title should vest with the person who enjoyed the benefit of the property. Ecclesiastical bodies answered this legislation by inventing the legal fiction of a use upon a use, whereby the title to real property was transferred to one physical person, for the use of a second physical person, for the use of the Church corporation. The common law would not recognize a use upon a use, voiding the limitation of the first use. But equity considered the second physical person as holding the property in TRUST for the Church, so that a trust was originally a use limited upon a use, but eventually a trust was said to have been created, even though there was no second use. Hence, legal title vests in the trustee and the equitable title in the *cestui que trust*.

Now the membership of certain ecclesiastical associations in the United States was so large that ownership in common and common management of the property became impracticable. Certain members, therefore, were selected as trustees to hold the property for the benefit of all.[88] These trustees have the legal title, yet the members of the society are the beneficiaries and have both the *jus habendi* and the *jus disponendi* for all legitimate purposes, while the former had only the bare legal title.[89] At first these individuals held this title individually. But the defects of the system became intolerable. Upon the death of a trustee, if he were a tenant in common, his interest passed to

[86] Blackstone, *Commentaries,* II, 327; Kent, *Commentaries,* IV, 290.
[87] Strong, *Relations of Civil Law to Church Polity, o. c.,* 82.
[88] Zollmann, *o. c.,* 49.
[89] Morgan *v.* Rose, 22 N. J. Eq. 583; Bridges *v.* Wilson, 58 Tenn. 458.

his heirs; if he had a life estate, it reverted to the original owner, and if he was a joint tenant, it went to the surviving trustees, but in any event, the legal title might be lost or pass into the hands of incompetents. The wisdom of incorporating the board of trustees was seen.[90] The theory of the law was not that the societies select persons to be a corporation, but when certain representatives had been chosen to offices recognized by law and usage, the law annexes *proprio vigore* the corporate capacity to the office.[91] This incorporation had its advantages, for on his removal by death, resignation, or otherwise, the law *ipso facto* divested the trustee of all power as a corporator and recognized his legally chosen successor.[92] The equitable title still continued in the unincorporated society, but the legal title was now in the corporate body, to wit, the board of trustees. Death of a trustee did not suspend the activity of the organization, for the corporate existence continued until another trustee was named. The same was true with reference to the fee.[93] The incorporation of boards of trustees was first provided for by special charters, but subsequently, by general incorporating laws.

The trustee corporation had numerous defects. Thus, it engendered needless litigation, which should have been disposed of by the ecclesiastical body itself. Again, the trustee corporation in question might be an independent unit and it might receive title by an absolute deed; here the only test to determine the proper disposition of the property was the religious persuasion of the members at the time of the grant,[94] but this was sometimes an impossible undertaking. Judgments, moreover, against the corporation were worthless, for the corporation as distinguished from the church and society had only the legal title.[95] Trustees,

[90] Earle *v.* Wood, 62 Mass. 430.
[91] Bailey *v.* M. E. Church, Freeport, 71 Me. 472, 477.
[92] Earle *v.* Wood, 62 Mass. 430.
[93] Zollmann, *o. c.*, 51.
[94] Wilson *v.* Livingston, 99 Mich. 594, 603.
[95] Lord *v.* Hardie, 82 N. C. 241.

as incorporators, were not allowed to contract debts; hence the creditor had no redress unless, perchance, he had a contract with the trustee individually.[96] Finally, every deed to the corporation had to contain an express declaration of trust, a clumsy process. It is manifest, then, why New York and certain other states so construed the incorporating statutes as to destroy purposely the trustee corporation theory.[97] The trustees were made mere agents of the members of the society, and the entire membership was included in the incorporation. In other words, the corporation aggregate was evolved. In New York this was accomplished by the judiciary, which utilized the inexact wording of the statute and presumed that as the statute in some places loosely called the members, incorporators, that this was actually intended and that the sovereignty vested not in the board of trustees but in the members themselves.[98]

From this examination of the nature of the trustee corporation, it appears that it may or may not have been condemned impliedly by the Sacred Congregation of the Council, depending upon who are to be the trustees, and upon the method by which they are chosen, or, at least, a majority of them. If the majority of them are to be laymen or if they or a majority of them are to be chosen by the congregation, then such corporations come within the prohibition. Otherwise, they would be very satisfactory forms of the ecclesiastical corporation. Actually, the former situation is the rule in the vast majority of the states; so that the corporation would come under the control of the laity of the parish, which has either the power to name at least a majority of the trustees, or else to direct their actions by recourse to equity.

It is this possibility of a reference of the issue to equity, which also militates against the Bishop's holding the dio-

[96] Bailey *v.* M. E. Church, Freeport, 71 Me. 472.
[97] Zollmann, *o. c.*, 57.
[98] Zollmann, *o. c.*, 54 to 58.

cesan property as trustee, and leads to this inevitable conclusion, that the ecclesiastical legal personality with certain safeguards is the only solution to the question: What is the best method of tenure and administration of Church property in the United States at the present time? It is true that in theory the Bishop as trustee can function in accordance with canonical principles and rules, and the separation of the legal and equitable title makes it possible for the parish affairs to be administered by the pastor for the good of the congregation and under episcopal supervision.[99] Since there is a trust relation, however, equity can always assume jurisdiction to disturb the trust. As a matter of fact, the majority rule is that the Bishop is a mere dry trustee, without actual power, and subject to the direction of the *cestuis*.[100] A bitter controversy on this very point arose about twenty years ago in Scranton, Pennsylvania, and came up before the Supreme Court of that state no less than five times.[101] The effect of this series of adjudication has been thus summarized by Zollmann:

> These cases taken together establish, as clearly as can be done, the relation of the Bishop toward the property of the congregations of his diocese. Outside of what ecclesiastical pressure he may be able to bring to bear and outside of the difficulties which he can cause by his refusal to convey, the property of a Catholic congregation is as much at its disposal as if it stood in its own name. The Bishop is merely the dry trustee of the legal title.[102]

In some of the states, therefore, special laws have been passed providing for the incorporation of certain denominational organizations, and in such instances the state has

[99] Zollmann, *o. c.*, 353.
[100] *Ibid.* 355.
[101] Mazaika *v.* Krauczunas, 229 Pa. 47, 52; Krauczunas *v.* Hoban, 221 Pa. 213, 226; Mazaika *v.* Krauczunas, 233 Pa. 138, 146; Novickas *v.* Krauczunas, 240 Pa. 248; Novicky *v.* Krauczunas, 245 Pa. 86.
[102] Zollmann, *o. c.*, 360.

gone as far as possible to facilitate the procedure by simply requiring the filing of an affidavit or certificate with the prescribed state officers.[103] These statutes were even adapted to the particular governmental structure of the various denominations, and the courts have upheld the constitutionality of such statutes.[104] Other states make no such provision but compel all denominations to go through the same procedure and adopt the same corporate organization as merely lay or business corporations. In two states,[105] the right of incorporation is refused to all religious organizations, but even there, agencies of the Church may incorporate.[106] Certain states, like Delaware, frown upon the corporation sole.[107] In others, this form of corporation has not been brought to the attention of the courts, as in Indiana.[108] In some the courts recognize a quasi-corporation sole by legal construction in the absence of statutory authority, as in Texas;[109] while in other states, the statutes specifically provide for this type of corporation, as in California.[110]

[103] Zollmann, *o. c.*, 24.
[104] St. Hyacinth Congreg. *v.* Borucki, 141 Wisc. 205; 124 N. W. 284.
[105] Virginia and West Virginia.
[106] Wilson *v.* Perry, 29 W. Va. 169.
[107] Union Church *v.* Sanders, 1 Houst. 100 (Del.).
[108] Dwenger *v.* Geary, 113 Ind. 106.
[109] St. Antonio *v.* Odin, 15 Tex. 539.
[110] Mora *v.* Murphy, 83 Calif. 12.

CHAPTER X.

OPERATION, POWERS AND PRIVILEGES OF THE ECCLESIASTICAL CORPORATION.

The legal procedure for the incorporation of religious bodies is well defined in the statutes of the various states. The first step in such incorporation is generally the determination of the agents, directors or trustees who are to make application to the state for the corporate charter. This application is to be prepared by the trustees at their first meeting. These trustees are either chosen by the organization or else selected in accordance with the stipulations of the incorporating statutes. This board then petitions the legal authorities by sending to the proper state officer an application signed, acknowledged and sworn to, stating the name, purpose, domicile or principal place of business of the corporation. The express requirements of the statute must be complied with, and all facts required to be expressed in the certificate must be stated.[1] The propositions agreed upon in the application are the basic principles upon which all later legislation by the corporate entity must be grounded, for the civil law regards it as a compact upon which the corporation is based and the document which sets out the relationship of the members to the corporation.[2] After presentation of this application, there is issued by the state a certificate or charter of incorporation. The trustees then duly record and file this in the prescribed place; the corporation thereupon comes into being. The control of the temporal affairs of the church then passes automatically into the hands of the trustees, and also the title to all church property, if there has been created

[1] Boush, *Rulings by Civil Courts governing Religious Societies,* § 7.

[2] Boyles *v.* Roberts, 222 Mo. 613; 121 S. W. 805; Lemp *v.* Raven, 113 Mich. 375; 71 N. W. 627; Harrison *v.* Hoyle, 24 Ohio St. 254.

the trustee type of corporation, or if it is the aggregate form, the title and the corporate sovereignty vest in all the members of the organization for whom the trustees act simply as agents or administrators.[3]

A *de jure* ecclesiastical corporation, as distinguished from a *de facto* corporation comes into existence if all these statutory requirements have been substantially complied with. What then is the difference between the *de jure* corporation and those which are simply *de facto or quasi?* The *de jure corporation* is one that the law regards as juridically perfect, since it has complied with the essential conditions which the law imposed for the incorporation. A *de facto* ecclesiastical corporation implies three elements, just as in the case of other private corporations, namely: first, a law under which it might have become a *de jure* corporation, secondly, a *bona fide* effort, however faulty, to organize under it, a colorable compliance with the statute, therefore, and thirdly, a user of corporate powers. A *quasi* corporation is not a corporation actually, but the law will consider it such for special limited purposes, for instance, for taking property. Thus, since 1731, the Pennsylvania statute declared that bodies religious not incorporated were corporations for the purpose of taking property;[4] a similar law was passed in Maryland in 1779;[5] in Massachusetts in 1911;[6] in Vermont in 1814;[7] and also in New Hampshire, Tennessee, and others.[8] But in Michigan such recognition is given only after a ten year user.[9]

In law, a *de facto* corporation is good as against all but the state, which alone can challenge the organization's

[3] People *v.* Fulton, 11 N. Y. (1 Kern) 94; Keith & Perry Coal Co. *v.* Bingham, 97 Mo. 196; 10 S. W. 32 (Mo.); Centenary Methodist Episcopal Church *v.* Parker, 43 N. J. Eq. 307; Gewin *v.* Mt. Pilgrim Baptist Church, 166 Ala. 345; 51 So. 947.

[4] Phipps *v.* Jones, 20 Pa. 260.

[5] Bartlett *v.* Hipkins, 76 Md. 5.

[6] Hamblett *v.* Bennett, 88 Mass. 140.

[7] M. E. Soc. *v.* Lake, 51 Vt. 353.

[8] Zollmann, *o. c.*, 62.

[9] Congreg. Church, Ionia *v.* Webber, 54 Mich. 571.

right to exist as a corporation and it does this only by a direct attack.[10] It may be suggested that this division of the ecclesiastical corporation into *de jure* and *de facto* is evidence of the private character of this class of corporations in the United States;[11] this distinction is not drawn in respect to public corporations.[12]

Where those who object to the corporate existence of an ecclesiastical legal personality have dealt with the organization as though it were *de jure* a corporation, then, with reference to such complainants, the courts will hold the corporation to be *de facto,* and hence a corporation so far as those dealings are concerned, and this even though the attempts at incorporation were very irregular; examples are: an inapplicable statute,[13] an unconstitutional law,[14] no notice of meeting to incorporate the organization,[15] omission of several statutory requirements from the certificate.[16] But a stricter view will be taken by the courts when the complainants have not acknowledged the corporate existence in their dealings with the organization; thus, where the certificate was not signed by the proper person,[17] and where a seal was omitted, and the recording delayed an unreasonable time,[18] it was held there was no *de facto* corporation.

A compliance with the statute as to matters not appearing in the certificate will be presumed from user under it, where the certificate has been duly acknowledged and recorded in the absence of proof to the contrary.[19]

[10] Klix *v.* Polish Roman Catholic Church, 137 Mo. App. 347; 118 S. W. 1171.

[11] Roberts, *Laws relating to Religious Corporations,* Introd. xi.

[12] Zollmann, *o. c.,* 69.

[13] St. John Baptist Greek Catholic Church *v.* Baron, 73 Atl. 422 (N. J.).

[14] Catholic Church *v.* Tobbein, 82 Mo. 418.

[15] East Norway Lake Lutheran Church *v.* Froislie, 37 Minn. 447; 35 N. W. 260.

[16] Fifth Baptist Church *v.* Baltimore & Potomac R. Co., 137 U. S. 568.

[17] Congregational Church, Ionia *v.* Webber, 54 Mich. 571; 20 N. W. 542.

[18] Ferraria *v.* Vasconcelles, 23 Ill. 456.

[19] All Saints' Church *v.* Lovett, 1 N. Y. Super. Ct. 213.

In an action by a religious corporation it must show itself to be a corporation *de facto*. Proof of the existence of a law, or a special charter, authorizing its incorporation, and user of corporate rights conferred will be sufficient for this purpose.[20] Colorable compliance is presumed. The fact of incorporation must be proved by the production of the original certificate. The record of a certificate can only be produced, when the non-production of the original is accounted for.[21]

One who has contracted with a religious corporation by subscribing towards building a place of worship, may deny its corporate existence, but if it be shown that such corporation exists *de facto*, he will not be permitted to take advantage of an imperfection in the record or certificate of incorporation.[22] And one who accepts an office in a religious society acting as a corporation, thereby admits it to be a body corporate, and in an action by it, he is estopped from denying its corporate existence.[23]

Upon the incorporation of a religious organization, the statute under which it was incorporated becomes the constitution of the society.[24] A religious corporation is a society; its charter, its constitution, and its privileges are dependent on whatever conditions are clearly expressed.[25] Hence the charter or constitution is the supreme law of the organization to which all else is subordinated.[26] The organization may draw up by-laws but it can not formulate any set of rules which can properly be termed a constitution.[27] The manner in which charter powers are to be exercised is left to the discretion of each particular corporation. The power to make by-laws for this purpose, where it is not

[20] M. E. Church *v.* Pickett, 19 N. Y. 482.

[21] Paddock *v.* Brown, 6 Hill. 530 (N. Y.).

[22] M. E. Union Church *v.* Pickett, 19 N. Y. 482.

[23] All Saints' Church *v.* Lovett, 1 N. Y. Super. Ct. 213.

[24] Zollmann, *o. c.*, 111.

[25] Juker *v.* Commonwealth, 20 Pa. 484, 495; Canadian Religious Association *v.* Parmenter, 180 Mass. 415; 62 N. E. 740.

[26] Langolf *v.* Seiberlitch, 2 Pars. Eq. 64 (Pa.).

[27] Zollmann, *o. c.*, 109.

expressly granted, will then be implied, unless it is expressly excluded by the terms of the charter.[28] While a by-law need not be reduced to writing,[29] it must not be contrary to the charter and must be reasonable.[30] The purpose of by-laws is to direct the internal action of the organization, as distinguished from the corporate constitution which sets forth the relation of the corporation to the state.[31] They may cover such things as membership and its forfeiture, and this even though the charter contains nothing on this point.[32] A majority vote of the corporation may repeal by-laws at any time. In fact a provision in a by-law that it shall not be repealed shall be declared null and void by the courts.[33] It has been held that a by-law which necessitates the assent of the Bishop for the election of lay trustees is valid and will be enforced.[34] An ecclesiastical corporation may be made up of members who belong to a single religious denomination but it would be unconstitutional, it has been held, for such a corporation to pass a by-law requiring the incorporators to adhere to this faith as a condition of membership in said corporation.[35] The rights given them by statute may not be disturbed by a religious organization though it may deprive them of spiritual favors.[36] Courts will sometimes construe corporate usages and practices as by-laws.[37]

Subscription promises may be enforced by an ecclesiastical corporation even though the promises have been made before incorporation.[38] The validity of such promises is not

[28] Curry *v.* First Presbyterian Congregation, 2 Pittsb. R. 40 (Pa.); Taylor *v.* Edson, 58 Mass. 522, 526.

[29] Miller *v.* Eshbach, 43 Md. 1.

[30] Calkins *v.* Cheney, 92 Ill. 463; Hussey *v.* Gallagher, 61 Ga. 86.

[31] Zollmann, *o. c.*, 88.

[32] Taylor *v.* Edson, 58 Mass. 522, 526.

[33] Wardens of Christ Church *v.* Pope, 74 Mass. 140, 142.

[34] St. Hyacinth Congregation *v.* Borucki, 141 Wisc. 205; 124 N. W. 284.

[35] People *v.* Franciscus Benevolent Society, 24 Ho. Pr. 216.

[36] People *v.* German Church, 53 N. Y. 103.

[37] Miller *v.* Eshbach, 43 Md. 1; Zollmann, *o. c.*, 116.

[38] Ref. Prot. Dutch Church *v.* Brown 29 Barb. 335; but see Presbyterian Soc. *v.* Beach, 8 Hun. 644; Snyder, *o. c.*, 30

affected by the fact that they are oral; they do not come within the Statute of Frauds.[39] Should incorporation be impossible, courts have gone as far as to hold a trust created with respect to the money willed for the benefit of a church.[40] Nor can contributions actually given to a church be assailed by the assignees in bankruptcy of the donor.[41] Some courts hold that it is the mutuality of the promises as between the various subscribers which constitutes the consideration for the subscriptions.[42] But necessary conditions must be fulfilled before the subscriber becomes liable where there is a conditional promise and the condition is not a mere condition subsequent[43] or has not been waived.[44] It is safer for a church to incorporate, however, before asking for subscriptions; thus, a note made in favor of an unincorporated organization may be declared void.[45] The various individuals who are jointly interested in the common enterprise of promoting the ecclesiastical corporation have no remedy for services rendered where there is no incorporation.[46] Where incorporation has taken place, there should be proper authorization of those who solicit subscriptions in order to avoid invalidity.[47] It has been held that an ecclesiastical corporation may contract with its members in the way of accepting stock subscriptions.[48]

The general rule is that actions must be brought in the name of the ecclesiastical corporation.[49] Thus, it has been held that an incorporator may not bring an action in his own name to set aside an order changing the corporate name; the corporation itself must be made a party.[50] Again,

[39] Methodist Episcopal Society *v.* Lake, 51 Vt. 353.
[40] Seda *v.* Huble, 75 Ia. 429.
[41] Carpenter *v.* Buttrick, 41 Mich. 706.
[42] George *v.* Harris, 4 N. H. 533.
[43] New Myer's Appeal, *In re,* 72 Pa. 121.
[44] Thompkins *v.* Dinnie 21 N. D. 305.
[45] Boutell *v.* Gowdin, 9 Mass. 254.
[46] Cheeny *v.* Clark, 3 Vt. 431; Zollmann, *o. c.,* 326.
[47] Leonard *v.* Lent, 43 Wisc. 83.
[48] Zollmann, *o. c.,* 103.
[49] People *v.* Fulton, 11 N. Y. 94; Bundy *v.* Birdsall, 29 Barb. 31 (N. Y.).
[50] Watkins *v.* Wilcox, 4 Hun. 220, aff'd. 66 N. Y. 654.

it is necessary to join the corporation itself where there is sought the appointment of a receiver of property of a religious corporation.[51] An ecclesiastical corporation has the same capacity to bring actions for the violation of its legal rights as a physical person. For example, it may bring an action of forcible entry and detainer in its own name.[52] Such an action may be brought even against the minister and members of the church where they had broken open the building to hold religious services.[53] It has been held that an ecclesiastical corporation may bring an action to quiet title,[54] to reform a deed,[55] and to compel conveyance.[56] It has the right of maintaining actions of ejectment.[57] And it may agree to consolidate with corporations of a similar nature.[58] The courts have recognized its right to bring tort actions for trespasses on church property;[59] for example, it may sue a railroad company for nuisance in disturbing the use of the church edifice and damages may be recovered both for the material depreciation of the property caused thereby, and for the inconvenience suffered by the members of the congregation as a result of the building's being rendered unfit for church services.[60]

But in some states the action must be brought in the name of the trustees and not in the name of the corporation.[61] Such a holding has reference to the trustee type of

[51] Groesbeck *v.* Dunscomb, 41 Ho. Pr. 302 (N. Y.).

[52] People *v.* Fulton, 11 N. Y. 94.

[53] People *v.* Runkle, 9 Johns 147 (N. Y.).

[54] First Baptist Church of San Jose *v.* Branhan, 90 Calif. 22; Davis *v.* Owen, 107 Va. 283; Lincoln, *o. c.*, 15.

[55] M. E. Protestant Church *v.* Adams, 4 Ore. 76.

[56] Enos *v.* Chestnut, 88 Ill. 590.

[57] Van Deuzen *v.* Presbyterian Cong. at Ft. Edward, 42 N. Y. (3 Keyes) 550; Lincoln, *o. c.*, 5.

[58] Zollmann, *o. c.*, 103.

[59] Second Congregational Parish in North Bridgewater *v.* Waring, 41 Mass. 304; Green *v.* Cady, 9 Wend. 414 (N. Y.); Penny *v.* Central Coal and Coke Co., 138 Fed. 769; Religious Congregational Society *v.* Baker, 15 Vt. 119; Cargill *v.* Sewall, 19 Me. 288.

[60] Baltimore & Potomac R. Co. *v.* Fifth Baptist Church, 108 U. S. 317; Boush, *o. c.*, § 79. First Baptist Church *v.* Schenectady & T. R. Co., 5 Barb. 79 (N. Y.).

[61] Ada St. Methodist Episcopal Church *v.* Garnsey, 66 Ill. 132.

corporation.

In the aggregate type of ecclesiastical corporation, the trustees are simply a board of directors.[62] Yet corporations belonging to this type may enter into contracts through a majority vote of the trustees. The other ways in which this form of corporation may act are, first, by a majority vote of the aggregate body, or secondly, through an agent duly authorized either by the trustees or the aggregate body or both.[63]

But what constitutes a quorum with reference to the incorporators of an aggregate ecclesiastical corporation? When the number of incorporators is indefinite, it seems that those present constitute a quorum if the corporate meeting has been regularly held and a majority of these are sufficient to pass binding resolutions.[64] There are adjudications that this rule applies even though the number which actually assembles is a minority of the whole, provided that there is no corporate law to the contrary.[65] Illegal votes which do not affect the result of the ballot do not invalidate the election.[66] But some courts hold that where the number of incorporators is definite a majority of this number must be present to constitute a valid assembly capable of passing authorized resolutions.[67]

If the ecclesiastical corporation belongs to the trustee type, the board of trustees, as distinguished from the members of the society, are alone incorporated. In such instances, the trustees in their official capacity have complete control with respect to the temporalities of the church and the society, there being three distinct elements in this form of corporation, namely, the legal corporation, the voluntary

[62] Attorney General *v.* Geerlings, 55 Mich. 562.

[63] M. E. Church *v.* Sherman, 36 Wisc. 404.

[64] Field *v.* Field, 9 Wend. 394; Snyder, *o. c.*, 25.

[65] Lincoln, *o. c.*, 316; *Cyc.* XXXIV, 1127, note, quoted in Barton *v.* Fitzpatrick, 187 Ala. 273; 65 S. 390; Madison Ave. Baptist Church *v.* Baptist Church in Oliver St., 2 Abb. Prac. (N. Y.) N. S. 254, aff'd. 31 N. Y. Super. Ct. 109.

[66] First Parish, Sudbury *v.* Stearns, 21 Pick. 148 (Mass.).

[67] Moore *v.* St. Thomas Church, 4 Abb. 51 (N. Y.).

association, and the spiritual society. Here the incorporated board of trustees becomes the trustee of the money and property belonging to the society, with such powers as may be at least implicitly approved by the society; the society in turn is the *cestui que trust* with both the *jus habendi* and the *jus disponendi.*[68] Thus, it is to this board of trustees that a pastor of a parish must look for the payment of his salary; but the trustees must not exceed their authority; for example, a court will grant a *writ of mandamus* to force the trustees to admit a minister rightfully appointed for the society by the Bishop.[69]

Trustees, in both the aggregate and trustee types of ecclesiastical corporation, may be either *de jure* or *de facto.* They are *de jure* when they are duly qualified in every way to hold office. There is no defect legally in their election or appointment. Thus, it has been decided that a majority vote of those members of the Church constituting a quorum assembled after due notice and cast at an election properly conducted according to the constitution, by-laws or customs of the church will be sufficient to make them *de jure* officers.[70]

Trustees are *de facto* when they are acting as officers under "color" of having been duly elected or appointed.[71] A court of law will inquire into the regularity of the election of trustees of a religious corporation to whom the property of the corporation is committed and will determine the qualifications of the voters who are allowed to vote at such an election. But when the trustees are irregularly elected, the validity of their acts can not be questioned in a collateral proceeding, for instance in an action involving corporate property.[72] The right of a *de facto* trustee to hold office can not be questioned, except, first, by a *de jure*

[68] Page *v.* Asbury M. E. Church, 78 A. 246 (N. J.); Boush, *o. c.*, § 51.

[69] People *v.* Steele, 2 Barb. 397 (N. Y.).

[70] Zollmann, *o. c.*, 394.

[71] East Norway Lake Norwegian Ev. Lutheran Church *v.* Halvorson, 42 Minn. 503, 506; 44 N. W. 663, 665.

[72] Bellport *v.* Tooker, 29 Barb. 256, aff'd in 21 N. Y. 267.

successor rightfully qualified, or secondly, by the attorney general of the particular state in a direct action by *quo warranto* brought upon his relation or upon the relation of a private individual.[73] It has been held that equity can not inquire into the validity of the election of the officers of a church duly incorporated but the remedy is by *quo* warranto.[74] In Maryland, under statute it has been held that *mandamus* is the proper remedy to determine the title to the office of trustee of a church.[75]

A religious corporation like any other is bound by the acts of its authorized agents in the scope of their authority and in matters that are within its corporate capacity and may, by the enactment of by-laws, or by the distribution of the exercise of its powers among its various officers or by conferring authority upon special agents, so charge itself as to become liable for the acts of individuals representing it and acting by its authority.[76] But it has been decided that an ecclesiastical corporation is not liable for injuries resulting from the negligence of an employee of a corporation where it was not alleged that said employee was not competent to do the work, or that there was negligence on the part of the corporate officers in his employment.[77]

The trustees of an ecclesiastical corporation are in joint possession of all the property of the church, real or personal and are charged with the duty of executing its contracts.[78] They are managing agents of the corporation and may bring an action for an injunction restraining certain members of the society from interfering with the possession and management of the corporate property.[79] In fact this

[73] Jackson *v.* Nestles, 3 Johns 115; Snyder, *o. c.*, 39; Zollmann, *o. c.*, 370; Commonwealth *ex rel.* Gordon *v.* Graham, 64 Pa. St. 339.

[74] Grant St. Reformed Presbyterian Church, Appeal of, 238 Pa. 419; Nelson *v.* Benson, 69 Ill. 27; Boush, *o. c.*, § 33.

[75] Clayton *v.* Carey, 4 Md. 26.

[76] Constant *v.* St. Albans Church, 4 Daly 305 (N. Y.).

[77] Lincoln, *o. c.*, 607; Haas Missionary Society of the Most Holy Redeemer, 6 Misc. 281 (N. Y.); McDonald *v.* Mass. General Hospital, 120 Mass. 432.

[78] Zollmann, *o. c.*, 394.

[79] Baptist Congregation *v.* Scannel, 3 Grant's Cas. 48 (Pa.).

power extends to the prevention of all unauthorized acts.[80] It has been adjudicated that a court can not take the property of a religious corporation out of the hands of trustees and put it into the hands of a receiver, i. e., not as an incidental proceeding in a suit by the state for the forfeiture of the corporation's charter.[81] Under the New York statute, it has been held that proceedings by a majority of the trustees of a religious corporation for a sale of its property are sufficient without a vote of the members of the corporate body; for the trustees are the agents of the corporation for this purpose.[82]

The ecclesiastical corporation has certain rights even as against the trustees. Thus the trustees of a religious corporation may not allow claims against the corporation which come within the operation of the Statute of Limitations.[83] Nor is an ecclesiastical corporation liable for all the debts which the trustees may have contracted.[84] Certain conditions are required in order that the trustees may bind the corporation:

I. MEETING OF THE TRUSTEES: The act must be authorized by a vote of the trustees at a meeting. The trustees, therefore, must act as a body and not simply individually to bind the corporation. Thus, it has been adjudicated that where the trustees borrowed money for which they tendered their promissory notes, in which the signers purported to be trustees, and where the note was given in behalf of the church, the corporation was not liable, for there was no authorization for this negotiation by a vote of the trustees at a meeting.[85] And it has been held that a promissory note which purported to be made by a

[80] Langolf *v.* Seiberlitch, 2 Pars. Eq. 64 (Pa.); Snyder, *o. c.*, 39.

[81] State *v.* Immanuel Presbyterian Church of New Orleans, 52 La. Ann. 1311; 27 So. 806; Boush, *o. c.*, § 204.

[82] Congregation Beth Elohim *v.* Central Presbyterian Church, 10 Abb. Pr. N. S. 484 (N. Y.).

[83] Orthodox Congregational Church, Union Village, *In re*, 6 Abb. N. C. 398 (N. Y.); Lincoln, *o. c.*, 823.

[84] Wesley Church *v.* Moore, 10 Pa. 273, 278.

[85] Dennison *v.* Austin, 15 Wisc. 334.

corporation and signed by its president, secretary, and treasurer was not recoverable against the corporation in the absence of proof that the note was authorized at a meeting of the board of trustees.[86] It has been held that a Roman Catholic Bishop did not bind the corporation, though a trustee, where it was proved that he had not been authorized to bind the corporation in securing the services of an architect.[87] The purpose of requiring the trustees to act as a board seems to be to insure that they may have the benefit of mutual deliberation and discussion.[88] This end is not obtained where the act is authorized by a majority of the trustees acting individually.[89] It was decided that a person supplying materials for certain repairs in a church edifice which had been ordered by individual members of the vestry could not maintain an action against the trustees of the property for the vestry had not acted as a body, although individual members had assumed to make the contract.

II. MAJORITY VOTE. In order that the corporation may be bound, the resolution must be passed at a meeting of the trustees by a majority vote. Nor does this major per cent refer to the number to which the board may have been reduced by accident, resignation or othrwise, but to the number prescribed by statute.[90]

III. OFFICIAL CAPACITY. In order that the meeting be sufficient, the trustees who are present must act separately in their official capacity,[91] and under official author-

[86] People's Bank *v.* St. Anthony's Church, 109 N. Y. 512; Cattson *v.* First Universalist Society, 46 Ia. 106.

[87] McGlynn *v.* Hoban, 42 Pa. Super. Ct. 478; Boush, *o. c.*, § 130.

[88] Columbia Bank *v.* Gospel Tabernacle Church, 127 N. Y. 361; 28 N. E. 29.

[89] Constant *v.* St. Albans Church, 4 Daly 305.

[90] Moore *v.* St. Thomas Church, 4 Abb. N. C. 51 (N. Y.); Snyder, *o. c.*, 14.

[91] Cammayer *v.* United German Lutheran Churches, 2 Sandf. Ch. 186 (N. Y.).

ity.[92] This means that the meeting must be called by one authorized to assemble the body.[93]

IV. SCOPE OF THE CORPORATE POWER. The trustees may not bind the corporation except through transactions which are within the scope of its corporate power.[94] The extent of this *scope* is to be determined by the statutes, constitutions and by-laws of the corporation.[95] Should the negotiation fall within this *scope* and yet not be within the regular scope of church activity, the ecclesiastical corporation will not be liable unless it can be proved that the person who acts for the corporation has been authorized by the corporation or at least notified by it with knowledge of all the circumstances.[96]

But trustees will be personally liable on contracts which they make unless they act as a board by a majority vote, therefore, and under express or implied authority from the society and within the powers conferred on it, and as mere agents, and indicate this clearly, and they must also act for a society which has a legal personality, i. e., a corporation.[97] When these conditions are complied with, however, they are not personally liable for corporate debts.[98] Thus, trustees are not liable for the contracts of a building committee unless authorized.[99] Nor is a building committee liable when the contract is made in the name of the society.[100]

There are certain things which the trustees of an ecclesiastical corporation may not do. They may not make a contract in their own name and then put the liability on the

[92] State *v.* Aucker, 31 S. C. Law (2 Rich. Law) 245.
[93] Ladd *v.* Clements, 58 Mass. 476.
[94] Miller *v.* Milligan, 6 Ohio Dec. 1000; Dennison *v.* Austin, 15 Wisc. 334.
[95] Wyncoop & Watkins *v.* Bellvue Congregational Society, 10 Ia. 185.
[96] Wilson *v.* Tabernacle Church, 59 N. Y. Supp. 148.
[97] Zollmann, *o. c.*, 394.
[98] People, *ex rel.* Howlett *v.* The Mayor, 63 N. Y. 291; Snyder, *o. c.*, 39.
[99] Devoss *v.* Gray, 22 Ohio 159.
[100] Stanton *v.* Camp., 4 Barb. 274 (N. Y.); Johnson *v.* Welsh, 42 W. Va. 18, but liable in Copeland *v.* Hewett, 96 Me. 525.

corporation and thus defeat a personal action brought by the other party to the contract.[101] An attorney who is one of the church trustees may not recover compensation for legal services rendered to the trustees where the work is done under circumstances which justify the belief that no charge was intended.[102] A church can not be bound by the action of the trustees beyond the express powers granted by its members, in the case of the aggregate corporation. The trustees of a religious corporation can not bind it by covenant unless duly authorized nor can they dispose of or encumber its real estate unless they are duly authorized.[103] The trustees of a religious corporation organized under statute and in conformity with the canons and discipline of the Catholic Church have no authority to permit an excommunicated priest to occupy the corporation's church edifice consecrated by its founders to religious worship according to the canons and discipline of the church.[104] Trustees can not bind the corporation for an adverse interest of their own.[105] There is no presumption that a treasurer of a religious corporation has power to borrow money, sign notes and bind the corporation. His authority must be established by evidence.[106] Trustees may not turn the property over to another body.[107]

In the case of an unincorporated church, its real estate is held by a trustee or trustees. The same is true in jurisdictions where trustees are the only members of the church corporation.[108] Even in states where the aggregate theory of the ecclesiastical corporation prevails, the possession of realty is in the hands of the trustees.[109] But where there

[101] St. Patrick's Roman Catholic Church *v.* Gavalon, 82 Ill. 170; Zollman, *o. c.*, 377.

[102] Cicotte *v.* St. Ann's Church, 60 Mich. 552; 27 N. W. 682.

[103] Klop *v.* Moore, 6 Kans. 27; Boush, *o. c.*, § 44.

[104] Immaculate Conception *v.* Murphy, 89 Neb. 524; 131 N. W. 946.

[105] United Brethren Church, New London *v.* Van Dusen, 37 Wisc. 54.

[106] Wilson *v.* Tabernacle Baptist Church, 28 Misc. Rep. 268 (N. Y.).

[107] St. Ann's Church, *In re*, 14 Abb. 424 (N. Y.).

[108] Church of St. Francis of Pointe Coupee *v.* Martin, 43 La. 62, 68.

[109] German Evangelical Congregation of Lafayette *v.* Pressler, 17 La. Ann. 127, 129.

is question of a legal personality, the ownership of the property is always in the corporation, and not even in the members.[110]

What are the powers of the ecclesiastical corporation with reference to the acquisition and alienation of real property? When the powers of such a corporation are not defined and restricted by its charter, or by any general law, its capacity to take, hold and dispose of real estate is precisely the same as that of a natural person and such a corporation may hold lands as a trustee; real estate may be granted to any religious corporation in trust for any specific use or purpose comprehended in the general object of its incorporation.[111] But the powers to purchase real estate for the use of ecclesiastical corporations are restricted to the pious uses for which the land may be held as are comprehended within the general object for which the society was incorporated.[112]

The question whether a religious corporation has capacity to take property in excess of the amount prescribed by its charter can be raised only by the state in a direct proceeding for that purpose. The question can not be brought up collaterally at the instance of a private individual who may be interested in the property, nor in a proceeding for the construction of a will.[113] The majority rule, therefore, is that if a corporation takes land by grant or devise, in trust or otherwise which by its charter it can not hold, its title is good as against third persons and strangers and the state alone can interfere. If the corporation exceeds the prescribed amount though it be by an original purchase, nobody but the state can interfere with the holding of the property which it acquires and it is a matter of which individuals can not avail themselves in any way.[114] But other

[110] First Baptist Society, Leeds *v.* Grant, 59 Me. 245; Lincoln, *o. c.*, 543.

[111] Tucker *v.* St. Clement's Church, 5 N. Y. Super. Ct. aff'd. 8 N. Y. 558.

[112] Boush, *o. c.*, § 60.

[113] Hanson *v.* Little Sisters of the Poor, Baltimore & St. Mary's Church, Hampden, 79 Md. 434.

[114] De Camp *v.* Dobbins, 29 N. J. Eq. 36, aff'd 31 N. J. Eq. 671; Conklin *v.* Davis, 63 Conn. 377.

states, with reference to the effect of statutes on deeds made in contravention of them to religious corporations hold that such deeds are absolutely void and capable of being attacked in a collateral proceeding.[115]

If an unincorporated society becomes incorporated, property owned by it passes to the new corporation.[116] But if lands be granted for pious uses to a corporation not in being, the right to the possession and custody of the lands remains in the grantor till the corporation intended shall come into existence.[117]

It has been held that the receipt of money under a will and the institution of legal proceedings to recover it are not to be regarded as the exercise of corporate franchises such as are forbidden by statute to any domestic corporations. Hence foreign religious corporations are entitled to recover bequests made in their favor by a testator in the state in question.[118]

It has been adjudicated that an ecclesiastical corporation may lease property and in the absence of any pecuniary consideration, the support of the Gospel will be deemed sufficient consideration in such a transaction.[119]

What are the powers of the ecclesiastical corporation to alienate its property? Its power to sell its real property is absolute save in New York, where a statute requires the assent of a court to such transactions.[120]

In New York, therefore, a religious corporation which has the title to its realty may determine when it should be sold and has the sole and exclusive power to enter into contracts for that purpose. It is not necessary that the consent of the court should precede the making of the contract, but such a contract of sale can not become effec-

[115] St. Peter's Roman Catholic Congregation *v.* German, 104 Ill. 440.

[116] Gewin *v.* Mt. Pilgrim Baptist Church, 166 Ala. 345; Lincoln, *o. c.*, 845.

[117] Shapleigh *v.* Pilsbury, 1 Me. 271.

[118] Ticknor's Estate, *In re.* 13 Mich. 44; Boush, *o. c.*, § 89.

[119] Ref. Prot. Dutch Church *v.* Veeder, 4 Wend. 494 (N. Y.).

[120] Zollmann, *o. c.*, 109.

tive without a court order which should be obtained before a conveyance is made.[121] But elsewhere in the absence of contract the corporation unless specially restrained by its charter has the inherent right without any express authority to dispose of its property,[122] and such disposition will be approved by the courts.[123]

The power of the ecclesiastical corporation to mortgage or lease its property, if not expressly given,[124] will be implied.[125] The courts will not be exacting in reference to the procedure which the corporation may choose to adopt. Thus, a mortgage given by a New York religious corporation was executed by all of the trustees except one who had resigned, but there was no order or resolution of the board directing the execution. The referee found that in executing the mortgage the trustees acted as a board of trustees, and that though all who signed it were not present at the same time, yet that a majority of the trustees were present part of the time when it was executed. The mortgage was held to be as binding as if a formal resolution had been previously passed.[126] With reference to leasing its property, it has been held that the church corporation had power to do this, thus, the power to lease its property for opera house purposes.[127]

It has been held that an ecclesiastical corporation may assign its property to trustees for the benefit of creditors, unless restrained by its charter or by statute.[128] But a church edifice is not liable to be taken in execution for the debts of the society.[129]

[121] Congregation of Beth Elohim *v.* Central Presbyterian Church, 10 Abb. Pr. N. S. 484 (N. Y.).

[122] Langolf *v.* Seiberlitch, 2 Pars. Eq. 64 (Pa.).

[123] Catholic Church *v.* Manning, 72 Md. 116; 19 Atl. 599; Zollmann, *o. c.*, 94.

[124] Zion Church of Sterling *v.* Mensch, 178 Ill. 225; 52 N. E. 858.

[125] Zollmann, *o. c.*, 101.

[126] South Baptist Society, Albany, *v.* Clapp, 18 Barb. 35 (N. Y.); Lincoln, *o. c.*, 418.

[127] Catholic Institute *v.* Gibbons, 7 Ohio Dec. 516.

[128] Lincoln, *o. c.*, 599; De Ruyter *v.* St. Peter's Church, 3 N. Y. 238.

[129] Bigelow *v.* Congregational Society, Middletown, 11 Vt. 283.

Ecclesiastical corporations enjoy immunity from taxation with respect to necessary property; but this does not mean that the church will be exempted even from special assessments.[130] The privilege of exemption from taxation refers only to the buildings whose primary purpose is to afford shelter to religious services and the land upon which these buildings are situated which is reasonably necessary for comfort and enjoyment. The privilege, therefore, extends beyond the area actually covered by the buildings.[131] But parsonages, cemeteries, and schools do not receive such an exemption unless definitely mentioned in the statutes.[132] The rule followed by all the states is that "property used directly, immediately, and exclusively for religious purposes is exempt from taxation without regard to the question of direct ownership." [133] But there is disagreement as to what constitutes taxation. It has been held, however, that the privilege did not relate to concurrent or alternate occupation of the buildings or property by the church.[134]

Whatever the principles of the matter and the rights of the state, the custom of not taxing such property is inveterate.[135] Various reasons have been given. It has been suggested that the fundamental grounds upon which all such exemptions are based is a benefit conferred on the public by such institutions and a consequent relief to some extent of the burden upon the states to care for and advance the interests of its citizens.[136] Religious bodies are tax exempt because the religious and moral culture afforded by them is deemed to be beneficial to the public and necessary to the advancement of civilization.[137] But the tax ex-

[130] Lefevre *v.* Detroit, 2 Mich. 586; Lockwood *v.* St. Louis, 24 Mo. 20; Chicago *v.* Baptist Theological Union, 115 Ill. 245; Harlem Presbyterian Church *v.* New York, 5 Hun. 442.

[131] Trinity Church *v.* Boston, 118 Mass. 164.

[132] Zollmann, *o. c.*, 281.

[133] Boush, *o. c.*, § 105.

[134] Philadelphia *v.* Barber, 160 Pa. 123.

[135] Nichols *v.* School Directors, 93 Ill. 61.

[136] Book Agents of M. E. Church *v.* Hinton, 92 Tenn. 188; 21 S. W. 321.

[137] People *ex rel.* Lady of Angels Seminary *v.* Barber, 42 Hun. 27 (N. Y.).

emption statutes are generally construed strictly,[138] so that the burden of proof rests with the one who claims the exemption,[139] although the liberal rule is adhered to by some of the states.[140]

Church corporations usually acquire property by deed or will,[141] but it is possible for them to obtain title to land in another way, namely, by adverse possession, after the running of the period prescribed by the Statute of Limitations.[142] Title to property acquired by ecclesiastical corporations through adverse possession is good even though statutes have not been complied with in reference to the acquisition of the realty. "A corporation acquired real property in 1863 and at the time of the commencement of this action had been in uninterrupted possession of it for more than forty years. The society was deemed to have acquired the title by adverse possession, notwithstanding the provisions of Art. 38 of the Maryland Bill of Rights which in effect requires the sanction of the legislature to conveyances to religious societies, which sanction had not been obtained."[143] Where a deed in contravention of state statutes conveys to an ecclesiastical corporation more land than the statute allows, some courts will consider such a deed as "good color of title" for purposes of adverse possession, so that an ecclesiastical corporation may, through adverse possession under such a deed, acquire more property than the statute allows.[144]

In general, then, incorporation of the congregation and possession a sufficient length of time will vest title in the corporation barring the rights of the original owner by adverse possession.[145] But the possession must be exclu-

[138] Zollmann, *o. c.*, 247.

[139] New Haven *v.* Sheffield, 30 Conn. 160, 171; 109 Me. 22; 82 Atl. 290.

[140] Poultney Congregational Society *v.* Ashley, 10 Vt. 241.

[141] Zollmann, *o. c.*, 413.

[142] Propagation Society *v.* Sharon, 28 Vt. 603; Bogardus *v.* Trinity Church, 4 Paige 178 (N. Y.).

[143] Dickerson *v.* Kirk, 105 Md. 638; Lincoln, *o. c.*, 521.

[144] Dangerfield *v.* Williams, 26 App. D. C. 508.

[145] Zollmann, *o. c.*, 413.

sive of the original owner, continuous in time, and under a claim of right.[146] Color of title is not essential.[147] "But where the church is unincorporated or its possession has been too short for the purpose of the statute, the original owner, if he has in any manner evidenced an intention to donate the property, will by such acts of dedication be estopped from disputing the possession of the church. He will, however, retain the legal title and even a contingent remainder in the equitable title."[148] Some courts have held that twenty years of naked possession by an ecclesiastical corporation is sufficient to confer title in fee simple.[149] The title acquired by adverse possession is good as against the world, save the state, and as to the state not void but merely voidable at its option.[150] While a religious corporation can not by a mere resolution divest itself of the title to real estate, a separation of a church into two societies and the transfer by the parent society to the new society of the church edifice and other property occupied by the latter will at least lay the foundation of a right to adverse possession, and if the new society afterwards becomes incorporated, this adverse possession continues in the corporation thus formed, and the right may thereby ripen into a complete title.[151]

In a general way, the operation, powers, and privileges of the ecclesiastical corporation in the United States have been presented in the above chapter. It remains to supplement the idea of corporate power with the antithetic notion of corporate limitation. This constitutes the subject matter of the succeeding chapter.

[146] Zollmann, *o. c.*, 403.

[147] Harpending *v.* Ref. Prot. Dutch Church, 16 Pet. 455 (U. S.).

[148] Zollmann, *o. c.*, 413.

[149] Harpending *v.* Reformed Prot. Dutch Church, 16 Pet. 455 (U. S.); Boush, *o. c.*, § 71.

[150] Humbert *v.* Trinity Church, 24 Wend. 587, 630.

[151] Ref. Church, Gallupville *v.* Schoolcraft, 65 N. Y. 134; Lincoln, *o. c.*, 522.

CHAPTER XI.

LIMITATIONS OF THE ECCLESIASTICAL CORPORATION

The fundamental rule is that an ecclesiastical corporation must act according to its nature.[1] It possesses only those powers which are expressly given to it and the statutes which confer this power are to be interpreted so as to exclude those rights which are not therein expressly or impliedly contained.[2] In other words a Church corporation must not act *ultra vires*.[3] There are certain powers which are prohibited to religious corporations. Thus, they may not engage in the banking business expressly, unless so authorized by charter. This activity would fall within the act which forbids unauthorized banking. It has been held that a note discounted in the transaction of such business would be illegal and void.[4] And adjudications indicate that a Church corporation created for the carrying on of religious worship and authorized to receive and hold lands and erect buildings for this purpose and no other may erect only such buildings as are directly and distinctly appropriate to the promotion of religion and necessary to the comfort and convenience of the congregation when engaged upon religious duties. Thus, the trustees would have no power to erect an office building.[5] An ecclesiastical corporation, therefore,

[1] Harriman *v.* The First Bryan Baptist Church, 63 Ga. 186; Roman Catholic Church *v.* Weighaus, 16 Ky. Law Rep. 446; Thompson *v.* West, 59 Neb. 677; 82 N. W. 13; Second Precinct in Rehoboth *v.* Catholic Congregational Church and Society, 140 Mass. 139; Zollmann, *o. c.*, 106.

[2] People *ex rel.* Freeman and White *v.* Hulbert, 46 N. Y. 110; Snyder *o. c.*, 25.

[3] Franke *v.* Mann, 106 Wisc. 118; 81 N. W. 1014.

[4] Huber *v.* The United Evangelical Protestant Congregation of Cincinnati, 16 Ohio 371; Harriman *v.* The First Bryan Baptist Church, 63 Ga. 186; Thompson *v.* West, 59 Neb. 677; 82 N. W. 13.

[5] Lincoln, *o. c.*, 600.

may not enter into any business relations with the outside world, except such as are immediately necessary for the proper management of its own concerns.[6]

There are numerous limitations imposed upon the religious corporation. The corporation has nothing to do with the Church, except as it provides for the wants of the Church.[7] For instance it can not prevent the Church from receiving or expelling whomsoever that body shall see fit to receive or expel.[8] It may not expel a member from the corporate body as distinguished from the Church for mere moral delinquency.[9] He must be given notice and an opportunity to defend himself.[10] A resolution passed by the corporation for the purpose of depriving members of the privileges secured to them as incorporators by the statute of the state is a mere nullity.[11] Under a statute authorizing the incorporation of a Roman Catholic congregation, it was held that the provision in the statute for the selection of two lay members by the congregation's committee was mandatory and that persons chosen by the congregation, without a committee were not entitled to hold office.[12] The right to share in the government of a corporation is a civil right which the law will protect and hence the civil courts may determine who are members of the corporation.[13] When a judgment and execution have been obtained against the corporation, it is the corporation which is liable and not the members.[14] A corporation is not necessarily

[6] Zollmann, *o. c.*, 103.

[7] Lincoln, *o. c.*, 321.

[8] *Ibid.*; Harbison *v.* First Presbyterian Society, 46 Conn. 529; Hardin *v.* Baptist Church, 51 Mich. 137.

[9] People *v.* German United Evangelical St. Stephens Church, 53 N. Y. 103.

[10] Jones *v.* State, 28 Neb. 495; 44 N. W. 658.

[11] People *ex rel.* Dilcher *v.* German United Evangelical Church, 53 N. Y. 103; Lincoln, *o. c.*, 112.

[12] State *ex rel.* Barry *v.* Getty, 69 Conn. 286; Lincoln, *o. c.*, 822.

[13] Lincoln, *o. c.*, 154.

[14] Richardson *v.* Butterfield, 6 Cush. 191 (Mass); Allen *v.* North Des Moines M. E. Church, 127 Ia. 96; Lincoln, *o. c.*, 603.

ecclesiastical because it is managed by persons who adhere to the doctrine of a particular creed.[15]

Religious corporations may not consolidate without legislative authority.[16] And where a majority of the trustees on the boards of both corporations are identical, no legally binding contract for a consolidation of the two corporations can come into existence.[17] But under modern incorporation acts, the power to consolidate is sometimes granted to ecclesiastical corporations on condition that they are of similar nature with purposes and machinery which are not essentially different.[18]

It is not necessary to belong to the parish corporation in order to have the right to own a pew.[19] The American civil law view is that a pewholder has an easement in and not a title to the freehold; his pew constitutes a property right of which he has exclusive possession, including the right of passing through the aisles of the Church. These principles are applicable to all religious denominations. Thus, it has been adjudicated that the title to pews in a Roman Catholic Church when conveyed to individuals was not held in any different way than in the Churches of other religious denominations.[20]

The powers of the religious corporation are limited in several ways with respect to property. It is only in so far as the rights of others are concerned that the rights of natural persons are restricted in the acquisition of property, but it is different with regard to religious corporations which are mere "creatures of the State."[21] Thus Maryland makes it necessary for the ecclesiastical corporation to obtain the legislative consent when the acquisition of realty

[15] Bradfield *v.* Roberts, 175 U. S. 291; Lincoln, *o. c.*, 683.

[16] Lincoln, *o. c.*, 633; Chevra Bnai Israel Aushe Yanove und Motal *v.* Chevra Bikur Cholim Aushe Rodof Sholem, 24 Misc. 189 (N. Y.).

[17] Stokes *v.* Phelps Mission, 14 N. Y. St. Rep. 901.

[18] Selkir *v.* Klein, 100 N. Y. Supp. 449.

[19] First Baptist Society, Leeds *v.* Grant, 59 Me. 245.

[20] Lincoln, *o. c.*, 463.

[21] Trustees *v.* Dickinson, 12 N. C., 189, 202.

is intended,[22] and New York by statute requires the assent of the court when a Church corporation endeavors to sell its real property.[23] "This latter law grew up from the passage of the Statutes of Queen Elizabeth restraining the power of corporations to alienate property. Colonists brought these laws to New York. A law was passed in 1806, and re-enacted in 1813 which authorized the chancellor to give an order of sale to corporations to do away with the cluttering up of the legislature with petitions for such orders. Later judicial construction was to the effect that this statute prohibited the sale unless this judicial assent was given."[24] It has been adjudicated that a New York religious corporation has the title to its real property, may determine when it should be sold and has the sole and exclusive power to enter contracts for that purpose. The only distinction which exists between its power of alienation and that possessed by other corporations is that the consent of the court is necessary.[25]

The general rule seems to be that the ecclesiastical corporation may hold as much land as is necessary to fulfil its purpose. Its power to acquire property is in some states limited by mortmain laws whose test is the amount of real estate.[26] But reasonable men may differ honestly as to the amount needed; hence the quantity has been specified in the different jurisdictions. The rule applies only to land held for the use of the corporation. The amount has varied from two[27] to forty acres.[28]

The principle of restricting the acquisitions of religious organizations is not confined to the ecclesiastical corporation, for in about half of the states there are restrictions against gifts to charity and religion in general; thus, one

[22] Grove *v.* Trustees, 33 Md. 451.
[23] Zollmann, *o. c.*, 109.
[24] Zollmann, *o. c.*, 96.
[25] Bowen *v.* Irish Presbyterian Congregation, 19 N. Y. Super. Ct. 245, 267.
[26] Zollmann, *o. c.*, 109.
[27] Dangerfield *v.* Williams, 26 App. D. C. 508.
[28] Kinney *v.* Kinney's Ex'r. 86 Ky. 610; 6 S. W. 593.

may in certain instances give only a part of his estate to charity. In some states, land can only be conveyed by deed to religious undertakings; in others, a will giving property to religious enterprises must be made out at least a few months before the demise of the testator.[29]

The Ohio statute prohibiting a religious society from holding more than twenty acres, however, was interpreted to apply to a single religious society and not to a denomination.[30] Under the Civil Code of California no religious body, corporation or society can take under a will, and the bequest of money is void.[31] The declaration of rights in Maryland which declared that every sale of land to a religious body without leave of the legislature should be void, except sales for not more than two acres to be used for a meeting house or burial ground, imposed no restriction on the power of the legislature granting such leave, but authorized it to declare limitations or not in its discretion both as to the extent and quality of the estate to be purchased and the purpose for which it should be used.[32] Churches in Virginia are not incorporated and under the policy of the law of that state can not be. The property they are allowed to hold and its use are designated by statute; this likewise controls the activity of the church trustees.[33] The constitutional and statutory provisions of the West Virginia policy prohibiting the holding of land by any church or religious denomination were not intended to and could not if they were so intended, affect the right of

[29] Milwaukee Protestant Home *v.* Becher, 87 Wisc. 409.

[30] Morgan *v.* Leslie, Wright 144, Ohio. Cf. Sec. 10020, *Ohio General Code*, 1926: "Lands and tenements *not exceeding twenty acres* that have or may be conveyed by devise, purchase or otherwise to any person or persons as trustee or trustees for the use of a religious society within this state, either for a meeting house, burying ground or residence for their preacher, shall descend, with the improvements and appurtenances, in perpetual succession, in trust to such trustee or trustees as from time to time are elected or appointed by any such religious society, according to their respective rules, customs, usages and regulations."

[31] Wright Estate, *In re*, Myr. Prob., 213 (Calif.).

[32] Catholic Cathedral Church *v.* Manning, 72 Md. 116; 19 Atl. 599.

[33] Globe Furniture Co. *v.* Trustees, Jerusalem Baptist Church, 103 Va. 559.

an owner of land in that state to convey or devise it in trust for sale for the benefit of a foreign religious denomination.[34]

A religious corporation which holds property charged with a trust for certain purposes can not divert it to other inconsistent uses, either by corporate action or by the trustees individually. It has been held that when such use is for the promotion of the doctrines and discipline of some particular denomination, courts will prevent a diversion to the support of a different and inconsistent one if but a single individual legally interested raises an objection.[35] Neither the corporation, therefore, nor a majority of the incorporators can divert trust property to the propagation of a different religious faith, for the doctrine of implied trusts would be here invoked.[36] Where a donor has dedicated property for the purposes of advancing any particular religious doctrine or faith, if conflicting claims arise as to its ownership or possession, the civil courts will examine and decide which of the rival claimants is holding to the faith, which the donor desired to favor,[37] and will restrain those who have departed from that faith from using the property.[38] This principle applies not only to gifts but to all acquisitions and is referable to both unincorporated and incorporated organizations.

Says a Wisconsin court:

> Where property has been acquired, whether by gift or purchase, for the maintenance and support of the faith of any recognized denomination or church, every member of the association acquiring it, corporate or unincorporated, has a right to resist its diversion to other antagonistic uses, whether secular or religious

[34] Boush, *o. c.*, § 63.

[35] Cape *v.* Plymouth Congregational Church, 130 Wisc. 174; Lincoln, *o. c.*, 605.

[36] Zollmann, *o. c.*, 60.

[37] Wallace *v.* Hughes, 131 Ky. 445; 115 S. W. 684.

[38] Bowden *v.* McLeod, 1 Ed. Ch. 588 (N. Y.); Peace *v.* First Christian Church of McGregor, 20 Tex. Civ. App. 85, 90; 48 S. W. 534; Cape *v.* Plymouth Congregational Church, 117 Wisc. 150, 156; Mt. Zion's Baptist Church *v.* Whitmore, 83 Ia. 138, 148; 49 N. W. 81; Zollmann, *o. c.*, 151.

> and hence those who hold the title or control, whether a corporation or the officers of the association, hold it charged with a trust to apply it to those uses for which it was acquired and not to inconsistent one.[39]

Such a diversion to another religious use can not be upheld on the grounds of the doctrine of *Cy Pres*. This doctrine will be invoked in determining the disposition of a charitable use. Courts of equity can not devote any portion of a fund dedicated to charitable uses to any object not contemplated by the donor. When property is given to a class of objects in general terms and also directed to be applied to one of them in special terms, if its application to that one becomes unlawful or impracticable, the doctrine of *Cy Pres* authorizes the court to devote it to one or more of those embraced in the general intent most analogous to the one especially named.[40] But this is not the situation comprehended in the case where property has been given to a specific denomination and where a diversion is attempted.

It is immaterial how many of the congregation agree to divert the trust fund. According to a Minnesota court:

> A minority have the right to insist upon carrying out the proposition for which the Church or society was organized and the majority will not be permitted to divert the common property to other uses, or use it for the support and maintenance of a doctrine or polity essentially at variance with its original constitution.[41]

The same rule applies even though a schism occurs:

> Where a congregation has been organized and holds its property as a constituent part of any particular religious denomination, or in subordination to the government of any particular Church, it can

[39] Marien *v.* Evangelical Creed Congregation,. Milwaukee, 132 Wisc. 650; Lincoln, *o. c.*, 525, 526.

[40] Mormon Church *v.* U. S., 136 U. S. 1; Lincoln, *o. c.*, 75.

[41] Schradi *v.* Dornfeld, 52 Minn. 465.

> not without just cause sever itself from such connection or government. If it does so it necessarily forfeits its rights and property to those of the organization who maintain the original status.[42]

Of course, there is no question with respect to the Catholic Church as to which faction is schismatic. But in regard to ecclesiastical corporations of other denominations, it is necessary to determine which party represents the legitimate succession of the old or original body.

All courts will not uphold this implied trust doctrine. Indeed, it has been bitterly attacked by certain authors on the ground that it locks up property and that where property is conveyed by a general deed to an ecclesiastical organization, it should be presumed that it is the donor's intention to devise it to religious purposes in such manner and in such way as the governing body of the organization whatever it may be shall under its constitution and rules determine, for the religious faith of the incorporators is subject to continual change.[43] But the proposition that a "*faith once adopted must not forevermore remain stationary*"[44] is simply an assumption. It is respectfully submitted that this may be true of non-Catholic ecclesiastical societies and corporations, but in order that the general statement may stand, it will be necessary to show that Roman Catholicism has also changed, and since the opponents of the implied trust theory have not succeeded in proving this the reason proposed in favor of the opposite doctrine must fall, at least with reference to Catholic ecclesiastical corporations. Indeed, it seems most inequitable to thwart the will of the donor by applying his bequest ultimately to a purpose not intended by him.

The principle of estoppel applies to the ecclesiastical corporation in several ways and constitutes a limitation.

[42] McAuley's Appeal, *In re*, 77 Pa. 397; Lincoln, *o. c.*, 524; McGinnis *v.* Watson, 41 Pa. St. 9.

[43] Alexander *v.* Slavens, 46 Ky. 351, 353; Gable *v.* Miller, 10 Paige 627, 640; Mack *v.* Kime, 129 Ga. 1; 58 S. E. 184.

[44] Zollmann, *o. c.*, 195.

Thus, a religious corporation like a natural person may lose title to real estate by adverse possession.[45] Where a religious corporation permits individuals to act as trustees and holds them out to the world as such, it will be estopped from questioning acts done by them within the scope of their authority.[46] It has been held that where a church corporation was aware of a mortgage when the loan was made, but allowed the proceeds to be spent for its benefit, without an expression of dissent to the plaintiff, the mortgager could not claim that the trustee had no authority to enter into the transaction in an action to foreclose.[47] A corporation was held liable in an action against it to recover money borrowed by its treasurer, without the knowledge of the trustees, the money being used for the benefit of the corporation.[48]

A corporation of the ecclesiastical type may cease to exist, first, by the expiration of the time specified in its charter, secondly, by a resolution to disband,[49] or thirdly. by failure for a long time to hold corporate meetings and elect officers.[50] The resolution to disband is followed by an application to the proper court for dissolution.[51] A majority of the trustees may make this application without authority from a corporate meeting when the society has ceased to hold meetings.[52]

The contingency of dissolution is covered in the various state statutes. Thus, the facts which constitute extinction are defined in Sec. 16 of the *Religious Corporation Law of New York,* chapter 52, i. e.:

> if it (the corporation) has failed for two consecutive years next prior thereto to maintain re-

[45] Reformed Church *v.* Schoolcraft, 65 N. Y. 134; Snyder, *o. c.*, 34.
[46] Lovett *v.* German Reformed Church, 12 Barb. 67 (N. Y.).
[47] Scott *v.* First Free Methodist Church, 50 Mich. 528.
[48] Wilson *v.* Tabernacle Baptist Church, 28 Misc. 268 (N. Y.).
[49] McRoberts *v.* Moudy, 19 Mo. App. 26.
[50] Lynde *v.* Hill, 31 Mass. 447.
[51] Third Methodist Episcopal Church, Brooklyn, *In re,* 142 N. Y. 638.
[52] Tobey *v.* Wareham Bank, 54 Mass. 440; Zollman, *o. c.*, 73.

> ligious services according to the discipline, customs and usages of such governing body, or had had less than thirteen resident attending members paying annual pew rent, or making annual contributions toward its support.

Such a state of affairs is tantamount to an inability to maintain ordinary services.[53]

It has been held that the incorporated governing body of a church can dissolve a church over which it has ecclesiastical jurisdiction and provide for the custody and control of its property if authorized by statute.[54]

Upon dissolution, the property and rights of the corporation vest in the members who may validly sell it in conformity with the customs they have tacitly or expressly adopted, provided these are in conformity with the state laws.[55] This is the view of the Louisiana civil law, but a different rule obtains in the common law states of this country. To quote from a decision of the United States Supreme Court:

> When a (religious) corporation is dissolved, its personal property, like that of a man dying without heirs ceases to the subject of private ownership and becomes subject to the disposal of the sovereign authority; whilst its real estate reverts or escheats to the grantor or donor, unless some other course of devolution has been directed by positive law, though still subject as we shall see hereafter to the charitable use.[56]

The members of the defunct ecclesiastical corporation may later reincorporate and take over possession of the property and administer the trust vested in the former corporation.[57] But the disbanding of an incorporated religious

[53] Westminster Church *v.* Presbytery of N. Y., 211 N. Y. 214.

[54] Westminster Presbyterian Church, West 23rd St. *v.* Trustees of Presbytery of New York, 127 N. Y. Supp. 851.

[55] Burke *v.* Wall, 29 La. Ann. 38.

[56] Mormon Church *v.* U. S., 136 U. S. 1.

[57] Congregation of Roman Catholic Church *v.* Texas and P. R. Co., 41 Fed. 564.

society following a sale of its property on foreclosure and the incorporation of a new society composed in part of the same persons and the purchase of the Church property by the new corporation from the purchaser on the foreclosure sale, does not make the new corporation liable for the debts of the first corporation.[58] The present New York statute does not seem to consider the situation of the reincorporation of Catholic corporate bodies.[59]

The subject of ecclesiastical corporate powers and limitations has been discussed from the non-denominational viewpoint because the holdings of the American civil courts with respect to one sect may be applied to all since all religions occupy a plane of equality in the United States. What the courts have decided in this matter with respect to Protestant sects may be regarded as binding upon ecclesiastical corporations for the promotion of Catholicism and *vice versa.* Nor has it been attempted to analyze the corporation sole, first, because that form of corporation is not common in this country, and secondly, there are not many principles of corporation law which may be applied to it.[60]

The examination of the status of the Catholic ecclesiastical corporation reveals limitations which apparently restrict the temporal interests of the Church in the United States. In the final chapter, after a short comparative legal study, it is proposed to evaluate the precise effect of the present corporate situation in this country and to consider the merits of possible solutions.

[58] Allen *v.* North Des Moines Methodist Episcopal Church, 127 Ia. 96.
[59] *Religious Corporations of New York,* chapt. 52, § 90, 91, 92.
[60] *C. J.* XIV, § 39, *Corporations.*

CHAPTER XII.

CONCLUSION.

From the foregoing study, it appears that legal personality is a basic factor in every legal system of occidental civilization, constituting an important vehicle for the adequate fulfillment of the aims of society, regardless of whether that society be lay or ecclesiastical, and irrespective of the different attitudes taken by the various juridical schemes. By way of pointing out a few of these differences, it may be said that there is a lack of uniformity between the lay and ecclesiastical viewpoints. Civil law in general tends not to acknowledge the divine right of the Church to utilize the medium of the *persona moralis* in the fullest sense, without at least some sort of reference to the State. But ecclesiastical law insists upon the divine, inalienable right of having its juristic personalities independent of the State. While civil law has generally tended to claim a degree of authority with respect to all juristic persons, including those of the ecclesiastical type, it seems that its attitude has been different at different times and in different places. Thus, the law of Rome, after the religious persecutions, conceded the right of the Church to create its moral personalities, but claimed the right to pass upon the question of whether or not such personalities might continue to exist. In other words, the State did not deny the Church the right to erect juristic persons, but asserted its authority by claiming the power either to put its stamp of approval upon them or to dissolve them in the event that they were deemed to be a source of injury to the State.[1] Civil law through part of the Middle Ages maintained a similar attitude.[2] But later on, the civil law of the con-

[1] *Supra* pp. 64, 65, 67.
[2] *Supra* chapters III, IV.

tinent began to deny the Church's right in this respect. Later English common law also insisted that moral personality could come only from the State. And the jurisprudence of the United States has followed the English common law in the matter. Lack of uniformity, therefore, prevails today generally between the viewpoints of Canon and civil laws in reference to legal personality.

Canon law has maintained a consistent position with respect to the creation and division of the *persona moralis*, but a further comparative study will discover that numerous conflicts exist among the different civil laws concerning juristic personality. Thus, whether the State had the exclusive right to create legal persons was a matter of dispute under Roman law.[3] The same is true in regard to the continental legal systems which are adaptations of the Roman law. Later on, continental civil law tended to accept only State authority in the erection of the legal personality.[4] But in the English common law of later development, it was definitely settled that only the State could create corporations, though in the early common law the Church had been conceded the right of erecting ecclesiastical moral persons.[5] In the United States, the theory of the corporation as a State Concession obtains in civil law.

Civil legal systems have also differed with respect to the divisions of the legal person. Thus, Roman law recognized only two types of moral personality, i. e., the corporation and the institution, the foundation being simply a subdivision of the latter. But English common law added a further type, namely, the corporation sole. Yet the common law of England,[6] while adding another form of juristic person to the Roman conception, made the Roman institution simply a species of the corporation. The Roman institution became an eleemosynary corporation.

[3] *Supra* pp. 66, 67.
[4] *Supra* chapter IV.
[5] *Supra* pp. 40, 41.
[6] *Supra* chapter III.

This country has accepted the English common law theory. Hence the Roman and Canonical conception of the institution has no exact counterpart in the American system of jurisprudence. It does not accept the doctrine whereby an aggregate of property is regarded as a separate, distinct artificial entity, with rights and duties of its own. In the American institution or foundation, there is always incorporation, as the incorporation of a college or hospital.[7] The American institution or foundation is an eleemosynary corporation. Those legal entities created for charitable purposes which the Romans called the *universitas bonorum* and Canon law looked upon as *persona moralis non collegialis* are in the United States non-pecuniary corporations. But the American non-pecuniary corporation implies incorporation while the Roman institution and the canonical non-collegiate moral person did not require this, since they were not aggregates of persons but of property. The term incorporation in this connection is to be understood as referring to the erection of a legal personality from an aggregate of physical persons. The American non-pecuniary corporation is practically always a non-stock corporation. A stock corporation has been defined as a corporation with capital stock divided into shares, authorized by law to distribute to the holders thereof dividends or shares of the surplus profits of the corporation.[8] The term non-stock corporation includes every corporation other than the stock corporation, includes, therefore, non-pecuniary corporations, as hospitals, asylums and other purely religious, charitable or benevolent corporations.[9] The American non-pecuniary corporation, therefore, takes the place of the Roman institution and the Canonical non-collegiate moral person. This legal philosophy is substantially a reflection of the English Common Law.

[7] *C. J.* XXVI, 1003, *Foundation.*
[8] Bouvier, *Law Dictionary,* II, 1039.
[9] Ihmes' Estate, *In re,* 154 Ia. 20.

But American jurisprudence differs from the Common Law in the former's definite tendency to relegate the corporation sole, which is admitted in theory but generally speaking denied in practice. Different principles therefore obtain with regard to the principles of juridical personality in the grand ensemble of aggregated, universal jurisprudence, but a broad perspective including in the sweep of vision the historical, philosophical and juridical essences respectively of this notion will justify the interpretation, first, that there is uniformity in the belief that societies can best sustain themselves and achieve their destinies by immortalizing, as it were, certain activities by a transcendentalizing process, through the mechanism known as moral personality, and secondly, that the extent of the power to create and destroy, to direct and control these legal entities is a measure of the degree of sovereignty possessed by a particular society, whose subjects these personalities may happen to be. Hence when two societies whose aims are not identical come into contact with each other, it seems inevitable that their relative dependence or independence may be measured by determining the powers and limitations of their juridical personalities. In brief, the relation of the State to the Church in any country may be expressed in terms of the powers granted to the ecclesiastical corporation by the State. This has been universally true. It is illustrated by the situation which obtains in the United States at the present time.

The status of the canonical juristic personality in this country will always be determined in ultimate analysis by the policy which the American people may choose to have this government assume towards the Catholic Church. Law has always yielded and always must yield to political compulsion, just as inevitably as the weak must succumb to the strong. It is, therefore, not proposed to attempt to bring forward a corporate theory by which the position of the Church might be benefited in the United States. Suffice it to say that while in American law there is no ecclesiastical juristic personality in the sense understood in Canon law, i. e., moral persons created by the Church and functioning without the authority of the State, nevertheless the conscience of the American people has dictated an equitable policy toward the Church by protecting her temporal interests and assisting her to achieve indirectly the results which would have followed from an unqualified recognition of her juridical personality.

It is possible to submit solutions in the nature of procedures by which the Church might endeavor to bring about a new era in her corporate status in the United States; thus:

(1) A plan providing for the change of the ecclesiastical corporation into a stock corporation might be defended by certain jurists. Under such an arrangement, non-transferrable shares of stock[10] might be issued to the incorporators, for instance the Bishop, Vicar-General, Rector and two laymen, the Bishop owning more than fifty per cent of the stock. Restrictions might be imposed whereby such stock could be held only by the successors in office of these incorporators. The advantages of such a stock arrangement, it is argued, would be, first, the possibility of its being put into operation in practically every state in the Union, secondly, the vesting of the controlling power in the hands of the Bishop in accordance with the spirit of Canon law, and thirdly, the certain identification of the interested members in the event of corporate dissolution, who would hold the property as trustees for the benefit of all the parishioners. But in practice such a plan would be limited, first, by the attitude of the people in the different states with regard to the coincidence of such a plan with public policy, for such a procedure under the states' incorporating laws might be looked upon by the

[10] *C. J.* XIV, § 1036, 1037, 1038, *Corporations.*

majority of the citizens as a legal trick, which would accordingly be promptly prohibited by the different state legislatures, and secondly, by the principle that "the director of a corporation acquires no additional authority to act for the corporation, from the fact that he owns a majority of the corporate stock,"[11] it having even been held that "the stockholders of a corporation at a general meeting can not, even by a unanimous vote, bind the corporation by contract; their action would at most be advisory and not obligatory upon the directors."[12] Hence, the control of the Bishop under such a scheme would be uncertain, and finally, the dissolution problem would not be remedied in the event that ecclesiastical corporations were to become stock organizations, for under the present plan of Church corporation, the statutes provide for reincorporation, and further if it should ever happen that the State was bent upon the escheating to the civil government of the funds of the dissolved corporation, no legal device could prevent such a disposition.

(2) Again, a program might be defended whereby an intensive movement would be launched in the various states to have them pass incorporating laws after the fashion of the approved New York plan, with resulting uniformity in the realm of the ecclesiastical corporation and in reference to the tenure of Church property. But such a recommendation would be open to the objection that it is doubtful whether the New York plan, for example, would be advantageous if transplanted to other states where the judiciary might choose to construe the incorporating statutes adversely, not following the interpretations of the New York courts, and besides, it is uncertain whether uniformity is desirable in the United States with its forty eight juris-

[11] Clement *v.* Young-McShea Amusement Co., 69 N. J. Eq. 347; 67 A. 82; Allemong *v.* Simmons, 124 Ind. 199; 23 N. E. 768; Cent. Dig., vol. 12, *Corporations*, § 1274, 1593, 1594.

[12] Insurance Bank of Columbus *v.* Bank of the U. S., 4 Clark 125 (Pa).

dictions, each one with varying local problems, which perhaps can be best met by the particular jurisdiction itself.

(3) Finally, it might be thought desirable to have the different states recognize the right of all Church organizations to erect and control their own legal persons without any reference to state authority. But this would imply a complete constitutional change and a revolutionary transformation in American psychology and theory of government.

The future security of the temporal interests of the Church in the United States will depend upon the fair-mindedness and sense of equity of the American people who may be expected to display these characteristics to judge from the experience of the past. The Church's activity *de facto* is not limited in this country or cramped by the refusal of this government to recognize her corporate personality. The phenomenal growth of the Church in the United States proves this. While it is to be admitted that the recognition of the Church's right to function through purely canonical moral persons, established and existing independently of the civil authority is the ideal arrangement and the plan to which Catholic theology can alone give unqualified assent, neverthless when such an arrangement becomes impossible, no better substitute can be presented than the policy which has been worked out by the American people. To invoke the eloquence of the late James Cardinal Gibbons: "But thank God, we live in a country where liberty of conscience is respected, and where the civil constitution holds over us the aegis of her protection, without intermeddling with ecclesiastical affairs. From my heart, I say: America with all thy faults, I love thee still. Perhaps at this moment there is no nation on the face of the earth where the Church is less trammelled, and where she has more liberty to carry out her sublime destiny than in these United States."[13]

[13] Gibbons, *Faith of Our Fathers*, 28.

BIBLIOGRAPHY.

A. A. S.—*Acta Apostolicae Sedis, Commentarium Officiale,* vol. XVII, Rome, 1925.

Acta et Decreta, Concilii Plenarii Baltimorensis II, Baltimore, 1877.

Acta et Decreta, Concilii Plenarii Baltimorensis III, Baltimore, 1886.

Angel and Ames, *Corporations,* 1846.

Annibale, Joseph d', *Summula Theologiae Moralis,* 3 vols. Rome, 1891.

Augustine, Charles, O.S.B., D.D., *A Commentary on the New Code of Canon Law,* 4th ed., 8 vols., St. Louis, 1921.

Ayrinhac, H. A., *General Legislation in the New Code of Canon Law,* New York, 1923.

Baart, P. A., S.T.L., LL.D., *The Tenure of Catholic Church Property in the United States of America* (Authorized Copy), Marshall, Mich., 1900.

Bachofen, Augustine, *Summa Juris Ecclesiastici,* Rome, 1910.

Barbosa, Agostino, *Pastoralis solicitudinis sive de officio et Potestate, Parochi,* Lugdini, 1665.

Barbosa, Agostino, *Tractatus Varii,* Lugdini, 1660.

Barillari, Mich., *Sul Concetto della Persona Giuridica,* Rome, 1910.

Beitel, Calvin G., *The Ecclesiastical Laws of Pennsylvania,* Philadelphia, 1904.

Bernard, Fernand, *First Year of Roman Law,* translated by C. P. Sherman, New York, 1906.

Binder, Julius, *Das Problem des juristischen Persönlichkeit,* Leipzig, 1907.

Blackstone, Sir William, Knt., *Commentaries on the Laws of England* (notes by John L. Wendell), 4 vols., New York, 1852.

Blat, Alberto, O.P., *Commentarium Textus Codicis Juris Canonici,* 5 vols., Rome, 1921.

Bondini, A., O.M.C., *De Personae Moralis Exstinctione,* Jus Pontificium, Rome, III, (1923).

Bonfante, Pietro, *Storia del Diritto Romano,* 2 vols., 1923.

Bouix, Marie Dominique, *De Capitulis,* Paris, 1882.

Boush, Christian M., *Rulings by Civil Courts governing Religious Societies,* Cleveland, 1915.

Bouvier, John, *Law Dictionary,* 2 vols., Boston, 1897.

Brabandere, P., de, *Juris Canonici et Juris Canonico-Civilis Compendium,* 2 vols., Brugis, 1866.

Brentano, L., *History of the Guilds,* London, 1870.

Brinz, Alois, *Lehrbuch der Pandecten,* Leipzig, 1895.

Buckland, W. W., *Elementary Principles of Roman Private Law,* Cambridge, 1912.

Buckland, W. W., *A Text Book of Roman Law,* Cambridge, 1921.

Cahill, James, *Consolidated Laws of New York,* Chicago, 1923.

Cappello, Felix, *Institutiones Juris Publici Ecclesiastici,* 2 vols., Turin, 1907.

Cappello, Felix, *Summa Juris Publici Ecclesiastici,* Rome, 1923.

Catholic Encyclopedia, 16 vols., New York, 1907-12.

Cathrein, Victor, S. J., *Philosophia Moralis,* Friburgi, Brisgoviae, 1911.

Cavagnis, Felix, S.R.R. Card., *Institutiones Juris Publici Ecclesiastici,* 3 vols., Rome, 1882.

Channing, Edward, *A History of the United States,* 5 vols., New York, 1909.
Chelodi, Joannis, *Jus De Personis,* Trent, 1922.
Cicero, Marcus T., *Letters,* edited by J. S. Waters, London, 1855.
Cocchi, Guidus, C.M., *Commentarium in Codicem Juris Canonici,* 6 vols., Turin, Rome, 1924, 1925.
Codex Juris Canonici, Rome, 1923.
Codicis Juris Canonici Fontes, Cura Emi Petri Card. Gasparri Editi, Romae, 4 vols., 1923-1926.
Coke, Lord Edward, *Institutes of the Laws of England,* by J. H. Thomas, Esq., 3 vols., Philadelphia, 1836.
Collectanea S. Congregationis De Propaganda Fide, 2nd ed., 2 vols., Rome, 1907.
Cooley, Thomas M., LL.D., *General Principles of Constitutional Law,* Boston, 1898.
Corpus Juris Canonici, Richter-Friedberg, Leipzig, 2 vols., 1879, 1881.
Corpus Juris Civilis, Coloniae Munatianiae, 1781.
Corpus Juris-Cyc. System, New York, 1919.
Creagh, John T., *Benefice* (*Catholic Encyclopedia,* II, 473).
Cummings and Gilbert, *Membership and Religious Corporations of New York,* Albany, 1907.
Cyclopedic Law Dictionary (Shumaker-Longsdorf), Chicago, 1922.
Dernburg, Heinrich, von, *System des Römischen Rechts,* 2 vols., Berlin, 1912.
Desmond, Humphrey, J., *The Church and The Law,* Chicago, 1898.
De Vareilles-Sommières, *Les Personnes Morales,* Paris, 1902.
Devoti, Joannis, *Institutionum Canonicarum,* 2 vols., Leodii, 1860.
Ecclesiastical Review, vol. XLV, Philadelphia, 1911.
Ephemerides Theologicae Lovanienses, Louvain, IV, 1927.
Ferrini, Contardo, *Pandette,* Rome, 1917.
Ferrara, Fr., *Le Persone Giuridiche,* Naples, 1907-1910.
Frère-Orban, Hubert, *La main morte et la charité, Paris* 1857.
Gibbons, James, Cardinal, *The Faith of Our Fathers,* Baltimore, 1898.
Gierke, Dr. Otto, *Political Theories of the Middle Ages.* Translated with an Introduction by Frederick William Maitland, Cambridge, 1900.
Girard, P. F., *Droit Romain,* Paris, 1924.
Harvard Law Review, vol. 24, Cambridge, 1910-1911.
Hohenlohe, Constantine, O.S.B., J.U.D., *Papstrecht und Weltliches Recht,* Munich, 1925.
Hölder, Eduard, *Natürliche und juristische Personen,* Leipzig, 1905.
Hunt, Sandford, *Laws Relating to Religious Corporations,* New York, 1876.
Ihering, Rud., *Geist des römischen Rechts,* Leipzig, 1891.
Kahl, Joh., *Lex. Magnum,* Geneva, 1683.
Kent, James, *Commentaries on American Law,* 12th ed., 4 vols., Boston, 1884.
Kettleborough, Charles, *The State Constitutions,* Indianapolis, 1918.
Kirch, Conradus, S.J., *Enchiridion Fontium Historiae Ecclesiasticae Antiquae,* Frieburg, 1910.
Kirsch, J. P., *Unam Sanctam,* (*Catholic Encyclopedia,* XV, 126).
Landon, Judson, *The Constitutional History and Government of the United States,* Boston, 1889.
Laurent, Francois, *L'Église et L'État en Belgique,* 3 vols., Brussels, 1858-62.
Laurent, Francois, *Principes de droit civil,* 33 vols., Brussels, 1869-78.
Lilla, Vicenzo, *Manuale di Filosofia del Diritto,* Milan, 1903.
Lincoln, Charles, Z., *The Civil Law and The Church,* New York, 1916.

Machen, Arthur, W., Jr., *Corporate Personality* (*Harvard Law Review*, vol. 24, p. 253).
MacCaffrey, James, *History of the Catholic Church in the Nineteenth Century*, 2 vols., Dublin, 1910.
Mansi, Joannes, D., *Sacrorum Conciliorum Nova et Amplissima Colleotio*, 51 vols., Paris and Leipzig, 1901-26.
Maroto, Philippo, *Institutiones Juris Canonici*, 2 vols., Rome, 1921.
Mayer, Otto, *Die juristische Personen und ihre Verwertbarkeit im öffentlichen recht*, Tübingen, 1908.
Muerer, Christian, *Die juristische Personen*, Stuttgart, 1901.
Michoud, Leon, *La Théorie de la Personnalité Morale*, 2 vols., Paris, 1906-09.
Milman, H., *History of Latin Christianity*, 8 vols., New York, 1889.
Mitteis, Ludwig, *Römisches Privatrecht*, Vienna, 1908.
Mommsen, Th., *De Collegiis*, (Marquardt), Leipzig, 1888.
Mommsen, Th., *Römisches Staatsrecht*, Leipzig, 1887.
Morey, William C., *Outlines of Roman Law*, New York, 1884.
Moulart, Ferdinand, *L'Église et L'État*, Louvain, 1895.
Page, William, *Ohio General Code*, Cincinnati, 1926.
Pauly-Wissowa, *Real-Encyclopadie*, Stuttgart, 1901.
Permaneder, Franz, M., *Handbuch des Kirchenrechts*, Landshut, 1856.
Pic, Paul, *Sociétiés Commerciales*, Paris, 1908.
Pollock and Maitland, *History of English Law*, 2 vols., Boston, 1895.
Raccolta di Concordati tra la Santa Sede e le Autorita Civili, Rome, 1919.
Reeves' History of England: W. F. Finlason, Amer. Ed., 5 vols., Philadelphia, 1880.
Reiffenstuel, Analecto, *Jus Canonicum Universum*, 7 vols., Paris, 1864-69.
Ricobono, S., *Fontes Juris Romani Ante-Justiniani*, Florence, 1909.
Riviere, J., *Le Probleme de l'église et de l'état au Temps de Philippe le Bel*. XIV. Louvain, 1927.
Roberts, Wm., H., *Laws relating to Religious Corporations*, Philadelphia.
Ruffini, Fr., *La classificazione delle persone giuridiche in Sinnibaldo dei Fieschi* (Innocenzo IV), Turin, 1898.
Santi, Franciscus, *Praelectiones Juris Canonici*, 4 vols., Rome, 1842.
Savigny, Friedrich Karl, *System des heutigen Römischen Rechts*, Berlin, 1840.
Scherer, Rudolf Ritter von, *Handbuch des Kirchenrechts*, 2 vols., Graz, 1886.
Schmalzgrueber, R. P., Francisco, S.J., *Jus Ecclesiasticum Universum*, 12 vols., Rome, 1844-45.
Schulte, D. Joh. Friedrich, *Die Juristische Persönlichkeit*, Giesen, 1869.
Schwabe, Max, *Die juristische Person und das Mitgliedshaftsrecht*, Basel, 1900.
Schwabe, Max, *Rechts-subject und Nutzbefugnis*, Basel, 1901.
Schwabe, Max, *Die Körperschaft mit und ohne Persönlichkeit*, Basel, 1904.
Second Plenary Council of Baltimore and Pastoral Letter, Baltimore, 1866.
Sherman, Charles Phineas, *Roman Law in the Modern World*, 3 vols., New Haven, 1922.
Smith, William, *Dictionary of Greek and Roman Antiquities*, 2 vols., London, 1890.
Snyder, William, L., *The Laws of the State of New York relating to Religious Corporations*, New York, 1879.
Sohm, Rudolph, *The Institutes of Roman Law*, translated by James Crawford Ledlie, Oxford, 1907.

Strong, Hon. William, *Relations of Civil Law to Church Polity*, New York, 1885.

Tacitus, Cornelius, *Annales*, translated by Church and Brodribb, London, 1871.

Tanquerey, Ad., *Synopsis Theologiae Dogmaticae*, 2 vols., Rome, 1922.

Taunton, Ethelred, *The Law of The Church*, London, 1906.

Taylor, Henry O., *Private Corporations*, Philadelphia, 1898.

Thesaurus Resolutionum Sacrae Congregationis Concilii, vol. 130, Rome, 1871.

Thomae Aquinatis, *Summa Theologica*, 6 vols., Rome, 1894.

Thorpe, Francis Newton, *The Constitutional History of the United States*, 3 vols., Chicago, 1901.

Toso, Dr. Alb., *Jus Pontificium*, Rome, 1922.

Tyler, Ransom, H., *American Ecclesiastical Law*, Albany, New York, 1866.

Vermeersch, A., S. J., *Periodica*, 7 vols., Brugis, 1913.

Vermeersch, A., S. J., *Supplementa et Monumenta*, Brugis, 1909.

Vidal, P. P. Petri, S.J., *Jus Canonicum Auctore P. Francisco Xav. Wernz, S.J., ad Codicis Norman Exactum*, vol. II, Rome, 1923.

Walde, Dr. Alois, *Lateinisches etymologisches Wörterbuch*, Heidelberg, 1910.

Walsh, William F., *History of English and American Law*, New York, 1923.

Waltzing, Jean Pierre, *Etude Historique sur les corporations professionnelles chez les Romains*, 4 vols., Paris, 1900.

Waterworth, J., *Canons and Decrees of the Council of Trent*, London, 1848.

Wernz, F. X., S. J., *Jus Decretalium*, 4 vols., Rome, 1905.

Willis, John, *Corporation*, (*Catholic Encyclopedia*, IV, 387).

Williston Samuel, *History of the Law of Business Corporations before 1800*, in *Selected Essays in Anglo-American Legal History*, III, n. 57, Boston, 1909.

Woywod, Stanislaus, O.F.M., *The New Canon Law*, New York, 1918; 2 vols., 1925.

Zollmann, Carl, LL.B., *American Civil Church Law*, New York, 1917.

TABLE OF CASES CITED.

Ada Street Methodist Episcopal Church *v.* Garnsey, 66 Ill. 132.
Alexander *v.* Slavens, 7 B. Mon. 351 (Ky.).
All Saints' Church *v.* Lovett, 1 N. Y. Super. Ct. 213.
Allemong *v.* Simmons, 124 Ind. 199.
Allen *v.* North Des Moines, M. E. Church, 127 Ia. 96.
Alna *v.* Plummer, 3 Greenl. 88 (Me.).
American Primitive Society *v.* Pilling, 24 N. J. Law 653.
Anderson *v.* Brock, 3 Greenl. 243 (Me.).
Attorney General *v.* Geerlings, 55 Mich 562.
Austin *v.* Thomas, 14 Mass. 333.

Bailey *v.* M. E. Church, Freeport, 71 Me. 472.
Baker *v.* Fales, 16 Mass. 488.
Baltimore & Potomac R. Co. *v.* Fifth Baptist Church, 108 U. S. 317.
Banks *v.* Phelan, 4 Barb. 80 (N. Y.).
Baptist Congregation *v.* Scannel, 3 Grant Cas. 48 (Pa.).
Barline *v.* Ramirex, 7 Philippines 41.
Bartlett *v.* Hipkins, 76 Md. 5.
Barton *v.* Fitzpatrick, 187 Ala. 273.

Bellport *v.* Tooker, 29 Barb. 256, aff'd in 21 N. Y. 267.
Bennet *v.* Taylor, 70 Hun. 51 (N. Y.).
Bigelow *v.* Congregational Society, Middletown, 11 Vt. 283.
Blair *v.* Odin, 3 Tex. 288.
Bogardus *v.* Trinity Church, 4 Paige 178 (N. Y.).
Bonacum *v.* Harrington, 65 Neb. 831.
Bonacum *v.* Murphy, 71 Neb. 463.
Book Agents of M. E. Church *v.* Hinton, 92 Tenn. 188.
Boutell *v.* Cowdin, 9 Mass. 254.
Bowden *v.* McLeod, 1 Edw. Ch. 588 (N. Y.).
Bowen *v.* Irish Presbyterian Congregation, 19 N. Y. Super. Ct. 245.
Boyles *v.* Roberts, 222 Mo. 613.
Bradfield *v.* Roberts, 175 U. S. 291.
Bridges *v.* Wilson, 11 Heisk, 458 (Tenn.).
Bundy *v.* Birdsall, 29 Barb. 31 (N. Y.).
Burke *v.* Wall, 29 La. Ann. 38.

Calkins *v.* Cheney, 92 Ill. 463.
Cammayer *v.* United German Lutheran Churches, 2 Sandf. Ch. 186 (N. Y.).
Canadian Religious Association *v.* Parmenter, 180 Mass. 415.
Cape *v.* Plymouth Congregational Church, 117 Wisc. 150.
Cape *v.* Plymouth Congregational Church, 130 Wisc. 174.
Cargill *v.* Sewall, 19 Me. 288.
Carpenter *v.* Buttrick, 41 Mich. 706.
Catholic Church *v.* Manning, 72 Md. 116.
Catholic Church *v.* Tobbein, 82 Mo. 418.
Catholic Institute *v.* Gibbons, 7 Ohio Dec. 516.
Cattron *v.* First Universalist Society, Manchester, 46 Ia. 106.
Centenary M. E. Church *v.* Parker, 43 N. J. Eq. 307.
Chase *v.* Cheney, 58 Ill. 509.
Cheeny *v.* Clark, 3 Vt. 431.
Chevra Bnai Israel Aushe Yanove und Motal *v.* Chevra Bikur Cholim Aushe Rodof Sholem, 24 Misc. Rep. 189.
Chicago *v.* Baptist Theological Union, 115 Ill. 245.
Christian Union *v.* Yount, 101 U. S. 352.
Church and Congregational Society in Greenland *v.* Hatch, 43 N. H. 393.
Church of St. Francis of Pointe Coupee *v.* Martin, 43 La. 62.
Cicotte *v.* St. Ann's Church, 60 Mich. 552.
Clark *v.* Brown, 108 S. W. 421, (Tex. Civ. A.).
Clayton *v.* Carey, 4 Md. 26.
Clement *v.* Young-McShea Amusement Co., 69 N. J. Eq. 347.
Columbia Bank *v.* Gospel Tabernacle Church, 127 N. Y. 361.
Commonwealth *ex. rel.* Gordon *v.* Graham, 64 Pa. St. 339.
Congregation Beth Elohim *v.* Central Presbyterian Ch., 10 Abb. Prac. (N. S.), (N. Y.).
Congregational Church, Ionia *v.* Webber, 54 Mich. 571.
Congregation of Roman Catholic Church *v.* Texas & P. R. Co., 41 Fed. 564.
Conklin *v.* Davis, 63 Conn. 377.
Constant *v.* St. Albans Church, 4 Daly 305 (N.Y.).
Copeland *v.* Hewett, 96 Me. 525.
Curry *v.* First Presbyterian Congregation, 2 Pittsb. 40 (Pa.).

Dangerfield *v.* Williams, 26 App. D. C. 508.
Dartmouth College *v.* Woodward, 4 Wheaton 518 (U. S.).
Davis *v.* Owen, 107 Va. 283.
Day *v.* Bolton, 12 N. J. Law 206.

De Camp *v.* Dobbins, 31 N. J. Eq. 671, affirming 29 N. J. Eq. 36.
Dennison *v.* Austin, 15 Wisc. 334.
De Ruyter *v.* St. Peter's Church, 3 N. Y. 238.
Devoss *v.* Gray, 22 Ohio 159.
Dickerson *v.* Kirk, 105 Md. 638.
Dillingham *v.* Snow, 5 Mass. 547.
Dismukes *v.* State, 83 Ala. 287.
District of Columbia *v.* Robinson, 30 App. D. C. 283.
Downes *v.* Bowdoin Square Baptist Society, 149 Mass. 135.

Earle *v.* Wood, 8 Cush. 430 (Mass.).
East Norway Lake Lutheran Church *v.* Froislie, 37 Minn. 447.
East Norway Lake Norwegian Ev. Lutheran Church *v.* Halvorson, 42 Minn. 503.
Enos *v.* Chestnut, 88 Ill. 590.

Feener *v.* Reiss, 90 N. Y. Supp. 586.
Ferraria *v.* Vasconcelles, 23 Ill. 456.
Field *v.* Field, 9 Wend. 394 (N. Y.).
Fifth Baptist Church *v.* Baltimore & Potomac R. Co., 137 U. S. 568.
Fink *v.* Umscheid, 40 Kans. 271.
First Baptist Church, San Jose *v.* Branhan, 90 Calif. 22.
First Baptist Church *v.* Schenectady & T. R. Co., 5 Barb. 79 (N. Y.)
First Baptist Church *v.* Witherell, 3 Paige 296 (N. Y.).
First Baptist Society, Leeds *v.* Grant, 59 Me. 245.
First Parish, Sudbury *v.* Stearns, 21 Pick. 148 (Mass.).
First Society, Waterbury *v.* Platt, 12 Conn. 181.
Franke *v.* Mann, 106 Wisc. 118.
Franklin St. Society *v.* Manchester, 60 N. H. 342.

Gable *v.* Miller, 10 Paige 627 (N. Y.), reversed, 2 Denio 492.
George *v.* Harris, 4 N. H. 533.
German Evangelical Congregation *v.* Pressler, 17 La. Ann. 127.
Gewin *v.* Mt. Pilgrim Baptist Church, 166 Ala. 345.
Globe Furniture Co., *v.* Trustees, Jerusalem Baptist Church, 103 Va. 559.
Goshen *v.* Stonington, 4 Conn. 209.
Grant St. Reformed Presbyterian Church, *Appeal of,* 238 Pa. 419.
Gray *v.* Goode, 44 Ind. A. 476.
Green *v.* Cady, 9 Wend. 414 (N. Y.).
Groesbeeck *v.* Dunscomb, 41 How. Prac. 302 (N. Y.).
Grosvenor *v.* United Society of Believers, 118 Mass. 78.
Grove *v.* Trustees, 33 Md. 45.

Haas *v.* Missionary Society of the Most Holy Redeemer, 6 Misc. Re. 281.
Hamblett *v.* Bennett, 6 Allen 140 (Mass.).
Hanson *v.* Little Sisters of the Poor, Baltimore and St. Mary's Church, Hampden, 79 Md. 434.
Harbison *v.* First Presbyterian Society, 46 Conn. 529.
Hardin *v.* Baptist Church, 51 Mich. 137.
Harlem Presbyterian Church *v.* New York, 5 Hun. 442.
Harpending *v.* Ref. Prot. Dutch Church, 16 Pet. 455 (U. S.).
Harriman *v.* First Bryan Baptist Church, 63 Ga. 186.
Harris *v.* Cosby, 173 Ala. 81.
Harrison *v.* Hoyle, 24 Ohio St. 254.
Heiss *v.* Vosburg, 59 Wisc. 532.
Hennessy *v.* Walsh, 55 N. H. 515.
Holcomb *v.* Leavitt, 124 N. Y. Supp. 980.

Holt *v.* Downs, 58 N. H. 170.
Huber *v.* The United Evangelical Prot. Cong. of Cin., 16 Ohio 371.
Humbert *v.* Trinity Church, 24 Wend. 587 (N. Y.).
Hundley *v.* Collins, 131 Ala. 234.
Hussey *v.* Gallagher, 61 Ga. 86.

Ihmes' Estate, *In re,* 154 Ia. 20.
Insurance Bank of Columbus *v.* Bank of U. S., 4 Clark 125 (Pa.).

Jackson *v.* Hopkins, 113 Md. 557.
Jackson *v.* Nestles, 3 Johns 115.
Johnson *v.* Welch, 42 W. Va. 18.
Jones *v.* State, 28 Neb. 495.
Juker *v.* Commonwealth, 20 Pa. 484.

Keith & Perry Coal Co. *v.* Bingham, 97 Mo. 196.
Kinney *v.* Kinney's Ex'r., 86 Ky. 610.
Klix *v.* Polish R. C. St. Stanislaus Parish, 137 Mo. App. 347.
Klop *v.* Moore, 6 Kans. 27.
Kniskern *v.* Lutheran Churches, 1 Sandf. Ch. 439 (N. Y.).
Krauczunas *v.* Hoban, 221 Pa. 213.
Krecker *v.* Shirley, 163 Pa. 534.

Ladd *v.* Clements, 4 Cush. 476 (Mass.).
Landrith *v.* Hudgins, 121 Tenn. 556.
Langolf *v.* Seiberlitch, 2 Pars. Eq. Cas. 64 (Pa.).
Lefevre *v.* Detroit, 2 Mich. 586.
Lemp *v.* Raven, 113 Mich. 375.
Leonard *v.* Lent, 43 Wisc. 83.
Lockwood *v.* St. Louis, 23 Mo. 20.
Lord *v.* Hardie, 82 N. C. 241.
Lovett *v.* German Reformed Church, 12 Barb. 67 (N. Y.).
Lucas *v.* Case, 9 Bush. 297 (Ky.).
Lynde *v.* Hill, 14 Pick. 447 (Mass.).

Mack *v.* Kime, 129 Ga. 1.
Madison Ave. Baptist Church *v.* Baptist Ch. in Oliver St., 2 Abb. Pract. (N. Y.), N. S., aff'd in 31 N. Y. Super. Ct. 109.
Mannix *v.* Purcell, 46 Ohio St. 102.
Marien *v.* Evangelical Creed Congregation, Milwaukee, 132 Wisc. 650.
Mazaika *v.* Krauczunas, 229 Pa. 47.
Mazaika *v.* Krauczunas, 233 Pa. 138.
McAuley's Appeal, *In re,* 77 Pa. 397.
McDonald *v.* Mass. General Hospital, 120 Mass. 432.
McGinnis *v.* Watson, 41 Pa. 9.
McGlynn *v.* Hoban, 42 Pa. Super. Ct. 478.
McRoberts *v.* Moudy, 19 Mo. App. 26.
Methodist Episcopal Church *v.* Adams, 4 Or. 76.
M. E. Church *v.* Sherman, 36 Wisc. 404.
M. E. Society *v.* Lake, 51 Vt. 353.
M. E. Union Church *v.* Pickett, 19 N. Y. 482.
Milford *v.* Worcester, 7 Mass. 48.
Miller *v.* Ahrens, 150 Fed. 644 (No. 583).
Miller *v.* Eshbach, 43 Md. 1.
Miller *v.* Milligan, 6 Ohio Dec. 1000.
Milwaukee Prot. Home *v.* Becher, 87 Wisc. 409.
Moore *v.* St. Thomas Church, 4 Abb. N. C. 51 (N. Y.).

Mora *v.* Murphy, 83 Calif. 12.
Morgan *v.* Leslie, Wright 144 (Ohio).
Morgan *v.* Rose, 22 N. J. Eq. 583.
Mormon Church *v.* U. S., 136 U. S. 1.
Mt. Zion Baptist Church *v.* Whitmore, 83 Ia. 138.

Nachtrieb *v.* Harmony Settlement, Fed. Case No. 10,003.
Nance *v.* Busby, 91 Tenn. 303.
Nelson *v.* Benson, 69 Ill. 27.
New Haven *v.* Sheffield, 30 Conn. 160.
New Myer's Appeal, *In re,* 72 Pa. 121.
Nichols *v.* School Directors, 93 Ill. 61.
Novickas *v.* Krauczunas, 240 Pa. 248.
Novicky *v.* Krauczunas, 245 Pa. 86.

Opinion of the Justices, *In re,* 214 Mass. 599.
Order of St. Benedict *v.* Steinhauser, 234, U. S. 640.
Order of St. Benedict *v.* Steinhauser, 179 Fed. 137.
Orthodox Congregational Church, Union Village, *In re,* 6 Abb. N. C. 398 (N. Y.).
Osgood *v.* Bradley, 7 Greenl. 411 (Me.).

Paddock *v.* Brown, 6 Hill. 530 (N. Y.).
Page *v.* Asbury M. E. Church, 78 N. J. Eq. 114.
Parish of the Immaculate Conception *v.* Murphy, 89 Neb. 524.
Pawlet *v.* Clarke, 9 Cranch 292 (U. S.).
Peace *v.* First Christian Church, McGregor, 20 Tex. Civ. App. 85.
Penny *v.* Central Coal and Coke Company, 138 Fed. 769.
People *ex rel.* Lady of Angels Seminary *v.* Barber, 42 Hun. 27 (N. Y.).
People *v.* Board of Education, 245 Ill. 334.
People *v.* Fulton, 11 N. Y. (1 Kern.) 94.
People *v.* Franciscus Benevolent Society, 24 Ho. Pr. 216.
People *v.* German Church, 53 N. Y. 103.
People *v.* Hulbert, 46 N. Y. 110.
People *v.* Runkle, 9 Johns 147 (N. Y.).
People *v.* Steele, 2 Barb. 397.
People *v.* The Mayor, 63 N. Y. 291.
People's Bank *v.* St. Anthony's Roman Catholic Church, 109 N. Y. 512.
Permanent Committee of Missions of the Pacific Synod of the Cumberland Presbyterian Church *v.* Pacific Synod of the Presbyterian Church, 157 Calif. 105.
Permoli *v.* Municipality, No. 1 of New Orleans, 3 How. 589 (U. S.).
Perry *v.* Tupper, 74 N. E. 722.
Philadelphia *v.* Barber, 160 Pa. 123.
Phipps *v.* Jones, 20 Pa. 260.
Ponce *v.* Roman Catholic Church, 210 U. S. 296.
Poultney Congreg. Soc. *v.* Ashley, 10 Vt. 241.
Presbyterian Society *v.* Beach, 8 Hun. 644, reversed in 74 N. Y. 72.
Propagation Society *v.* Sharon, 28 Vt. 603.

Reformed Church, Gallupville, *v.* Schoolcraft, 65 N. Y. 134.
Reformed Prot. Dutch Ch. *v.* Brown, 29 Barb. 335.
Reformed Prot. Dutch Church of Schenectady *v.* Veeder, 4 Wend. 494 (N. Y.).
Religious Congreg. Soc. *v.* Baker, 15 Vt. 119.
Reynolds *v.* U. S., 98 U. S. 145.
Richardson *v.* Butterfield, 6 Cush. 191 (Mass.).

Robertson *v.* Bullions, 11 N. Y. 243.
Roman Catholic German Church *v.* Weighaus & Bros., 16 Ky. Law Rep. 446.

St. Andrews Church *v.* Shaughnessy, 63 Neb. 792.
St. Ann's Church, *In re,* 14 Abb. Prac. 424 (N. Y.).
St. Antonio *v.* Odin, 15 Tex. 539.
St. Hyacinth Congreg. *v.* Borucki, 141 Wisc. 205.
St. John Baptist Greek Catholic Church *v.* Baron, 73 Atl. 422 (N. J.).
St. Louis Institute of Christian Science, *In re,* 27 Mo. App. 633.
St. Patrick's Roman Catholic Church *v.* Gavalon, 82 Ill. 170.
St. Peter's Roman Catholic Congreg. *v.* Germain, 104 Ill. 440.
Santos *v.* Holy Roman Catholic Church, 212 U. S. 463.
Schradi *v.* Dornfeld, 52 Minn. 465.
Schweiker *v.* Husser, 146 Ill. 399.
Scott *v.* First Free Methodist Church, 50 Mich. 528.
Second Congregational Society *v.* Waring, 24 Pick. 304 (Mass.).
Second Precinct in Rehoboth *v.* Catholic Congregational Church & Soc., 23 Pick. 139 (Mass.).
Seda *v.* Huble, 75 Ia. 429.
Selkir *v.* Klein, 100 N. Y. Supp. 449.
Shannon *v.* Frost, 3 B. Mon. 253 (Ky.).
Shapleigh *v.* Pilsbury, 1 Greenl. 271 (Me.).
Slaughter House Cases, 16 Wallace 36 (U. S.).
Smith *v.* Pedigo, 145 Ind. 361.
Society for the Propagation of the Gospel *v.* New Haven, 8 Wheaton 464 (U. S.).
South Baptist Society, Albany *v.* Clapp, 18 Barb. 35 (N. Y.).
Speidel *v.* Henrici, 120 U. S. 377.
Stack *v.* O'Hara, 98 Pa. 213.
Stanton *v.* Camp, 4 Barb. 274 (N. Y.).
State *v.* Aucker, 31 S. C. Law (2 Rich. Law) 245.
State *v.* Getty, 69 Conn. 286.
State *v.* Immanuel Presbyterian Church, New Orleans, 52 La. Ann. 1311.
State *v.* Trustees of Township, Nine, 7 Ohio St. 58.
Stebbins *v.* Jennings, 10 Pick. 172 (Mass.).

Taylor *v.* Edson, 4 Cush. 522 (Mass.).
Taylor *v.* Public Hall Co., 35 Conn. 430.
Terrett *v.* Taylor, 9 Cranch 43 (U. S.).
Third M. E. Church of Brooklyn, *In re,* 67 Hun. 86, aff'd. in 142 N. Y. 638.
Thompkins *v.* Dinnie, 21 N. D. 305.
Thompson *v.* West, 59 Neb. 677.
Ticknor's Estate, *In re,* 13 Mich. 44.
Tobey *v.* Wareham Bank, 54 Mass. 440.
Trinity Church *v.* Boston, 118 Mass. 164.
Trustees *v.* Dickinson, 12 N. C. 189.
Tucker *v.* St. Clements Church, 5 N. Y. Super. Ct. 242, aff'd. in 8 N. Y. 558.
Turner *v.* Burlington, 16 Mass. 208.

Union Church *v.* Sanders, 1 Houst. 100 (Del.).
United Brethren Church, New London, *v.* Vandusen, 37 Wisc. 54.

Van Deuzen *v.* Presbyterian Congregation at Ft. Edward, 42 N. Y. (3 Keyes) 550.

Wallace *v*. Hughes, 131 Ky. 445.
Wardens of Christ Church *v*. Pope, 8 Gray 140 (Mass.).
Watkins *v*. Wilcox, 66 N. Y. 654, affirming 4 Hun. 220.
Watson *v*. Avery, 2 Bush. 332 (Ky.).
Watson *v*. Garvin, 54 Mo. 353.
Watson *v*. Jones, 13 Wallace 679 (U. S.).
Wehmer *v*. Fokenga, 57 Neb. 510.
Wesley Church *v*. Moore, 10 Pa. 273.
Westminster Church *v*. Presbytery of New York, 211 N. Y. 214.
Westminster Presbyterian Church of W. 23rd St., *v*. Trustees of Presbytery of N. Y., 127 N. Y. Supp. 851.
Weston *v*. Hunt, 2 Mass. 500.
Wilson *v*. Johns Island Presbyterian Church, 2 Rich Eq. 192 (S. C.).
Wilson *v*. Livingstone, 99 Mich. 594.
Wilson *v*. Perry, 29 W. Va. 169.
Wilson *v*. Tabernacle Church, 59 N. Y. Supp. 148.
Winebrenner *v*. Colder, 43 Pa. St. 244, 252.
Wright's Estate, *In re,* Myr. Prob. 213 (Calif).
Wyncoop & Watkins *v*. Bellvue Congregational Society, 10 Ia. 185.

Yanthis *v*. Kemp, 43 Ind. A. 203.

Zion Church, Sterling *v*. Mensch, 74 Ill. App. 115, aff'd. in 178 Ill. 225.

UNIVERSITAS CATHOLICA AMERICAE

Washington, D. C.
Facultas Juris Canonici
1926-1927
No. 39

DEUS LUX MEA

TITULI

Quas

AD DOCTORATUS GRADUM

In

JURE UTROQUE

Apud Universitatem Catholicam Americae

Consequendum
Publice Propugnabit

BRENDANUS FRANCISCUS BROWN, A.B., LL.M., J.U.L.

OMAHA, NEBRASKA.

HORA IX-XI DIE XXIV MAII A.D. MCMXXVII.

ROMAN LAW.

I. The Sources of Roman Law.
II. The *Jus Civile* and the *Jus Gentium*.
III. The Family.
IV. Slavery.
V. Personality.
VI. *Mancipatio* and the Nature of *Res Mancipii*.
VII. Citizenship.
VIII. Loss of *Status* (*Capitis Diminutio*) and Its Effects.
IX. *Cura*.
X. *Tutela*.
XI. The Juridical Personality of Corporations and Institutions.
XII. Adoption.
XIII. Adrogation.
XIV. Marriage.
XV. Emancipation.
XVI. Ownership.
XVII. Easements.
XVIII. Possession.
XIX. Usufruct.
XX. Pledge, Mortgage, Lien.
XXI. Prescription.
XXII. Obligation.
XXIII. Matrimonial Impediments.
XXIV. Inheritance.
XXV. Wills.
XXVI. Trusts.
XXVII. Trial *in Jure*.
XXVIII. Trial *in Judicio*.
XXIX. Proceedings after the Trial.
XXX. *Extraordinaria Cognitio*.

INTERNATIONAL LAW.

XXXI. The Monroe Doctrine.
XXXII. Piracy and International Law.
XXXIII. Protectorates and Spheres of Influence.
XXXIV. Mandates.
XXXV. Extradition.
XXXVI. The World Court.
XXXVII. Pan Americanism.
XXXVIII. Intervention.
XXXIX. Mediation and Arbitration.
XL. Jurisdiction over Vessels.

ECCLESIASTICAL LAW.

XLI. De Ecclesia, Societate Perfecta.
XLII. De Forma Ecclesiastici Regiminis.
XLIII. De Potestate Suprema in Ecclesia.

XLIV. De Episcopatu.
XLV. De Relatione inter Ecclesiam et Statum.
XLVI. De Concordatis.
XLVII. De Historia Juris Canonici ante Gratianum.
XLVIII. De Corpore Juris Canonici.
XLIX. De Historia Juris Canonici post Corpus Juris Canonici.
L. De Codice Juris Canonici.

LI.	Canones 1-6	De Ambitu Codicis.
LII.	Canones 8-24	De Legibus Ecclesiasticis.
LIII.	Canones 25-30	De Consuetudine.
LIV.	Canones 31-35	De Temporis Supputatione.
LV.	Canones 36-62	De Rescriptis.
LVI.	Canones 63-79	De Privilegiis.
LVII.	Canones 80-86	De Dispensationibus.
LVIII.	Canones 87-102	De Personis.
LIX.	Canones 329-333	De Nominatione et Institutione Episcoporum.
LX.	Canones 334-349	De Juribus et Obligationibus Episcoporum.
LXI.	Canones 451-454	De Parochis.
LXII.	Canones 492-498	De Erectione et Suppressione Religionis, Provinciae, Domus.
LXIII.	Canones 499-517	De Superioribus et de Capitulis.
LXIV.	Canones 518-530	De Confessariis et Cappellanis.
LXV.	Canones 531-537	De Bonis Temporalibus Eorumque Administratione.
LXVI.	Canones 542-571	De Novitiatu.
LXVII.	Canones 572-586	De Professione Religiosa.
LXVIII.	Canones 592-612	De Obligationibus Religiosorum.
LXIX.	Canones 613-625	De Privilegiis Religiosorum.
LXX.	Canones 637-645	De Egressu e Religione.
LXXI.	Canones 738-744	De Ministro Baptismi.
LXXII.	Canones 782-785	De Ministro Confirmationis.
LXXIII.	Canones 786-789	De Subjecto Confirmationis.
LXXIV.	Canones 1012-1016	De Matrimonio.
LXXV.	Canones 1035-1042	De Impedimentis in Genere.
LXXVI.	Canones 1043-1057	De Dispensationibus in Genere.
LXXVII.	Canones 1067-1080	De Impedimentis Dirimentibus.
LXXVIII.	Canones 1094-1103	De Forma Celebrationis Matrimonii.
LXXIX.	Canones 1118-1132	De Separatione Conjugum.
LXXX.	Canones 1133-1137	De Matrimonii Convalidatione.
LXXXI.	Canones 1138-1141	De Sanatione in Radice.
LXXXII.	Canones 1337-1348	De Sacris Concionibus.
LXXXIII.	Canones 1552-1554	De Judiciis.
LXXXIV.	Canones 1556-1568	De Foro Competenti.
LXXXV.	Canones 1608-1626	De Officio Judicum et Tribunalis Ministrorum.
LXXXVI.	Canones 1646-1654	De Actore et de Reo Convento.
LXXXVII.	Canones 1726-1731	De Litis Contestatione.
LXXXVIII.	Canones 1754-1791	De Testibus et Attestationibus.
LXXXIX.	Canones 1825-1828	De Praesumptionibus.
XC.	Canones 1892-1897	De Querela Nullitatis contra Sententiam.
XCI.	Canones 1960-1992	De Causis Matrimonialibus.

XCII.	Canones 2147-2167	De Modo Procedendi in Remotione et Translatione Parochorum Inamovibilium et Amovibilum.
XCIII.	Canones 2186-2194	De Modo Procedendi in Suspensione ex Informata Conscientia Infligenda.
XCIV.	Canones 2195-2198	De Natura Delicti Ejusque Divisione.
XCV.	Canones 2199-2211	De Imputabilitate Delicti, de Causis illam aggravantibus vel minuentibus et de juridicis delicti effectibus.
XCVI.	Canones 2215-2219	De Poenarum Notione, Speciebus, Interpretatione atque Applicatione.
XCVII.	Canones 2220-2225	De Superiore Potestatem Coactivam Habente.
XCVIII.	Canones 2226-2235	De Subjecto Coactivae Potestati Obnoxio.
XCIX.	Canones 2236-2240	De Poenarum Remissione.
C.	Canones 2245-2254	De Censuris in Genere.

Vidit Facultas Juris Canonici:

PHILIPPUS BERNARDINI, S.T.D., J.U.D., Decanus.
LUDOVICUS H. MOTRY, S.T.D., J.C.D., a Secretis.
VALENTINUS T. SCHAAF, O.F.M., J.C.D.
FRANCISCUS LARDONE, S.T.D., J.U.D.
MANUEL DE OLIVIERA LIMA, L.L.D.

Vidit Rector Universitatis:

THOMAS J. SHAHAN, S.T.D., J.U.L., LL.D.

BIOGRAPHICAL NOTE

Brendan Francis Brown was born at Sioux City, Iowa, October 19, 1898. He was graduated successively from St. Peter's Parochial School, Creighton University High School, and Creighton University College of Arts and Sciences, Omaha, Nebraska, receiving the degree of Bachelor of Arts in June, 1921. In September of the same year, he began the study of law at Creighton University College of Law, Omaha. He received the degree of Bachelor of Laws from that institution in 1924, and shortly after was admitted to the practice of law in the State of Nebraska. While at Creighton he was an instructor in English, History, and Latin.

In July, 1924, he was awarded a Knights of Columbus Scholarship by the Catholic University of America for graduate work in its law department. He received the degree of Master of Laws from the Catholic University of America, in June, 1925, the subject of his thesis being, "The Roman Conception of Juristic Personality." The same year he was admitted to the District of Columbia Bar.

In November, 1925, he qualified for the Baccalaureate in Canon and Civil Laws, and attended the lectures of Doctors Philip Bernardini, Valentine Theodore Schaaf, and Hubert Louis Motry on Canon Law, of Doctor Francesco Lardone on Roman Law, of Doctor Manoel de Oliviera Lima on International Law, and of Donald A. MacLean on Analytical Jurisprudence. He received the degree of Licentiate in Canon and Civil Laws in June, 1926, the subject of his thesis being, "The Canonical Juristic Person, with special reference to its status in the United States." The same year the Catholic University of America awarded him one of the three Frederick Penfield Scholarships to be used for post-graduate study either in the United States or abroad. He elected to spend the first year under this award at the Catholic University of America. In order to qualify for the Doctorate in Canon and Civil Laws he wrote the present dissertation. He became a member of the faculty of Civil Law of the Catholic University of America in the fall of 1926.

www.ingramcontent.com/pod-product-compliance
Lightning Source LLC
LaVergne TN
LVHW050241080826
844660LV00012B/574

* 9 7 8 0 8 1 3 2 2 2 2 8 8 *